Gendering Addiction

Gendering Addiction

The Politics of Drug Treatment in a Neurochemical World

Nancy D. Campbell
Rensselaer Polytechnic Institute, US

Elizabeth Ettorre
University of Liverpool, University of Plymouth, UK

palgrave
macmillan

First published 2011 by
PALGRAVE MACMILLAN

Palgrave Macmillan in the UK is an imprint of Macmillan Publishers Limited, registered in England, company number 785998, of Houndmills, Basingstoke, Hampshire RG21 6XS.

Palgrave Macmillan in the US is a division of St Martin's Press LLC, 175 Fifth Avenue, New York, NY 10010.

Palgrave Macmillan is the global academic imprint of the above companies and has companies and representatives throughout the world.

Palgrave® and Macmillan® are registered trademarks in the United States, the United Kingdom, Europe and other countries.

ISBN 978–0–230–22855–9

This book is printed on paper suitable for recycling and made from fully managed and sustained forest sources. Logging, pulping and manufacturing processes are expected to conform to the environmental regulations of the country of origin.

A catalogue record for this book is available from the British Library.

Library of Congress Cataloging-in-Publication Data
Campbell, Nancy D. (Nancy Dianne), 1963–
Gendering addiction: the politics of drug treatment in a neurochemical world/Nancy Campbell, Elizabeth Ettorre.
p. cm.
Includes index.
ISBN 978–0–230–22855–9 (alk. paper)
1. Women drug addicts—Rehabilitation—United States. 2. Women—Drug use—United States. 3. Drug abuse—Treatment—United States. 4. Sex discrimination against women—United States. I. Ettorre, Elizabeth, 1948– II. Title.
HV5824.W6C347 2011
616.86'06082—dc22 2011013739

10 9 8 7 6 5 4 3 2 1
20 19 18 17 16 15 14 13 12 11

Printed and bound in the United States of America

With gratitude and respect, we dedicate this book to our feminist mentors, Donna J. Haraway and Susanne MacGregor

Contents

List of Figures

Acknowledgements

Nancy D. Campbell would like to thank the Office of the Provost of Rensselaer Polytechnic Institute for granting the sabbatical leave that it took to finish this book in fall 2010. She also gratefully acknowledges the NSF RAMP UP Career Campaign Award that enabled the collaboration and the writing of the initial proposal. She gratefully acknowledges all those she interviewed for this book, including Carol Boyd, Vivian Brown, Norma Finkelstein, Loretta Finnegan, Lynn M. Paltrow, Nancy Paull, and Beth Glover Reed for their path-breaking work on behalf of drug-using women. She thanks Ned Woodhouse, Grace Campbell Woodhouse, and Isaac Campbell Eglash for affording her the time and space to write. Elizabeth (Betsy) Ettorre would like to thank Rensselaer Polytechnic Institute for the grant that was used to travel to the US and write the initial book proposal at Wiawaka Women's Retreat, Lake George, NY. A special thanks to the lovely women who were working there and/or visiting there at the time. Betsy also wishes to thank all of the women interviewed for the UK side of the study, including Virginia Berridge, Dorothy Black, Anne Delargy, Annas Dixon, Viv Evans, Cindy Fazey, Susanne MacGregor, Faye Macrory, Fiona Measham, Shirley Otto, and Betsy Thom. Betsy thanks Irmeli Laitinen for her support in the writing process. Both Nancy and Betsy are grateful to those who made it possible to present our work in progress: Carol Boyd and the University of Michigan Institute for Research on Women and Gender and the Substance Abuse Research Center; the Association for Feminist Epistemologies, Methodologies, and Science Studies; and Margrit Shildrick, Azrini Wahidin, and Deborah Steinberg who organized the seminar 'Estranged Bodies' funded by the Economic and Social Research Council, UK and sponsored by the Universities of Queen's (Belfast), Warwick and Liverpool. Given that we found the writing of this book a pleasurable feminist experience in the sharing of our ideas, we recommend this way of working to feminist scholars everywhere.

Introduction: Making Gender Matter: Drug-Using Women, Embodiment, and the Epistemologies of Ignorance

This book brings to bear the ideas of feminist sociology of knowledge, situated knowledge and ignorance, and standpoint epistemologies (Figueroa and Harding, 2003; Haraway, 1988; Harding, 1991, 1998, 2006, 2008; Hartsock, 1984; Smith, 1990) upon a basic injustice that has grave consequences for the human rights of drug-using women. Despite concerted efforts since the 1970s, most women who need drug treatment in the US and UK still do not get it – because it is delivered in ways they cannot take up. This book is about ongoing attempts to meet a basic need that has not been met. Why not?

We argue that knowledge-making practices in the drug research and treatment arena make it resistant to acknowledging the gendered, classed, and racialized power differentials that structure the lives of drug-using women. Without such knowledge, we argue that what we need to know about women's specific needs will continue *not* to be known. We craft a critical historical and sociological framework showing how feminist knowledge production became a promising route for overcoming the pervasive 'epistemology of ignorance' that prevails in this arena.[1] Why have women drug users been marginalized so consistently in treatment and policy circles? Why has it been so difficult for feminists to carve out spaces in which to create, support, and sustain 'gender-aware', 'gender-sensitive', or 'gender-responsive' drug treatment during the latter part of the twentieth century? Why, knowing that so many women still cannot get what they need in terms of healthcare and economic and social support, do we persist in criminalizing them – as if prosecuting women will make the situations for which they are held responsible anything but worse? Finally, knowing that criminalization takes a huge toll on poor women, particularly those who are members of racial-ethnic and sexual minorities, why do we lack the political will to bring about reproductive justice for all?

Multiple 'epistemologies of ignorance' work along gendered, sexualized, classed, and racialized lines to make knowing 'what women need' difficult to discern in this domain. These epistemologies define 'what women need' in popular women's culture as divorced from feminist political thought, which is typically viewed as a destabilizing force. We examine the historical emergence of 'feminist drug treatment' and 'feminist drug research' in the broader context of the women's health, reproductive rights, and sexual rights movements. Women who used drugs and alcohol in socially problematic ways were among those women who were initially invisible to these social movements. Even within the women's movement, women's drug and alcohol use and abuse were considered emblematic failures of gendered performativity (Ettorre, 2007) – drug-using women were seen as 'failures' as women. Drug-using women are not epistemologically credible; they continue to be constructed as wilfully wayward women who are morally corrupt and 'deviant' in socially unacceptable ways (Campbell, 2000). With the current relocation of the site of 'addiction' from the body to the brain, the dynamic we trace in this book produces an 'embodied deviance'[2] (Ettorre, 2007: 29) that is today represented as one among many forms taken by new forms of 'neurochemical deviance'.

Neurochemical deviance is seen as both productive of drug-using subjects – as causative, as productive of *problematic subjects and identities* – and as the long-term effect of a drug-using lifestyle. In effect, addiction research explores how drug-using bodies are variously configured as 'causal forces' under different social conditions.[3] Weinberg (2002) argues that when looking at the body as a materially incarnate social force, addiction researchers should recognize that while the visible 'symptoms' of addiction consist in social and cultural transgressions, the underlying 'nature' of addiction is usually located in bodily pathology, deficit, or vulnerability (1). Thus, drug users are viewed as materially constituted subjects whose very embodied 'essence' is to be marked as deviant, abject, and 'other', and they are thus positioned as deserving the very social exclusions that exacerbate their otherness. Public policy may be used to create a more inclusive climate that locates drug-using women within the social body – or to further exacerbate social distance.

While the cultural logics of 'neurochemical selves' in 'psychopharmacological societies' (Rose, 2007) are somewhat new, the cultural figures of the abject, feminized drug user are drawn from an older lexicon shaped by governing mentalities described by Nancy Campbell (2000), which offers an account of how the 'figures' of drug-using women have been 'used' in US drug policy discourse. Similar 'figures' have been used in the UK to depict women drug users as embroiled in 'malign constellations of abusive partners/ pimps, failures of the care system and coercion into street prostitution' (MacDonald, Shildrick, and Simpson, 2007: 168). Now marked as 'embodied deviants' whose very brains differ in structure and function from those of the 'normal', women so marked are considered fatally flawed at the level of neurochemical selfhood and neurobiopolitical citizenship. This book documents the 'difference' that gender makes in the lives of drug-using women, and in conclusion returns to take up the question of what difference gender makes in a neurochemical era.

'Gendering addiction' is our name for a precise vector of analysis that encourages the elaboration of critical feminist theory and reflexive research practices in the drugs field. As feminists, we attempt to delve into the conceptual and epistemological cauldrons that produce, construct, and resist difference, as well as sameness and reconciliation. We argue that 'gendering addiction' can be accomplished without essentializing women, who hail from a wide range of racial-ethnic formations, class, sexualities, abilities, ages, and other forms of difference, and who engage in a vast array of types and practices of substance use. We avoid essentialism in our own historical and sociological work by characterizing the knowledge paradigms that have structured policy, clinical practice, and knowledge production. At first we planned to 'recycle' the classical and postmodern[4] paradigms that Elizabeth Ettorre (2007) outlined in earlier work delving into the tensions in our knowledge awareness of the overall significance of gender and drugs. Keen to flag up key notions and related research practices characterizing these paradigms, Ettorre contended that the postmodern paradigm was more conducive to feminist, emancipatory, and anti-oppressive stances, while the assumptions of the classical paradigm were rather obsolete. However, in this book we reconsider these paradigms as co-constitutive, co-occurring, and concurrent 'modes of knowledge' based on different forms of expertise, skills, education, experiences, vocabularies, and disciplines (see Figure I.1). The classical mode of knowledge roughly corresponds to what Campbell (2000) termed the 'governing mentalities' of discourse on drugs issuing from scientific, therapeutic, and policy communities concerned with controlling drug users.

Governing mentalities are the dominant conceptual frames in which truth-claims about how to govern the unruly 'make sense', and are composed of assumptions and images that structure the apparatus of

Classical mode	Postclassical mode
Epistemology of ignorance in which there are no gendered bodies	Epistemology of embodiment based on recognition of gender
Theory of addiction: Chronic, relapsing brain disease suffered by an individual **brain** abstracted from social circumstances	Theory of addiction: Arises from adaptive relationship situated within social contexts, cultural geographies, and local economies that make drug use likely
Power differentials and inequalities are not recognized	Power differentials and inequalities are recognized
Modernist rehabilitation moulds individual subjects to conform with dominant social norms	New Social Movements for civil rights, women's rights, human rights; 'new'-style identities, self-modulation is 'postdisciplinary'
Epidemiological	Epistemological
Deterministic	Non-deterministic
Resistant to gender-sensitivity	Gender-sensitive; emphasizes agentic corporeality
Target of intervention: brain and behaviour of sick, maladjusted, misbehaving individual	Target of intervention: relationships between person, drug, and social context
One drug of choice	Poly-substance, pick 'n' mix scene
Drug use is most salient aspect of identity	Many intersecting salient aspects of identity, including gender, race, class, sexuality, ability/disability
Anti-social	'Truly social'
Abstinence is the condition for re-entry into full citizenship and human rights	Non-conditional: all have full citizenship and human rights regardless of drug-use status, which cannot be used as conditional basis for denying rights
Universal, one-size-fits-all treatment approaches	Cultural competence and specificity, treatment situated within community
Addicts, ex-addicts, and non-addicts are the full sum of possible identities	Consumers, survivors, recovering persons, people are not either/or but in a process
Driven by deviance amplification and moral panics	Resistant to deviance amplification, critical of moral panics

Figure I.1 Modes of knowledge

knowledge production within each mode. The classical mode also maps onto Elianne Riska's account of the central role of *medicalization* in sociological theories of social control and feminist theories of patriarchy. The feminist epistemological mode, on the other hand, corresponds to the role of *biomedicalization* in post-structuralist theories of the gendered ways in which relational constructions of bodies marked masculine and feminine work in post-disciplinary societies.[5] In shifting towards a post-structuralist analysis of a body 'governed' not only through discursive inscription and definitional processes, but now through self-definition and an 'empowerment model' that encourages active navigation of the health system, Riska demonstrates the influence of both the women's health and consumer's movements within the current regime of *biomedicalization* (2010: 148–53). Forms of 'empowerment' and 'agency' also differ between disciplinary and post-disciplinary societies, medicalized and biomedicalized regimes, and classical and epistemological modes of knowledge. Forms of embodiment – and the meanings attached to the corporeal and moments when the 'corporeal irrupt[s] into consciousness' (Shildrick, 2002: 4) – differ in their proximity to vulnerability, abjection or monstrosity, and otherness, and in their capacity to evoke ambivalent responses that range from tolerance to empathy to disgust.

We aim to show how different forms of embodied deviance, including those now understood as embodied in the neurochemistry of 'the brain', arise out of disciplinary and post-disciplinary societies and are translated into treatment and public policy. Arising as it did out of the social organization of knowledge and control central to disciplinary society, the 'classical paradigm' or mode of knowledge locates and responds to addiction as a disease of individual bodies and brains. Proponents of this governing mentality have sought to mould individuals to conform with dominant social norms through work discipline, vocational and recreational therapies, and health routines consistent with abstinence. Today, however, this mode finds its culmination in an emerging range of pharmacotherapies aimed at modulating 'neurochemical selves', suggesting that the governing notion of agency is shifting away from abstinence and towards forms of consumption favoured in post-disciplinary societies (Vrecko, 2009: 219). As pharmacotherapies for addiction become more available, older forms of modernist 'rehabilitation' and 'normalization' have given way to the current ambition of 'modulation' and even 'self-modulation'. Addict subjects are convinced to modulate themselves by targeting specific activities and practices such as drug use 'behaviours' or 'maternal habits', emphasizing for women drug users the 'positive aspects of motherhood' (Klee, 2002: 149). All drug users are told to seek expert help through pharmacotherapy for modulating specific parts of their brains and neurotransmitter systems. Drug use has been claimed to alter the structure and function of the addict's brain, sometimes in permanent and irreversible ways.[6] While the 'fragmentation' of the subject targeted for technological intervention may appear to be *less* subject to social or disciplinary control, the form of control goes *deep* in seeking to rearrange bodily and neurochemical processes, often at the molecular level. 'Gender' is located within neurochemical and hormonal processes: while there are no gendered bodies in this knowledge paradigm, there are sex-differentiated brains. This paradigm or mode of knowledge has moved towards a neurochemobiological determinism accompanied by a fundamental neglect of social processes, except insofar as they affect gene expression or other aspects of brain structure or function. This mode of knowledge is deeply 'anti-social', despite its former commitment to converting 'deviant bodies' into conformance with dominant social norms.

The 'epistemological paradigm' is a 'contending mentality' that focuses on knowledges of embodiment in recognizing how social power differentials position 'addicts' and acknowledging the pervasive 'epistemologies of ignorance' that structure knowledge practices in the drugs arena. This mode responds to a pressing need for new knowledge about social relations in post-disciplinary societies stratified by race, class, gender, and other modes of difference, but also stratified, increasingly, by health status and categorization within multiple biomedical diagnoses and classificatory systems. Calls for new knowledges may seem utopian – however, we remind our readers that the women's health movement has successfully mobilized conceptual and practical tools enabling the production of new knowledges that changed patterns of ignorance about the embodied deviance of women's bodies. We argue that the women's health movement enabled a shift between the classical governing mentalities and the new epistemology we see taking shape to get underway. In practical terms, however, the governing mentalities of drugs, drug control, and scientific research undertaken for the sake of social control remain dominant in ways that make it difficult to create and sustain gender-specific treatment that drug-using women are able to take up. As a result, the shift between the classical modes of knowledge and the post-disciplinary mode has been uneven, contested, and is almost nowhere complete. Given that drug-using women typically occupy subordinate social locations, they are often passed over by feminist movements for health equity, reproductive rights, and sexual freedom due to the stigma and moralizing surrounding drug and alcohol use which exist in these movements.[7] We argue that the epistemologies of ignorance that persist within otherwise liberatory feminist movements can be remedied through an approach rooted in feminist knowledge produced on the basis of embodiment, generating a sense of agentic corporeality, and paying attention to lived realities that are structured by and through power differentials.

The need for feminist theory and research practice in the drugs field

Campbell (2000: 223) contends that feminist theory is a 'critical practice' capable of dislocating careless adherence to the governing mentalities embedded in prevailing patterns of thought, perception and practice in any policy domain. Feminist theorists are compelled 'to return to a set of normative commitments based on the recognition of social inequality, economic dislocation and political exclusion' (Campbell, 2000: 223). With these ideas in mind, we as feminist theorists want not only to create innovative ideas about women drug users but also to begin to transform formative notions concerning the 'social location' of women drug users (Figueroa and Harding, 2003: 31). Our theoretical work is aimed at creating a society that is more reflexive about difference and which acknowledges the multiple and intersecting marginalities inhabited by drug-using women.

We want especially to cast doubt on normative beliefs and practices based on wilful ignorance of these realities – we see these as shaped in both marginalized and privileged spaces – and we would like those who hold these normative beliefs about the limits of drug-using women's agentic corporeality and subjectivity to feel uncomfortable about adhering to them. We would further like to show how normative beliefs about drug-taking comprise an epistemology of ignorance similar to Charles W. Mills' sense of the racial contract operating as an agreement not to know, to '*mis*interpret the world' and yet act as if this misrecognition constitutes a true account (1997; see also Tuana, 2004; Tuana and Sullivan, 2007). The whole point of identifying how epistemologies of ignorance work within modes of knowledge is not only to make feminist observations and construct feminist theories, but also to begin to affect changes that actively address the social, structural, and cultural relations that continue to single out and stigmatize 'addiction'. Feminist theory can help shape effective 'cultures of action' within political movements (Klawiter, 2008: 44). We document how women's treatment advocates constitute an 'epistemic culture' that has struggled on the margins of the larger drug treatment infrastructure and the public policy framework and research apparatus that sustains it.

A major problem has been the ways in which education, research, and theorizing (including feminist theorizing) have been used as weapons of colonization (Humm, 1992; Rich, 1980) to reinforce the 'imperializing' trajectory of Western knowledge systems (Harding, 2006: 12; 2008: 153). In the dominant academic and governmental arena of the drugs field, feminism has never been taken as seriously as it should be, nor has it been considered a viable research concern or a realistic therapeutic option within the major treatment modalities. Perhaps an anecdote from one of our respondents can illustrate what we mean: after decades of emphasizing that confrontational style 'therapeutic communities' (TCs) can damage women who have been traumatized in their past or present lives, an agency providing women's treatment within the US criminal justice system was asked to implement a model based upon the TC modality. What does this type of wilful mishearing mean? Why do punitive, hurtful and confrontational 'therapies' continue to be advanced even where there has been active and vocal women's advocacy to draw attention to the misfit between dominant practices and women's needs? In our field, both biomedical and criminal justice models predominate; the masculinist focus of these models has been highly visible and extremely well defended, if not rigidly adhered to. Within this masculinist focus are embedded 'mis-beliefs' such as the notion that women's struggles for liberation and equality have enabled women's incorporation into majority culture such that they can now be ignored in their specificity. Such 'mis-recognitions' make it seem as if the need for women's liberation passed with the movements of the 1960s and 1970s. Usually those who hold these misinterpretations do not attempt to expand their ways of thinking to include women at the margins, including black and ethnic minority women, transgender and lesbian women, indigenous women, working-class women, disabled women, etcetera. It is our view that until social justice is attained for *all* women, both those at the centre and those on the margins, feminism will still be needed as a source of embodied, cultural, intellectual, and political resistance in order to challenge the overwhelmingly masculinist focus in the academic research and clinical practice arenas of the drug addiction field.

Gender – An essential (not essentializing) notion for understanding drug cultures

The long history of women's treatment has simply not been documented. Our first chapter tells the story of women's treatment in the post-World War II US – what we call 'proto-feminist' responses to the growing number of women and girls who showed up addicted to a variety of licit and illicit substances prior to the Second Wave feminist movement. Our second chapter takes up the early 'maternalist' programmes initiated by medical professionals in the midst of the women's movement of the 1970s. Despite some women's movement attention to women's alcohol and drug problems, Ettorre recalls that when she started working as a sociologist in the drugs field in the 1970s, women drug users were completely hidden from view (2007: 5–6). Indeed, when she was carrying out a study of all 30 of the Alcohol Treatment Units (ATUs) then operating in England (Ettorre, 1984, 1985a, 1985b, 1985c, 1988), she encountered only *one* woman patient in her research travels to all of these units. She recalls:

> I remember the experience vividly. I had been ushered in to meet with staff at a Northern ATU and through an observation mirror I could see a group session going on. There in a group of all male patients and a male therapist was a middle aged very slim woman slumped in a chair. She looked dejected and miserable. I was so excited to see my first woman patient that I needed to calm myself down and not overlook how miserable she looked.

Women drug users were marginalized and stigmatized, while being silenced and were the targets of social injustice. To mark International Women's Year, Orianna Josseau Kalant edited a now classic text, *Alcohol and Drug Problems in Women* (1975). In her Introduction, Kalant argued that research on women and substance misuse was a 'non-field', stating quite openly that the subjects of choice in addiction research areas were most frequently males, ranging from rats to college students (1980: 1). Her point was not to replace male with female rats or male with female college students in research designs, protocols or scientific investigations, but to emphasize how overlooked sex differences were apt to be. This was, as she said, extremely frustrating.

More than 30 years on, it is still extremely frustrating to note that in comparison to studies of men and drugs use, studies of women and drugs use remain relatively few (South and Teeman, 1999). Indeed, studies like Marsha Rosenbaum's classic *Women on Heroin* (1981) stand in 'splendid isolation' (Pearson, 1999: 482). Despite an increase in gender related or even gender specific research, women remain 'the second sex' in diagnostic definition, theory development, and clinical trial involvement (Stein and Cyr, 1997: 993). This empiricist and at times reductionist type of work is qualitatively different from in-depth, qualitative, exploratory studies of female drug users (see, for example, Friedman and Alicea, 2001) which display a sympathetic, if not empathetic, non-deterministic position. As we document, the federal funding apparatus in the US that evolved in the early to mid-1970s has funded research on women as well as services for them – but never to the extent that women needed. This can also be said for the UK.

The third chapter of this book looks closely at programmes that briefly but successfully overcame the long-established resistance to gender sensitive or feminist approaches by researchers and treatment providers in the drugs field. While most of these programmes are no longer in existence, a few of them are and we provide some examples of the kinds of changes they have had to make in order to survive into the present. While researchers accept gender as a quirky specialty in the drug world, it has been more difficult for the overall treatment infrastructure to acknowledge the centrality of gender in shaping the lives of women drug users that must therefore be taken into account by the form that treatment takes. In clinical research, gender tends to be a one-dimensional demographic or epidemiological concern, used as a basis for superficial counting exercises which are used to prove that treatment settings are 'gender sensitive'. Contemporary work that draws attention to the intricacies of gender (Raine, 2001) and underscores how within the gendered environment of drug use, women 'do drugs' differently from men (Measham, 2002) has been promising. Similarly, emergent treatment approaches that concentrate on creating a 'trauma-informed' treatment infrastructure have seemed promising in the US context, as does the UK focus on 'hidden harms' (i.e., child abuse, child neglect, domestic violence, etc.) associated with drug and alcohol abuse (Advisory Council on the Misuse of Drugs (ACMD) 2003, 2007a, 2007b; Stella Project 2002). However, such approaches typically take as paramount the goals of child welfare, as opposed to the needs of drug-using women. An interesting approach was initiated in London in 2003 when the Stella Project was created for survivors of domestic violence and abuse, their children and perpetrators of domestic violence affected by problematic substance use. Project workers decided to incorporate sexual violence into the scope of its work 'in recognition of the level of sexual violence experienced by ***women*** in particular who access drug and alcohol treatment services and in recognition of the research highlighting drug and alcohol use as coping mechanisms for experiences of trauma'.[8]

Access to drugs, knowledge of drugs, use of drugs, and help for misuse of drugs – all involve hidden and sometimes not so hidden gendered processes, including infringements upon women's dignity and human rights.[9] For example, Ettorre and Riska (1995, 2001; Riska and Ettorre, 1999), found that experiences of psychotropic drug use and misuse differed for men and women drug users. Psychotropic drug users contextualized their experiences in gendered ways that revealed how hidden gendered strategies, gendered expectations, gendered norms, gendered styles, and gendered rules of engagement exist in the drugs world and that these gender issues and dynamics are not easy to uncover. These gender issues are particularly difficult to discern in positivist empirical work emphasizing 'sex differences' and subscribing to dominant notions of women's biological vulnerabilities (Campbell, 2000) at the expense of understanding differences of social power and gendered social processes that organize women's lived experiences as well as knowledge production about these experiences. Similarly, robust findings on the gendered genetics of alcoholism have remained confined, and have not yet been meaningfully translated into treatment programmes. However, naturalistic explanations that rely *solely* on pharmacological or neurochemical aspects of drug use without acknowledging the impact of gendered understandings on drug use practices are becoming more visible.[10]

Many studies of drug cultures demonstrate that what is male or characterized as masculine takes priority over what is female or characterized as feminine (Perry, 1979). Power differentials and social hierarchies pervade drug-using cultures and treatment systems, most of which were designed originally for men and have been slow to change their methods to meet the needs of women – needs that have now been voiced but subordinated or deferred for nearly four decades. Undeniably, work carried out within the past decade accentuates the importance of gender sensitive and/or feminist perspectives for treatment and policy (Friedman and Alicea, 2001; Kandall, 1996; Klee, Jackson, and Lewis, 2001; Raine, 2001; Sterk, 1999) and developments on the level of theory (Boyd, 1999; Campbell, 1999, 2000; Denton and O'Malley, 1999; Evans, Forsyth, and Gauthier, 2002; Ettorre, 2007; Henderson, 1999; Hunt, Joe-Laidler, and Evans, 2002; Irwin, 1995; Measham, 2002; Murphy and Rosenbaum, 1999; Wright, 2002). Clearly if so many investigators find gender of pivotal importance to understanding drug cultures (Measham, 2002), and yet the wide-ranging significance of gender is still not taken into account in treatment, there would appear to be a gulf between knowledge and practice. There is also a significant disciplinary divide in which social scientists tend to be more attuned to gender than are so-called natural or neuroscientists, who are just beginning to acknowledge the importance of 'social factors' within their turn to 'epigenetics' as a promising form of knowledge for understanding how social factors influence patterns of drug use.[11]

Simultaneous modes of knowledge: The classical governing mentality and the emerging postclassical/epistemological mode

To characterize the two very different modes of knowledge through which we are 'gendering' addiction in this book, we must first note that these arise out of two different epistemological frameworks and yet are co-constitutive. We contended above that the postclassical mode is more gender sensitive and conducive to multiple feminist, emancipatory, and anti-oppressive stances, while the classical mode is rather obsolete and overly essentialist, both towards drug effects and populations of drug users. Let us now look critically and more closely at these two modes of knowledge, which are co-occurring rather than chronological epistemologies. Neither mode of knowledge or paradigm displaces the other, although the 'classical' is currently the more dominant in that it sets the parameters within which authoritative knowledge production about drug use and treatment takes place. In recent decades this dominance has been secured by the redefinition of addiction as a 'chronic, relapsing brain disease' and a concurrent emphasis on neuroscience as the form of knowledge highest on the hierarchy of credibility when it comes to drug addiction.

Naturalization of parameters set by the classical mode of knowledge

The classical governing mentalities define drug addiction as a 'chronic, relapsing brain disease' tractable to the tools, techniques, and practices of clinical diagnosis and epidemiology. Experts, whether researchers, policy makers, or clinicians, focus on how the disease of 'addiction' spreads, what causes it, its prognosis and what its health consequences might be. With some exceptions, these experts prefer individualistic, causal explanations of disease; their level of analysis tends to be on the 'sick', 'maladjusted', or 'bad' individual rather than on the communities and social and cultural geographies in which drug markets expand as other opportunities contract, in which the social practices of doing drugs structure the society in ways that drive out other activities or 'inclinations'. Often, universalizing statements reflect the view that drugs are inherently evil, their effects undermining individual health and leading to the disintegration of community and society (Coomber and South, 2004: 13–14). In particular, drug use is supposed to lead to or even to cause antisocial behaviour, if not serious crimes. Drugs are believed to make people do treacherous things which justify overwhelming, punitive responses from those in the criminal justice system. Furthermore, interventions in the criminal justice system in the UK have been more successful in attracting young, white male users, and there is a shortage of broader drug services for women serving custodial sentences (Becker and Duffy, 2002: 20). Recently, the UK National Treatment Agency for Substance Misuse noted that there has been a 'striking shortfall' of women in drug treatment programmes, a situation that has 'existed for some years' (NTA, 2010: 3).

Within the classical mode, stereotypes and myths based on exaggeration and distortion of the effects of drugs abound (Hammersley and Reid, 2002: 13). However, such myths can be viewed as 'socially functional' for a wide range of groups: 'illegal actors' such as those involved in the production and trafficking of controlled drugs have their prices go up; drug users themselves get convenient explanations for their drug use that become an everyday part of drugs folklore. Ex-drug users replace addiction to drugs with addiction to groups against drugs as they are seen to re-integrate into society (Hammersley and Reid, 2002: 14). Social institutions connected with police, the criminal justice system, customs and excise, the pharmaceutical business, the white, dominated male and mainstream press, and religious and moral groups benefit, as individualized and often psychopharmacological responses to drug use have become a veritable 'industry' and profitable enterprise in our neo-liberal societies. In this process, gender issues are made invisible, naturalized, or reduced to matters of brain structure and function in ways that further naturalize gender and sex differences (Reid and Hammersley, 2000: 171).[12]

Psychiatrists and other mental health specialists have had a major hand in confirming the set of assumptions underlying this idea of addiction and developing an epidemiological focus (Edwards, 1978) and, more recently, an ecological one (Edwards, 2004) that privileges disease and intervention systems, respectively. Their 'thank you theory' operates on the basis that when the patient is cured he or she will thank the therapist even though the patient was an unwilling participant (Bean, 2004: 231). In the UK, important players in the treatment, intervention, and prevention of drug use include general practitioners, specialist 'addiction' psychiatrists, professionals working within a health and welfare or criminal justice framework (Duke, 2009), and organizations from both the statutory and non-statutory sectors (Mold, 2008; Mold and Berridge, 2010). While the more recent inclusion of 'generalists' in the drug treatment framework can be considered innovative and a movement away from the strictly psychiatric approach that has predominated in the UK, there is a tension among treatment providers between the goal of total abstinence versus ongoing maintenance of drug use. This tension may be attributed to the shifting policy response from focusing on addictions, to public health concerns and diseases linked to injecting drug use to the current focus on problem drug users (PDUs) involved in criminal behaviour (MacGregor, 2010: 12). On the other hand, in the US, the 12-step recovery programme, which is abstinence based, is a good example of a dominant treatment modality that reinforces popular notions of drug addiction as a disease without really defining what kind of disease it is, an idea which upholds what we are calling the classical paradigm. Despite the focus on 'mutual aid' central to the recovery orientation, the target of intervention remains the individual whose drug use is the most prominent aspect of his/her identity. Similarly, the neuroscience paradigm emerging in the US illustrates addiction as a 'chronic, relapsing brain disease' in ways that use the tools and techniques of neuroscience but converge with the dominant mental health paradigm by lodging addiction within the brain (Campbell, 2007, 2010). In the UK, official discussions around 'marked tolerance to brain effects' (ACMD, 2000: xiv, 12–13) and the neurotoxicity of drug use (ACMD, 2005) help stabilize neuroscientific accounts as authoritative. Reflecting on the notion of addiction as a chronic relapsing disease in the UK context, Professor Cindy Fazey, the leading UK expert on international drug policy (and the first woman to do a PhD on drug use in the UK) noted:

> Chronic relapsing disease was what addiction was always called ... to say it's a brain disorder is going into the realms not only of psychopharmacology but biology ...I have seen it [chronic relapsing disease] written down many times ... that [has been] ... around I would say from the fifties.[13]

Within the classical mode of knowledge, grand theories or narratives such as the 'chronic, relapsing brain disease' explain the roots of drug use in neurochemical terms, but acknowledge that the 'disease' manifests as deviant social behaviour that stigmatizes and marginalizes users (van Wormer and Davis, 2003: 50). Undeniably, drug users are morally reprimanded and culturally disciplined for having a 'disease of addiction' that is somehow embedded in their brains and bodies (de Belleroche, 2002) or is perhaps stamped in their genetic code (Peters and Preedy, 2002). The target of intervention is the brain and the behaviour of the sick, maladjusted, misbehaving individual. Even if social and cultural factors are taken into account, these factors are presented in a deterministic way as a part of 'neurobiological fine tuning' (Hill, 2000: 461).

The classical mode of knowledge is driven by 'moral panics' and, in turn, spirals of 'deviance amplification'. As Stanley Cohen (1972) contends moral panics usually include deviance amplification spirals, which involve 'media hype' or an increasing cycle of coverage when reporting of antisocial behaviour or 'undesirable' events, such as drug use (Cohen, 1972). Interestingly enough, the concept of deviance amplification requires that actual levels of 'deviant activity' be measurable by the analyst in order to show that it has increased, a possibility which Richard Hammersley (2001) contests.

Such 'hegemonic' moral panics (McRobbie and Thorton, 1995) emerge from positions of privilege and are generated by the media to remind the entire population of drug users' deviance. 'Timewasters', 'slackers', or 'social malingerers' are thus separated out from the cultural mainstream occupied by 'productive citizens' whose neurochemistry has not gone awry or whose brains have not yet misfired. Whether or not 'wars on drugs' are media-stimulated, 'armistices' appear to redefine the boundaries of containment, surveillance, and control (Ben-Yehuda, 1994). 'Armistices' mean that another different group of drugs users may have their passports confiscated by the 'powers that be' or that punitive strategies are used to keep drugs users in line by arresting their treatment providers, as in the Wintercomfort case in Cambridge, England (Shapiro, 2000; Flemen, 2004).

Here in the classical mode of knowledge, drug use subsumes all other forms of difference and becomes the most salient dimension of identity. Expertise can thus be constituted without attention to 'intersectionality', despite the existence of practitioners of 'biographical medicine' (Armstrong, 1979) in the UK drugs field (Mold, 2008) who are supposed to have a holistic view of their patients. Indeed, issues such as race, ethnicity, class, gender, disability, and age tend to be dismissed or overlooked in the interest of maintaining the hegemony of the 'West over the rest' (Littlewood, 2002; Harding, 2006). Middle class, young, white, male, Western concerns take priority in this monolithic perspective (Coomber and South, 2004: 15). Few question the incarceration of women offenders, the grave impact that this has on poor black and ethnic minority women or that in the US the proportion of African-American females who were incarcerated was seven times higher than for white females

(Roberts, Jackson, and Carlton-Laney, 2000: 903). Additionally, there is no conception of disability beyond drug use – it is believed that drug use is a drug user's main disability and that this disability is self chosen and indicates moral failure despite higher rates of disability among the drug-using population (NTA, 2009a: 5). If you are a disabled person who cannot walk, see, or hear, you have an even more difficult time as a drug user (Li, Ford, and Moore, 2000), and are more likely to be or have been a victim of violence.

In the classical mode of knowledge, there continues to be a tendency to 'treat' single substances within a hierarchy of drugs, despite evidence that most substance abusers have relationships with multiple drugs (Ettorre, 1992). Abstinence (not harm reduction) is considered key to rehabilitation (Mertens and Weisner, 2001; Westermeyer and Boedicker, 2000). Prohibition is the ultimate goal as even small amounts of 'drug exposure' are understood to alter the brain. In this mode of knowledge, drug users appear to share political, social, and human 'rights' *only* if they stop using drugs: their 'welfare takes precedence over their wants' (Seedhouse, 1998: 192–3). Only ex-users have rights and even these rights are somewhat limited (Smart, 1984). Women users appear to have fewer rights than men, especially if they are expectant mothers (Daniels, 1996; Murphy and Rosenbaum, 1999). Here, the governing mentality or cultural production of ideas and images related to women's illegal drug use in the classical mode of knowledge is masculinist to its very core. A pervasive 'ideology of sacred maternity that sacralizes motherhood at the expense of women's subjectivity' (Klassen, 2001: 775) ultimately targets pregnant drugs users as archetypal 'bad mothers' (Gomez, 1997; Ladd-Taylor and Umansky, 1998; Woliver, 2002). While women's drug and alcohol use during pregnancy is far from new, since the 1980s efforts to criminalize women's behaviour during pregnancy have intensified, particularly in the US where treatment capacity for pregnant women lags far behind documented need. Criminalization has deterred pregnant women not only from seeking drug and alcohol treatment, but also from seeking prenatal care and other forms of basic maternal healthcare.[14]

The models of deviance and pathology that emerge from the classical mode of knowledge tend to silence individuals by focusing on pathologies or syndromes, and failing to take into account the important relationships between drug use and the broader social contexts in which it is embedded (Friedman and Alicea, 2001: 3). Gender sensitive theories that analyse difference, domination, and subversion as a way of looking at drug users' conditions and experiences challenge these obsolete models but are often nowhere to be found in this paradigm. Indeed the state of knowledge about gender and drugs to emerge from this paradigm was so under-developed that in 1974, when one of the earliest Women's Drug Research Projects in the US was funded at the University of Michigan in Ann Arbor, there were fewer than 20 articles on the topic.[15] Extant studies were marred by epistemological flaws in ways recounted by Beth Glover Reed:

> The only studies we found when we went looking said that women were more deviant than men, sicker than men, and less motivated to recover than men. Then we really went into those studies to ask why they were making these conclusions.... The 'more deviant than' was really tied to sexual abuse and questions they weren't asking the men. Women were telling them about sexual abuse because many of them were prostitutes to support their habits. Many of them had been raped or abused as kids. So these researchers, who had no feminist standard for this – and weren't asking these questions of the men and the men weren't volunteering that information – were then calling the women 'more deviant'. The 'not motivated' was that they didn't come into treatment and they didn't stay in treatment. When you look at it, there were no resources for women. People were stigmatizing them and the treatment didn't work for them. It wasn't helping them, it was harming them. The treatment was making them worse. I would say that was the state of the literature.[16]

Similarly, when UNESCO commissioned Fazey in 1976 to prepare a report and critically annotated bibliography on research into the aetiology of alcohol, nicotine, opiate, and other psychoactive substance use, she found that out of 2,144 references, only 51 referred specifically to women and only 1 in 42, or 4.2 per cent, focused on women (Fazey, 1977). Around the same time Gloria Litman, who worked at the Addiction Research Unit at the time, wrote a UK-based article asking what we really know about women and found that very little work mentioned 'the alcoholic woman' except as a side statistic (see Litman, 1975 and 1986).

This under-developed state of knowledge was due not only to the assumptions of the prevailing knowledge paradigms, but also to the type of social science then practiced. Prior to the emergence of the women's movement and women's and gender studies, its so-called intellectual arm – much of the literature emphasized gender roles and thus owed a good deal to the somewhat deterministic sociological paradigm of

Talcott Parsons, in which gender roles were naturalized, with women perceived as 'expressive' and men as 'instrumental'.[17] Thus, increased numbers of women in the workforce and in higher education placed a 'strain' upon women's roles – a 'strain' attributed to feminism itself. Women who turned to drugs or drinking to handle 'role strain' were thus 'treated' through the application of proper doses of femininity or maternalism – taught to better handle women's roles in a socially expected manner. After all, women and girls were seen as more apt to be relatively docile, to conform in general according to expectations, to be 'good' (Parsons, 1942: 605). The first generation of women's treatment programmes, created by pioneering women examined in the first chapter of this book, were based on ideas that women who were guided towards more appropriate and 'proper' discharge of gendered obligations within the parameters of prevailing forms of femininity would no longer need to turn to drugs or alcohol in order to manage role strain.

Soon after the first generation of women's treatment programmes came about, feminist activists embarked on a very different analysis of where women's drug and alcohol problems came from and how they should be treated. Attempts to bring intersectionality into view under the rubric of multiculturalism in the 1970s and 1980s and the clinical practice of 'cultural competence' evolving in the 1990s all contended with the above-noted tendencies towards amplifying women's deviance in the context of an assumed but unstated male norm. Attention to gender and to pregnancy, always closely linked in the drugs field, has simmered beneath the level of awareness for the past four decades. The women's movement was initially a catalyst for the development of comprehensive treatment services. The women's health movement mobilized women's physicians and also neonatologists to attend to drug-using women.

The stigmatized issues of alcoholism and illicit drug addiction mattered relatively little in the overall context of the women's health movement. However, attention to legal psychotropics among middle-class women became significant in both the US and the UK. Ruth Cooperstock, a Canadian medical sociologist and feminist who carried out pioneering work on psychotropic drug use (Cooperstock, 1978a, 1978b, 1979; Cooperstock and Lennard, 1979; Cooperstock and Sims, 1971; Cooperstock and Parnell, 1982), helped to bring the issue to attention within medical sociology and beyond. Cooperstock worked as a scientist in the Epidemiology and Social Policy Research Department of the Addiction Research Foundation (ARF) in Toronto. Professor Betsy Thom, Professor of Health Policy, School of Health and Social Sciences at Middlesex University in England, remembers working with her in the late 1970s:

> While I was [working] with Margo [Jeffries at Bedford College, London] Ruth Cooperstock visited ... I really liked Ruth ... she worked with me on a little thing that I was doing ... we published a paper together but it was her doing. She helped me a lot and that's how I got interested in women and psychotropic drug use ... I ... remember .... it was talking to her that gave me an interest in women's health ... in the addiction ... context because [of] her work on psychotropic drug use ... she wrote a number of very good papers ... I went ... and stayed with her in Toronto and ... we [my family] spent a week with her. I was working on this little paper that got published but it was exciting for me you know to work with her and to do this and she was very kind.[18]

In the UK, a visible, but brief drug-related moral panic was fuelled when in 1985 television journalists Nick Ross and Esther Rantzen of BBC 1's *Drugwatch* programme launched the 'Just Say No' campaign. Rantzen had earlier highlighted benzodiazepine use in the *That's Life* series of BBC 1 programmes in the early 1980s, resulting in publication of a popular book (Lacey and Woodward, 1984). At the same time, addiction to benzodiazepines and licit drugs came into public focus when women such as TRANX founder, Joan Jerome (1991)[19] and Shirley Trickett (1986), a State Registered Nurse (SRN) and founder of the tranquillizer support group, 'Come Off It' took the public stage. When BBC 1's *That's Life* programme mentioned TRANX in June 1983, thousands of calls were received by the organization (Jerome and Bilgorri, 1991: 98; Melville, 1984: 153). Women involved in the licit tranquillizer issue tended to make clear distinctions between 'iatrogenic' and 'self-induced' addictions: the former being their addiction to legitimately prescribed medications, and the latter being the addictions of 'those illicit, heroin, or "hard" drug addicts' (Jerome, 1991: 98).

Similarly, in the US a distinction was drawn between addiction to 'medical' and 'nonmedical' substances. In light of reports that benzodiazepines such as Valium might be 'addictive', David Herzberg (2009) argues, 'depression partisans' successfully countered the 'Valium panic' and paved the way for a triumphalist onslaught of public discourse on antidepressants that has prevailed since the early 1990s.[20] Herzberg demonstrates that panic over whether Valium might be addictive reinforced existing divisions between licit and illicit drugs in ways that rendered women active on the prescription psychotropics issue unlikely to become vocally critical of the 'War on (Illicit) Drugs'. Thus was attention to illicit drug-using women obscured *except* in the context of high public visibility during moral panics, such as the concern about 'heroin mothers' in the 1970s or the maternal crack-cocaine scare of the late 1980s and early 1990s (Campbell, 2000). This pattern fits overall historical trends. During periods when gendered 'deviance amplification' is spiralling, attention to women's drug consumption is negative and stigmatizing, often focusing on women's individual deficits as women and as mothers. Yet even in such typically punitive contexts, there sometimes emerge women's advocates who typically deploy what post-colonial theorist Gayatri Spivak has called 'strategic essentialism' to draw attention to the needs of under-served women.[21] Often turning to feminist empiricism in order to document their claims about the scope and extent of a particular drug problem, feminist scholars in this arena have been self-aware – and carefully post-positivist – about the limits of positivism for making knowledge claims about a group constituted through 'deviance' from social norms and gendered expectations. Simultaneously, women's advocates have sought to expand the available treatment capacity by documenting under-treatment and women's historical lack of access to treatment. While we found these attempts proved more sustainable in the US than in the UK, we wrote this book to help keep women on the drug treatment agenda even during periods when there are not intense 'moral panics' concerning drug-using women. We write in support of the creation of a sustainable women's treatment infrastructure in both countries.

Feminist denaturalization as a contending epistemological mode of knowledge

Alongside the classical mode of knowledge is what we can refer to as a feminist, postclassical, post-disciplinary, or post-positivist epistemological paradigm (Campbell, 1999, 2000; Coomber and South, 2004; Ettorre, 1992, 2007; Measham, 2002; Measham, Aldridge, and Parker, 2001; Monaghan, 2001; Murphy and Rosenbaum, 1999; Parker, Measham, and Aldridge, 1995; Parker, Williams and Aldridge, 2002; South, 1999; Waldorf, Murphy, and Reinarman, 1991). Within the postclassical mode of knowledge, more useful ideas arise for gender-specific drug treatment because there is explicit recognition that persistent social inequalities, such as race, ethnicity, class, gender, and sexuality, structure drug consumption cultures and thus should be addressed once women are in treatment contexts. Recognition of differences of social power and gendered, as well as gendering, processes are made. Simply, the importance of 'context' (Coomber and South, 2004) and 'social location' (Figueroa and Harding, 2003: 31) in producing and reproducing women's drug use are appreciated, and the feminist level of analysis is on the collective, cultural, and social rather than on the individual's 'deviant' brain, body, or behaviour. No one discipline dominates the epistemological paradigm: the quest for understanding appears inter-disciplinary and developing cultural and social awareness, as well as sustainable treatment and prevention programmes, are viewed as crucial routes to improved knowledge and treatment outcomes.

Most, if not all social scientists, anthropologists, and historians working within this mode of knowledge would agree that the social practices that unite people into a community are important within cultures of consumption centred on drug-taking (Douglas, 1987: 4). The importance of understanding drug-taking rituals tends to take precedence over using stereotypes and upholding social myths. Rituals are viewed as scripted performative moments and enactments of embodied identities (Langman, 2003: 225). As sociologist Randall Collins shows, '[B]odily experiences themselves differ depending on the social ritual in which those experiences are enacted' (2004: 304). He argues that the variety of 'undifferentiated arousal is very large, allowing for large range of social interpretation' that is in turn shaped by social interaction rituals that are then experienced as the 'bodily effects' of drugs. Drawing upon this insight, women drug users may share an enthusiasm for the acute effects of drugs (Erickson et al., 2000: 773). However, in these performative moments and enactments of their embodied identities, women drug users can be seen to enact pleasure side by side with negative emotions and 'dis-pleasure'. Thus, within this paradigm the material, gendered practices of drug taking may be experienced as ambivalent, but pleasure is taken into account (Valentine and Fraser, 2008). Also, intersectionality becomes discernible within this mode of knowledge as the importance of developing approaches based on social inequalities such as race, class, and gender are recognized and valued. Difference is treated as the foundation of exclusion and therefore privileged as a theoretical category, a site of political practice, and a location from which to make claims for the enactment of human rights that are not contingent on whether or not a user has stopped using drugs.

The postclassical mode of knowledge begins to deal with ethics and the basic human rights of drug users (Ettorre, 1992: 57). Moral panics are replaced by conscious awareness of the cyclic nature of 'drug eras' (Johnson and Manwar, 1991; Musto, 1999; Reinarman, 1994). Subsequent conceptual movements towards a more participatory and relational view of bearing witness to the social injustices that drug users face allow for the experience of drug use to be transformed into a testimonial to everyday discrimination. Here, the testimony of drug users is able to emerge as a dialogical form of address. Simply, this requires attentive and ethical forms of listening (Ahmed and Stacey, 2001: 6) if it is to be incorporated into the repertoires of those helping or treating drug users.

Moreover, this paradigm focuses on how drug use is shaped into a 'cultural problem' that reflects 'disreputable pleasures' (O'Malley and Valverde, 2004). Professional experts are needed as much as drug users themselves. Drug users are the 'lay' experts who have a voice because they experience drug use and the social practices and problems related to it. Drug users are also seen as the consumers of drugs that become intertwined with the cultures of everyday life (Ruggerio, 1999). Theorists critical of a 'War on Drugs' note that what was once a largely innocuous, consensual, consumer market has been transformed into what is routinely described in policy terms as a war zone (Pearson, 1999: 478).

Consumption cultures are poly-drug cultures where users may or may not consume their drugs of choice, but at the very least they consume a substance that makes them feel high or provides psychotropic effects. Howard J. Parker and Fiona Measham (1994) call this the 'pick 'n' mix' scene. In the postclassical mode of knowledge, proponents recognize that this realm of consumer culture in contemporary society is a site for the reproduction of social inequalities and a fortification of normativity. Consumption of drugs flourishes within a society 'addicted itself to the sorry tension between individual excess and social control' (Ferrel and Sanders, 1995: 313). These drug cultures have a particular impact on young people (Ettorre and Miles, 2001), given that their lives are all about occupying distinct social spaces in the routes of consumption, reproduction, and production, all of which are located in specific gender, sex, class, and race contexts (Griffin, 1997). Furthermore, the policing of drugs consumption and the role of schools in policing drugs impact on young people's perceptions of drug consumption as a risky business in an environment where the availability of drugs is a normal part of the 'leisure-pleasure landscape' (Parker, Measham, and Aldridge, 1995: 25).

Rather than employing the grand theories embedded in the classical paradigm, those writing within the postclassical mode of knowledge construct local and particular narratives of normalization with a reconsideration of the agentic subjects, objects, and authors of research. These narratives focus on consumers, survivors, or users with specific needs and demands that may conflict with local policies of containment and control, shaped by overarching national surveillance systems such as the police, Customs, 'community epidemiology', and social services. Community-based services within the context of multi-agency responses have become the order of the day in both the US and the UK (Teeman, South, and Henderson, 1999). Relevant government departments and local government take the lead in supporting drug misusers' re-integration into society in both the US and the UK (HMG, 2008: 31).[22] The local emphasis enabled the development of Afrocentric treatment principles (Roberts, Jackson, and Carlton-Laney, 2000: 903); treatment sensitive to indigenous people (Segal, 2001); or holistic approaches which address womens' relationship dynamics, communication skills, assertiveness, and vocational skills (Sterk, Elifson, and Theall, 2002). Elements of 'cultural competence' are also central to the evolution of women's treatment in the US, although the emphasis on local responsibility has made women's access to and content of care highly variable from state to state. Although the federal agency the Substance Abuse and Mental Health Services Administration (SAMHSA) can refer individuals to community-based treatment, its main responsibility is to administer the state funding scheme, the Substance Abuse Prevention and Treatment Block Grant programme. SAMHSA has adopted the tenets of the classical paradigm and sought to infuse the states with Evidence-Based practices (EBPs) based upon it.[23] The National Treatment Agency for Substance Misuse (NTA) in the UK has adopted the same tenets and upholds the suite of guidance on clinical practice with drug users from the National Institute for Health and Clinical Excellence (NICE), the heart of EBP in the UK.

Within this mode of knowledge, drug users may be transgressors but only in so far as their 'rule breaking' is part and parcel of being poor, unemployed, homeless, disabled, victims, and/or perpetrators of violence. Thus, social exclusion is viewed as a key factor in shaping the transgression of drug use (Pearson, 1999). In this paradigm, safer sex and harm minimization strategies are more than catchwords – they are practices that self-aware users will exploit with their significant others, within their peer groups, and/or in public, rave, dance, or consumer settings.

For us, the postclassical mode of knowledge appears as the most responsive to social inequalities because of its fluid, discursive methods and the expansive scope granted to all things social and cultural. Within this paradigm, there are recognizable 'bio-struggles' in which individuals such as drug users attempt to break from the clutch of governing mentalities and disciplinary powers vis-à-vis drug use. These pharmacologically and biologically mediated struggles unleash the development of new bodies and pleasures which have the potential to undermine the construction of normalized subjects (Best and Kellner, 1991: 58). Regardless of this radical deployment of bodies, a postclassical mode of knowledge should include within its epistemological focus a vision of the future which does not: (1) deconstruct or debase gender as an issue (Maynard, 1994: 19), nor (2) deny that 'subjugated knowledges' can be an important part of transforming our social worlds (Harding, 1987: 188–9).

The two modes of knowledge we have described co-exist in the drugs field today. At times, the differences between them may not appear in such a sharp contrast. However, general tendencies do appear, as each represents a general body of thinking or epistemological system that has emerged over the years. Sometimes, they overlap, sometimes they diverge, and sometimes they even contradict each other. No doubt different epistemologies of ignorance can be seen to structure each one. Nevertheless, our contention is that the postclassical/epistemological mode of knowledge is more humane than the classical given that the voices of drugs users are heard rather than stifled; social inequalities and power differentials are more readily acknowledged as having effects on *who* drug-using women are than passed over or disavowed. Difference is able to become a clear theoretical category as well as a site of resistance. We build upon Campbell's work in *Using Women* (2000) and Ettorre's work in *Re-visioning Women's Drug Use* (2007) to develop an anti-oppressive and anti-essentialist stance from within a postclassical paradigm in which gender is conceptually central, and drug use and treatment are understood from a feminist embodiment approach.

Embodiment: Upholding corporeality and inscribing gender

Social behaviour at all times manifests through the fleshy human form; thus society is shaped by the body as a means of expressing who we are and who we ought to become. How drug-using bodies move in societies is shaped by complex cultural and social values, norms, and practices, including those of law, medicine, and policy. This drug-using, fleshy, material, human body provides the focus for regulatory techniques carried out on individuals within the material conditions that shape the possibilities they face as political subjects. In our analysis of women, drugs use, and drug treatment, we place the body at the core of a political struggle (Turner, 1996: 67). Bodies need to be seen as sites where the epistemologies of ignorance, knowledge of drugs, women's use, femininity, negative stereotypes, reproductive functions, discourses of risk, administration practices, physiological and pharmacological responses, treatment regimes, and affect converge and not as gender neutral, non-finite deterministic structures. One problem to be overcome by our work is that drug addiction is thought of as an individual pathology that renders bodies and brains 'deviant' or 'sick'. The individualization of the problem obscures how gendered performances and socially situated ideas about appropriate kinds and levels of treatment are 'embodied processes'. Thus, this work is simultaneously about the need for a renaissance of the body in our knowledge work and the restoration of 'epistemological' existence to our abandoned corporeal frames. Our work is about upholding corporeality – making the firm contention that the body exists and should be lodged centrally in the drugs arena and drugs discourse, and yet 'denaturalizing' the body and seeing it as an effect of knowledge production practices.

The move towards 'denaturalization' undercuts current tendencies to centre a decontextualized brain abstracted from the body exemplified by the 'Keep Your Brain Healthy' (Don't Use Drugs) campaign mounted in the US by the National Institute on Drug Abuse (NIDA) in 2000. This has been typified by the UK government's national anti-drug campaign, Talk to FRANK, which in 2004 mounted the 'Brain Warehouse' TV advertisement. This public service advertisement focused on a warehouse full of brains with eager customers; the catchphrase was, 'The more you mess with cannabis, the more you mess with your mind', implying that drugs damage your brain (see Home Office website www.homeoffice.gov.uk/drugs/). In scientific contexts dominated by neuroscience, there is no such thing as a robust social construct of gender or the significance of culture. Rather the documentation of sex differences in neurochemistry and neural organization takes place at a significant distance from 'the body'. In such contexts, the work we are trying to do in order to reclaim the centrality of the body – while simultaneously refusing to essentialize the body – takes a step towards understanding why the drugs field has traditionally been so gender insensitive, as we document in the pages of this book.

For us as feminists, bodies do matter and we are aware how gendering and racializing are deeply related to one's assimilation or manipulation of social location within a neo-liberal, global order. Recognizing that bodies of female and/or BME (Black and Minority Ethnic, as people of African and Asian descent are called in the UK) drug users do matter in this assimilation or manipulation is about recognizing that beliefs in, discourses about, and tools of modern technologies impose and embody novel social relations for these marginalized groups on a global scale. Most importantly, the drug field cannot escape this type of coding, that is to say, technologies and scientific discourses about drugs and drug use can be tools for imposing compulsory meanings and the continued exploitation on the basis of race, gender, ethnicity, and class. While drug users will be pressed into constant normativity, those with the ability to read 'webs of power' may champion their own survival and social justice, and exhibit forms of 'resistance consciousness'. But we are a long way from this type of liberatory situation for drug users, as we must first understand why negative stereotypes of women users have been consistently maintained as the basis for 'justifying' policy interventions that neglect the role of gender and racial-ethnic formation in structuring drug use, drug treatment, and drug research.

We challenge traditional views of addiction vis-à-vis women, while at the same time contesting the 'epistemology of ignorance' which prevails in this field to such an extent that multiple attempts to 'gender addiction' have gained so little traction over the past few decades that they are rarely sustainable. In effect, we have exposed the need for feminist theory and practice in the field and argued why gender sensitivity is important. We also propose that in comparison to the classical mode of knowledge, the postclassical mode of knowledge includes more useful ideas that arise for gender-specific drug treatment. This is because the postclassical paradigm deals more effectively with relentless social inequalities which at time appear as 'abject difference'. As we privilege difference, we privilege all types of drug users, both women and men, who are entitled to be equally unlike, different or dissimilar from the embodied norms of white, male, heterosexual, able, Western bodies typically assumed to be 'addicts'. In the postclassical epistemological mode, difference is imperative and far too important to be left solely to neuroscientists. Given the 'conceptual acrobatics' (Reinarman, 2005) which exist in the drugs field, we need to make 'addiction specialists', both researchers and clinicians alike, feel uncomfortable when they reject the kinds of difference-centred or feminist, embodiment, agentic approach we propose. The UK coalition government has stated a key research priority as 'to further strengthen our knowledge of drug use and needs among a number of groups, including young people, BME groups, families, and drug-using offenders' (HMG, 2010: 13). Yet embodiment and social factors tend to get lost in this 'policy speak', which governs the drug and alcohol research and treatment domains. We wrote this book to keep concrete attention to 'embodiment' alive in our neurochemical era and to counter the abstract relocation of 'addiction' to 'the brain'.

Part I
Reinventing the Wheel

1

Getting Gender on the Agenda: A History of Pioneers in Drug Treatment for Women in the United States and the United Kingdom

Drug and alcohol treatment have long challenged the public health infrastructures designed to deliver them. This chapter unfolds a proto-feminist history of treatment and research programmes focused on women that evolved in the mid-twentieth century. The chapter covers the history of how the treatment of women's drug and alcohol use were spoken about prior to the rise of a feminist social movement specifically centred on women's health and body politics.

Paternalism: Pervasive in early treatment programmes for women in the United States

The early 1950s brought warnings of a 'frightening wave' of addiction engulfing thousands of boys and girls in New York City and state.[1] The common explanation for women's lower drug use relative to men's advanced in *The Road to H* (1964), the classic social psychiatric study of heroin use in the period, was that 'females are less likely than males to express their tensions in ways that are detectably and flagrantly violative of prevailing social codes' (Chein et al., 1964: 300). While the press deployed the lurid vocabulary of 'moral panic' and played up the novel aspects of the post-war 'epidemic', professionals referred to it as the 'second peak of an old problem'.[2] Child psychiatrist Lauretta Bender, head of the Bellevue Hospital Psychiatric Division from 1934 to 1956, argued that focusing on adolescent addiction deflected from children's real problems: 'gross social neglect', family breakdown, lack of resources, and the 'boredom, neglect, and social malaise that characterizes our age' (Bender, 1963: 192). Noting the paucity of research on female adolescent addicts, Bender cited Dorris Clarke, Chief Probation Officer of the New York City Magistrate Court, who had taken up the 'question of the girl' at a conference (New York Academy of Medicine, 1951). Clarke was convinced that girls were initiating drug use at rates higher than their male counterparts: 'There is absolutely no question but that more and more females are turning to the use of drugs and more and more females are going into prostitution to support their drug habit.... We have to give serious consideration to the fact that more and more of our girls, *in contrast to our boys*, are turning to the use of narcotics' (New York Academy of Medicine, 1951: 139). Although no data to this effect was documented, Bender noted that female arrestees indicated that many girls who used narcotics were not caught and cited the greater number of narcotic cases heard in the Women's Court and the Girl's Term Court since 1950. For those dealing directly with girls, it was clear as early as 1951 that the New York City and state treatment facilities for addicted women and girls were insufficient.

That spring New York state prisons and reformatories that housed girls undertook a survey to identify narcotics users among the incarcerated population. Out of more than 300 girls in New York State prisons and reformatories, 65 girls were identified as narcotics users, segregated, and subjected to a psychiatric and sociological treatment regimen that included occupational therapy and aftercare at the Westfield State Farm. The Westfield experiment replied to the odd fact that the New York state drug problem was framed from the outset as one of addicted adolescent females. New York State Attorney General Nathaniel Goldstein stated his suspicion that 'right here in New York City was a great incidence of narcotic addiction, especially among girls' (American Bar Association (ABA), 1957). A month later he dispatched Eleanor Uris, an assistant attorney general and former public schoolteacher in the New York City schools, for a month-long information-gathering trip to the Women's Prison and Reformatory at Westfield State Farm in Bedford Hills, Westchester County, New York.[3] Goldstein had visited the site, finding four unoccupied brick buildings that could be used to 'segregate the drug addicts at Westfield State Farm from the other inmates, a step which I believe to be most advisable. The mingling of addicts and non-addicts in the institution serves to arouse the curiosity of non-addicts, so at the first opportunity they use drugs. The proof of this is the fact that several of the girls who were non-users, were returned to the institution as parole violators for the use of drugs while on parole' (New York State Narcotics Investigation, 1951–2: 476–7).[4]

The Westfield Farm experiment enabled New York State to do pioneering work in establishing the first *state* institution dedicated to the treatment and rehabilitation of drug addicts, among whom, Goldstein warned, 'we find so large a proportion of teenagers'. When Uris went to Westfield to gather tape-recorded testimony crucial for the hearings in the summer of 1951, she interviewed all 65 women categorized as 'drug addicts' there. She also found a 'relatively constant' population of ten or so infants. Of the women, slightly more than half were ages 16–20, and most were there for status offences and minor crimes. Uris interviewed a 25-year-old musician who was a recent graduate of Oberlin College, describing her as a 'cultured intelligent girl who is a college graduate and a talented musical arranger and composer', who had also twice enlisted in the Army (in which drugs were available through medical kits). She had been prescribed Demerol at age 20 for a kidney ailment and bladder infection. At the height of her addiction, she was paying more than $200/week for drugs on the streets of New York and Cleveland. Shortly after her six-week stint at the federal narcotic hospital in Lexington, Kentucky, she had returned to New York City and resumed prostitution, which led to her arrest in January 1951. Another interviewee, a 19-year-old ex-model, also associated with musicians out of her 'craving for excitement' (451). A 17-year-old girl related her opinion that, 'Many young addicts would turn themselves in for help if they were treated as being ill rather than being criminals' (468). Her sentiments were echoed by many young addicts – a number of female witnesses in the 1955–6 federal hearings on the 'Illicit Narcotics Traffic', criticized the lack of treatment available to women in prison (Campbell, 2000).

In retrospect, the New York State Attorney General admitted that the Westfield experiment failed to end the girls' addiction, a failure that he attributed to the 'ancient vintage' of the drug problem, which he felt could not be cured 'overnight'. Westfield superintendent Henrietta Additon noted that segregation had been incomplete: the 'drug girls' had been housed where they could evoke the 'curiosity and interest of the non-drug girls' (ABA, 1957: 80). Some used the experiment's failure to proclaim the inevitable failure of treatment, but Additon felt it simply did not go to the heart of the matter, which was the drug-using girls' desire to get others to use drugs in order to 'build up their belief in themselves' and allay their 'despondency and fear' (ABA, 1957: 91–2). Most of the 'drug girls' came from poor Puerto-Rican communities, lacked vocational training, and had learnt the habit from their boyfriends. Additon also blamed unstable, working-class family configurations for providing 'no real family life or supervision' because all members were 'working outside the home' (ABA, 1957: 93). Such condemnation of working-class life within urban ethnic enclaves was typical of the social science of the time.

Unsettled was the question of criminalization, decried by many public officials who dealt closely with addicts. Judge Anna Kross, Commissioner of Correction for the City of New York, noted a high number of female addicts among prisoners in the Women's House of Detention. 'During my twenty years on the bench [1933–54], I gradually saw this constant growing, continuous growing, increase of narcotics as far as women were concerned' (ABA, 1957: 418). Rates of addiction among this population were now as high as 50–60 per cent: 'They spread everything. I have made no bones about it', she said, extending this contagiousness to prison life itself making 'better criminals out of them at all levels' (ABA, 1957: 419). She concurred with a controversial report of the New York Academy of Medicine, which had in 1955 argued that addicts were 'sick' persons, rather than criminals, who should be maintained through a system of low-cost clinics managed by the federal government. For Kross, addicted women were 'sick people' who became criminals 'because of the inadequate way in which they are treated' (ABA, 1957: 419).

Others argued that there should be no dichotomy between punishment, treatment and rehabilitation: 'Punishment is a normal process in the State's structure, and there is no reason it can't be done in a rehabilitative way, the same way as when a parent punishes a child' (ABA, 1957: 682). Despite its punitive elements, parole could be used to promote 'health and normal social living' by getting parolees 'emotionally attached' to 'values the community considers acceptable' (ABA, 1957: 694). Drug users must convert their 'undisciplined lives,' according to probation officer Arch Sayler, to 'clean, honest, temperate and industrious lives' (ABA, 1957: 855). The rehabilitative aspects of social discipline were considered capable of combating the 'self-indulgence' embodied by drug addicts of all genders, but this project assumed a perniciously gendered form in cases where addicts were responsible for dependent children. Paternalism was pervasive in these days before the women's movement.

'Spare us the pregnant ladies': Early mentions of pregnant drug users

In a rare mention of children born to drug-addicted women during the 1950s, John Stanton, Chief of the Narcotic Bureau in the City of Buffalo, noted that the 'out-of-wedlock' children born of 'mothers having the habit' were causing 'not only a police problem but a welfare problem' (ABA, 1957: 971). The 'welfare problem' was not new – for at least the past decade, it had been acutely felt at the federal narcotic farm in

Lexington, Kentucky, one of the only places in the entire country that accepted addicted women for treatment and rehabilitation. Within two years of opening its doors to women in 1941, the institution faced overcrowding in the women's quarters, despite the prevailing assumption at the time that male relatives protected their mothers, wives, and sisters from coming to the attention of authorities. According to a letter of 8 July 1941 from Justin K. Fuller, of the Federal Bureau of Prisons, the women's annex opened to 'fill a long felt need presented by a considerable group of female volunteers and probationary addicts who largely through the protection given them by relatives have not come into direct conflict with the law in such a way as to merit sentenced incarceration'. Although Lexington's population of women rarely exceeded 300, there were constant complaints about the lack of capacity from administrators. Additionally, women presented special 'complications' that led administrators to cast them as distinctly troublesome and undesirable patient/inmates.

Throughout the 1940s, James Lowry, Chief Medical Officer at Lexington, complained bitterly to his superiors in Washington about the problems women presented the institution. On 16 October 1946, he wrote a letter strongly urging all female offenders be sent to Alderson, the women's prison in West Virginia, because it was better equipped for dealing with them. In a memo sent to all US Marshals on 8 June 1948, James V. Bennett, head of the Federal Bureau of Prisons and one of the chief architects of the narcotic farms, stated that authorities should stop sending women to them. This, apparently, did not happen, as Lowry continued to complain about the administrative headaches presented by pregnant women. On 28 December 1954, he wrote a letter begging the Director of Prisons to make him a happier man in the new year by: '(1) not sending unsuitables [poor candidates for treatment]; (2) keeping the number of informers to a minimum; and (3) by sparing us the pregnant ladies'. Many 'pregnant ladies and babies' were sent to Lexington within days or weeks of delivery. Delivery was costly, as Lexington had no obstetrical facilities or nurseries (although it boasted a full surgical suite and offered otherwise comprehensive healthcare services). Delivery elsewhere was costly even if no complications arose, 'but they do', continued Lowry. 'What really gives us trouble is getting an agency from whence the lady came to accept the baby ... most of the babies stay here for months. (We have a charming Negro baby, age 2 months now, that is looking for a good home if you know of one.)' With this sarcastic comment, this letter closed, but the issue was far from over. In the early 1950s Lexington was overrun by a series of demographic shifts that fundamentally changed the institution's character. These are often spoken of in terms of racial-ethnic shifts and the precipitous decline of the median age of admission from men in their high thirties to their early twenties or teens, but it was also the case that more women and girls comprised the ranks of those addicted to opiates. Addicted women were portrayed as more desperate and furtive than their male counterparts, hiding a secret vice beneath the trappings of domesticity and femininity. Although their number appeared small, an important demographic shift was underway. Prior to World War II, most addicted women had been white, middle-class, and native-born, whereas post-war addicts were younger, poorer, more 'delinquent', and more likely to be women of colour (Pescor, 1944). Addicted white women in the New York City House of Detention outnumbered women of colour 4:1 before World War II, but the ratio was reversed by the late 1950s, a rapid transformation that became more robust over time (Brummit, 1963).

While it was typical for the time for the babies of drug-using women to be removed from their mothers and put up for adoption in the jurisdiction from whence the mothers had come, it is also evident that there were some infants and young children with their mothers at Lexington. In early 1955, Lowry again wrote to Bennett about the underlying economics of the problem: 'The pregnant ladies are a problem since there are too few babies to justify an obstetric and nursery service and there are too many for our funds for consultation, etc., to support during deliveries and hospital care in town' and suggested that judges be instructed to delay sentencing until after delivery, as 'placement of the babies would certainly be easier if the woman had her baby in her home town'.[5] For the next few years, Bennett issued annual memos to federal marshals recommending that 'female inmates who are pregnant, informers, large-scale traffickers, those with custodial or disciplinary problems, or those previously declared unsuitable for treatment NOT be sent to Lexington'.[6] Given this list it is easy to see how closely female addicts were associated with the most deviant of addicted persons.

Like most of his contemporaries, however, Lowry held inconsistent views. On 2 June 1955, he testified in New York City in federal hearings on the 'Illicit Narcotics Traffic'. Contrary to his lamentations concerning pregnant addicts, Lowry asserted that male addicts lost their male functions and female addicts became 'sterile and unable to have any children', maintaining that addicts became abnormal in their sexual and reproductive functions and used drugs to satisfy their needs for 'sensations akin to sexual orgasm'. Addicts, according to Lowry, sought in drug effects something others found in 'normal' sexual and reproductive roles. The addict could not occupy familiar gender roles because addicts had 'lower resistance than normal to the disagreeable aspects of living and a higher than normal resistance to pleasure. Little things annoy this individual. He becomes almost hysterical at some incident that would not even disturb a normal person, and he does not enjoy simple pleasures' (1955). Addiction appeared to be a male pathology borne of dissatisfaction with normalcy: 'addicts don't want to be normal; they want to be what they call high.... It is not enough for him to be normal' (1955). Such ideas do not transpose easily onto the task of making sense of women's drug problems; Campbell (2000) investigated the cultural illogic involved in these early state and federal responses to women's addiction. What was known about the treatment of women's drug problems obscured the realities confronted by drug-using women. Covering over women's realities, including structural and domestic violence, mental illness, trauma, stigmatization, and marginalization – neither the therapeutic practices nor the early knowledge base accommodated or accounted for women and girls using drugs or alcohol except as flagrant violations of their feminine roles.

United States pioneers in women's drug and alcohol treatment

Treatment and research on women's relationships to alcohol and drugs was slow to start prior to the emergence of the Second Wave feminist movement – despite some glimmers of early recognition. The experiences of two US women who pioneered work on women in the alcohol field illustrate how slow the uptake was in absence of an organized movement. Edith Gomberg was a clinical psychologist in the Connecticut state system who began researching and writing about women alcoholics in the mid-1950s.[7] Sheila Blume was a physician who had benefited from the 5 per cent women's quota that enabled her admission to the Harvard Medical School Class of 1958. She spent most of her career working in New York State, which developed targeted women's programmes as early as the 1950s. However, such programmes were set up along masculinist lines with little or no exploration of what drug-using women might need from their own perspective or from a knowledge based developed about them. Women's advocates had to work very hard to gain treatment programmes that took seriously women's gendered roles in social reproduction, and much of that work did not come until the Second Wave women's movement in the mid-1970s. Given that context, it is all the more remarkable that the women profiled in this chapter – Gomberg and Blume in the US, and Dorothy Black in the UK – accomplished much of their pioneering work in the area during the decades preceding the emergence of that movement. While they are now recognized as feminist foremothers, they worked to draw attention to women's issues without the benefit of the collective actions and infrastructures described in the next chapter.

'Why bother'? The response of treatment professionals to women alcoholics

Becoming a physician at a time when women were still formally excluded from medicine, Blume was trained as a paediatrician. Her interest in the treatment of alcoholism, drug addiction, and gambling addiction drew her towards psychiatry. In 1962 Blume took a job at the Central Islip State Hospital, a 10,000-bed state mental facility on Long Island. Earlier that that year, New York State had started the first inpatient alcohol rehabilitation programme at Central Islip, which also housed the first inpatient alcohol detoxification unit in the state hospital system. In her oral history interview with *Addiction* (2006), Blume related how she had attempted to treat an alcoholic mother of six at the start of her career:

> The alcoholic woman was the real challenge. She was desperate to stop drinking. There was nothing therapeutic in the hospital for her except that it protected her from access to alcohol. She had only our sessions together. So she and I set out like two babes in the woods to try to figure out what to do. After a couple of weeks, I went to the chief of service and said I needed some help, and he started me on my career with his two-word answer, 'Why bother?'.
>
> (Blume, 2006: 34).

In 1962, before the women's health movement and activism around patients' rights changed doctor-patient relations, this is a remarkable story in which a female physician and her patient embarked on finding some form of treatment that would work. Blume learnt with and from her patients, also crediting Marty Mann's book, *The New Primer on Alcoholism* (1968).[8] The patient needs to which Blume was responding seemed genuine, leading her to persuade the hospital to allow women to attend meetings of Alcoholics Anonymous (AA), which had formerly been for men only. There were very few if any alcohol treatment programmes for women. In 1966 Blume was offered a job directing the alcohol unit at Central Islip (The Bowery was included in the catchment area for this hospital so there was a substantial patient base). She accepted the job on condition that she be allowed to develop the first women's unit in the state of New York, which she did with federal aid from the National Institutes of Mental Health, at the time the federal agency responsible for drug and alcohol treatment. Blume worked to integrate the sex-segregated facilities at Central Islip. In her eyes, women had to fight their way into detox, treatment, and AA programmes, all of which had been set up for men as if women alcoholics did not exist.

> I was always interested in women because their problems were routinely overlooked. Research would discuss this and that in alcoholics but the studies were only conducted in the male population. Sometimes they did not even mention the sex of the subjects – it was just assumed to be male. From these studies, broad generalizations about alcohol were made and women were left out. All the treatments were developed based on men, and women were squeezed into the mold.
>
> (Blume, 2006: 35)

While such laments became common during the Second Wave women's movement, they were not common in the mid-1960s. Running a detox unit, a rehab unit, and a 'quarter-way house', Blume started a day hospital, assuming that its main appeal would be to male '"down and outers" – people who were no longer employable but who were motivated to stay sober'. To her surprise, although 'male old-timers' showed up for the van in The Bowery, and came out to spend the day at the hospital, one of the main groups to benefit was housewives with children who could not come to an inpatient rehabilitation programme due to gender constraints. 'They just loved coming to the day hospital, never missed a day, and most got well' (Blume, 2006: 34).

Going on to become the president of the American Society of Addiction Medicine (ASAM) and the New York State Commissioner for the Division of Alcoholism and Alcohol Abuse from 1979–1983, Blume continued to advocate for women (1981a; 1981b). Ironically given its role as a bellwether state in the treatment of addiction, New York State was one of the last states to comply with the federal mandate to merge alcohol and drug programmes into a single state agency; when Blume was commissioner, there was a separate state agency concerned with 'narcotic drugs' and the merger did not happen until the 1990s. As commissioner, Blume worked to reduce women's barriers to treatment.

For instance, she personally found it problematic that the State of New York considered habitual drinking or drug-taking de facto evidence of child neglect and felt it should not be the basis for revocation of parental rights in absence of specific evidence of neglect. Because fear that their parental rights will be terminated if they seek treatment has been one of women's main barriers to treatment, Blume personally crusaded to change the law in New York state so that specific evidence of neglect had to be presented. This became a model law that was supported by organizations such as Children of Alcoholics. She also worked to ensure that warning labels appeared on alcoholic beverage containers so as to raise consumer awareness of the dangers of drinking during pregnancy.[9] Throughout her career, Blume saw connections and overlaps between women's alcoholism, pathological gambling, chemical dependency, and eating disorders – most importantly, the consideration that gendered expectations of caring for others might play a role in precipitating or sustaining women's addictions.

'Poor patients': Unworthy women, gender, and alcohol

A clinical psychologist by training, Edith [Lisansky] Gomberg grew up in Brooklyn, New York, as Edith Silverglied. She interned in the New York State hospital system, at Rockland State in Orange County, although much of her early work on alcoholism took place in the Connecticut state system. Gomberg did her doctoral work at Yale from 1943 to 1949. She worked as a clinical psychologist at the Yale Plan Clinic and the Connecticut Commission on Alcoholism Clinics in New Haven, Hartford, Waterbury, Bridgeport, and Stamford. Her work with the state of Connecticut was not yet focused on women, although there is archival evidence that she noticed the lack of treatment capacity for women alcoholics. After she married and moved to Hartford, Connecticut, she took a state job as a way to retain her connection to alcohol research.

Gomberg conducted her initial work on women and alcohol as a research assistant and lecturer at the Yale University Center of Alcoholism Studies. In a chapter titled, 'The Clinical Psychologist in a Clinic for Alcoholics' (1954), she wrote about the emergence, in the past decade, of clinics operating as part of a 'new public health approach towards the problem of alcoholism'. A new, state government-sponsored programme funded by a percentage of revenue from state liquor licenses, the Connecticut Commission on Alcoholism was set up by the Connecticut state legislature in recognition of the fact that alcoholism was 'an illness and a public health problem. It was the first time a major government agency approached the problem of alcoholism with a broad rehabilitation program' (Lisansky, 1954: 210). She surveyed eight Connecticut clinics, in which psychologists mainly performed diagnostic testing (using Rorschach, Wechsler-Bellevue, and Sentence Completion tests), conducted therapy and did research. In this chapter, Lisansky made no mention of gender or sex roles but did document what was essentially a harm reduction approach to alcoholism (Room, 2004).

Soon after, Lisansky was awarded an Elizabeth Avery Colton fellowship from the American Association of University Women to study alcoholism in women. This study resulted in her first publication on women in 1957, titled 'Alcoholism in Women: Social and Psychological Concomitants', an article she would reference throughout her career as her first findings in women.[10] 'The research problem of sex differences in psychopathology is a neglected one' (Lisansky, 1957: 588). Continuing to write on the theme of neglect, her writings can be used to document how pervasive was the 'epistemology of ignorance' at the time. Following these early publications, Gomberg developed an interest in the aetiology of alcoholism and increasingly published on alcoholism in women (1979). She joined the faculty of the University of Michigan in 1975. Her involvement with federal alcohol research increased after the formation of the National Institute on Alcohol Abuse and Alcoholism (NIAAA) in 1970, and she testified before Congress on the need for further research on the social aspects of alcohol in the early 1980s. To Gomberg, 'gender' translated into the socially determined 'double standards' for men's and women's drinking and drug-taking, with greater social sanction or tolerance directed towards women's 'medicinal' use of psychoactive substances (Gomberg, 1982). Undoubtedly the women's liberation movement propelled her career, although she, as an older woman than many, had an ambivalent response to the movement. In 'Femininity and Women's Alcohol Abuse', a paper Gomberg presented at the 92nd American Psychological Association meeting in Toronto, she argued that the focus on the male has a rational footing in alcohol studies because 'there is no society we know of where women drink more alcoholic beverages than men do' (1984: 1). She noted shifts over time in terms of whether women had social sanction to drink, locating that within her awareness of the feminist historical literature on the 'cult of true womanhood', and her pointed critique of 'class bias, a view of womanhood as seen from middle class America' (1984: 2). In this paper Gomberg was evidently defending against feminist charges that her work was less concerned with privilege or power than it should have been, while also displaying her own views that in the early days of the feminist movement, there was a naïve assumption that the 'traditional female role and the assigned tasks of wife/housewife/mother produce frustration and depression' (1984: 4), which ultimately translated into women becoming 'hidden', 'invisible', or 'closeted' alcoholics. This naivety, according to Gomberg, arose from 'feminists' considering fulfilment to reside only in 'self-actualizing work', and not realizing that 'a very large proportion of women are in the workplace, not to actualize themselves, but because they need the money' (1984: 5). She argued that working women were often over-burdened by 'dual role exhaustion' and continual over-responsibility (1984: 6). This latter point fits well with the emphasis on women's over-responsibility for both biological and social reproduction, and consequent concern with women's drug and alcohol use when women are not perceived able to meet these demands (Campbell, 2000).

While Gomberg found sex role theory somewhat promising for understanding female alcohol abuse, she found the burden fell too heavily on psychodynamic explanations. For her, femininity was as much a 'biological role' as a social role (1984: 9). This would have been a distinctly unfashionable claim in the 1980s, when debates about biological essentialism within the feminist movement were at their sharpest. Yet Gomberg was no essentialist, but held out against what she saw as a tendency to deny women's 'biological role' and wrote, in direct riposte to Blume (1981), that

> As a feminist, I am often turned off by the emphasis on the gonads which exists in discussing female alcoholism. First it was the menopausal depression, now it is the premenstrual syndrome. Women may be, as students say to me, more 'in touch with their bodies' than men but that does not explain the preoccupation of the alcoholism field with the 'fetal alcohol syndrome' which exists, albeit for only a small proportion of women alcohol abusers. The FAS issue has become more of a crusade than a scientific debate and controversy has even flared up in *Science*, the journal which got the scoop on behavior therapy with alcoholics as well as the debate over whether pregnant women may drink at all.
>
> (1984: 9)

Gomberg had long urged caution in interpreting similar patterns of birth defect as FAS, arguing that early studies targeted women over age 30 and children who were all later- or last-born offspring in large families. 'We know nothing of the families into which these birth-defect children are born – only that they are "living on welfare"' (1975: 6). She went on about the lack of knowledge of the intellectual or psychiatric status of the women to whom these children were born – her guess was that it was 'low intellectually or disturbed psychiatrically' (1975: 6).

Her scepticism about FAS was based on the seeming lack of a sizable number of 'defective children' born to alcoholic women who came to treatment – to clinics, hospitals, AA, and doctor's offices. The 1975 'State of Knowledge' paper delved into the aetiology of women's alcoholism, looking at multilayered physiological, psychological, and sociological factors. Data sources for physiological sex differences included metabolic functioning, hormonal status, obstetrical and gynaecological problems, and new findings concerning 'similar patterns of birth defect' in children born to alcoholic women. Urging caution, Gomberg was sceptical of the existence of what would come to be called FAS. Extrapolating data from a handful of cases to *all* women alcoholics would lead to the expectation that there would be a 'sizable number of 'defective children, offspring of the women who come to outpatient clinics, hospitals, AA, and doctor's offices' out there. Written in the margins by Gomberg's hand, she notes, 'and we don't seem to' (1975: 6). Excessive amounts of anything – salt, nicotine, or aspirin, the common substances she listed – would affect the foetus. Scepticism notwithstanding, Gomberg believed that physiological factors entered into the complex aetiology of women's alcoholism. However, she did not simply advocate physiological or biological understandings of the condition she spent her life studying. Instead she put her understanding in terms of psychological 'vulnerability', a term that later came to have great salience but that meant very little to alcohol or addiction researchers in the mid-1970s. Vulnerability she defined in psychological terms – as a combination of 'disruptive early life experiences' that produced a vulnerable person who had difficulty forming 'healthily interdependent' relationships because of underlying trust issues and trouble with impulse control (1975: 7). These problems were masked by 'hyperfemininity' that covered over resentment during adolescence and created excessively high expectations about what marriage might mean in the 'fantasies of our vulnerable, hyperfeminine young lady' (1975: 7). In such a context, alcohol becomes a 'potent weapon to fight back at a frustrating world' (1975: 8).

In 1984 Gomberg declared that femininity was defined 'differently by different subgroups in different societies and at different times', believing that 'we are born with a biologically determined gender, and over this, is laid layers of learning' (she did, after all, do an internship with

Julian B. Rotter, father of social learning theory, at the Norwich State Hospital). She saw gender as a 'socialization process in which we are taught what the female role prescriptions are, what we are assigned to do in terms of work, men, other women, responsibilities, social behaviors, etc.' (1984: 10). Drinking was simply one among these learnt social behaviours, but one that had biological effects that made it impossible to come to valid conclusions about women and alcoholism by generalizing from studies in men. She then summarized the data on gender and age differences, finding great variability but making some conclusions. In the end of this paper, which synthesized her knowledge by the mid-1980s, she underlined the importance of genetic and biological antecedents, 'but to deny the significance of sex role and societal definitions of acceptable and unacceptable feminine behavior in the etiology of alcoholism is unacceptable' (1984: 27).

Feminist activity had peaked, according to Gomberg, in the 1970s. In a 1986 paper for an American Psychological Association (APA) roundtable on 'Liberation and Libations', she recalled the 'handwringing' predictions that an increase in women's alcoholism might be one of the 'costs' of equality. She noted the paucity of data showing consistent results in terms of whether or not women's employment increased or decreased women's drinking. That there were more women in treatment was evident; however, Gomberg argued against the view that there was any real increase in heavy drinking. Her opinion was that there had been a change in the pattern of women's drinking: 'the frustrated, disappointed housewife-closet drinker seems to appear less frequently among the women we see clinically and the workplace women appear more. These changes, one must remember, reflect where women are at this point in history' (1986: 1).

Social drinking, however, had increased, according to Gomberg, by the mid-1970s. 'Equal rights apparently include the equal right to social drinking because that's what the statistics tell us' (1975: 10). As women were increasingly surrounded by 'models' – alcoholic relatives and husbands – they had begun to learn that alcohol could be used as a coping mechanism. Gomberg always put this very strongly in terms of a gender imbalance: 'Women seemed to "catch" alcoholism from their husbands much more readily than men catch alcoholism from their wives' (1975: 10). Such transmission was what Gomberg meant when she used the term 'social etiology': it was a way for her to talk about differential power within gendered social relations.

Women also exhibited 'telescoped development', one of Gomberg's main conceptual contributions and a finding borne out empirically.

What it meant was that women alcoholics looked different from men: women began drinking later (close to age 30), went through less distinct phases than did men, and showed up for treatment after fewer years of drinking (1975: 10). Why did women come to treatment at all? Often their behaviour precipitated a family crisis, and they were pressured by husbands, concerned children, physicians, employers or co-workers to seek treatment. The real gender difference in which Gomberg was interested was whether this difference in women's relationships affected their prognosis in treatment:

> [W]ith men, we will look at his work record, days missing, accident reports, and so on – and his family life, too. For our woman patients, we look to her relationships with her husband, her family, her children, and how she feels about herself – and this is, for many of our women clients, the major measure of her recovery. *We are looking at her work record.* In liberating ourselves from unjust discrimination, let us not lose sight of the fact that for most women at this moment in history, that is where recovery lies.
>
> (1975: 15).

Gomberg's work on the life cycle sprang from a useful generalization: where alcohol and drug use are more socially sanctioned, 'women are bigger users; where drug use is least sanctioned, males are the bigger users' (1980: 1). As women travelled through the life cycle, they drink and use legal and illegal drugs for different reasons at different times. By the early 1980s, Gomberg was raising questions about the lack of studies on black and minority women, lesbian women, and women in prison, but in her work she tended to generalize existing data to show how common problems of social isolation, low self-esteem and even self-hatred, and more familial and social problems crossed such groups. Here again, we see the gendered division between male legal and occupational problems, versus women's social, familial, and marital relationship problems (1980: 8). Noting that middle-aged or 'middle life' alcoholic women are the ones about which the most is known, Gomberg emphasized that very little was known about those who carry the 'triple stigma of being old, female, and alcoholic' (1980: 9).

Age became a research focus for Gomberg in the 1980s, a fertile period when she travelled widely, lectured often, and testified to Congress on numerous occasions. On 11 March 1981 she testified before the US House Subcommittee on Health and the Environment, chaired by Henry A. Waxman (D-CA), who raised several questions pertaining to age: whether or not the effects of alcohol vary with age and how this would affect older Americans; whether alcohol use or abuse by older Americans posed 'special diagnostic problems for physicians'; what was known about older American's use of prescription and over-the-counter medications; and what research was warranted to study the effects of alcohol upon the elderly.[11] The subcommittee was also concerned with the NIAAA alcoholism research agenda and extramural funding programme, a topic on which Gomberg had very definite thoughts. She was severely critical of the narrowing of the federal research agenda of the nine federally-funded Alcoholism Research Centers, rhetorically asking Representative Waxman: 'Is it sensible in the face of so many social problems connected with alcohol to have only one of the nine ARC's a social science research center?' Clearly Gomberg believed the answer was no. She questioned the decision to emphasize biomedical research to such an extent that she felt her list of research priorities was 'an exercise in futility'. As she had argued in testimony to Waxman's subcommittee, even excellent biomedical knowledge was insufficient to 'really solve the social, economic, legal and personal problems posed by abusive use of alcohol'.[12] She argued forcefully for a research agenda that emphasized 'special populations' – the 'relative vulnerability of minority people, women, young people leaving home, people in the labor force, and older people'. Gomberg acknowledged that 'in a sense, we are all members of 'special populations' – but for her, employers' over-emphasis on getting white, male alcoholics aged 35–55 into treatment translated directly into under-utilization of treatment by so-called special populations. The discourse of vulnerability – clearly a physiological, psychological, and social matter in Gomberg's thinking – would ultimately be both extended and reduced to notions of 'biological vulnerability' (cf. Campbell, 2000).

Early assumptions about alcohol and drug-using women derived from the notion that they made 'poor patients'. This notion was deeply gendered, having everything to do with conventional notions of masculinity and femininity and the ways in which these fit into ideals of productive citizenship. In Gomberg's testimony to the US Senate Subcommittee on Alcoholism and Drug Abuse on 27 July 1981, she noted that the original rationale for alcoholism treatment was rehabilitation of 'Skid Row men' to meet wartime manpower needs. 'But there was another rationale: alcoholic persons received short shrift in general hospitals and clinics because they were difficult to work with, because they broke appointments, because they were not 'good' patients'.[13] Not being a 'good' patient translated into moralistic attitudes that such persons were undeserving, unworthy, and low priority. According to Gomberg, such attitudes were still prevalent in the early 1980s, but the federal government 'made a great step forward' in creating the NIDA and the NIAAA (Gomberg considered alcohol dependence part of 'drug dependence'). She argued against going backwards to a moment when 'alcoholics and drug dependent people were last in line to be helped and to be studied'.[14] When asked if federal research dollars had been appropriately used, she again took exception with a 'disproportionate amount of research monies ... granted to the biomedical sciences at the expense of the social sciences'.[15] Advocating increasingly for the use of research on social norms for prevention programmes and predictive models, Gomberg went from research on women and gendered norms to thinking clearly about how group norms and social setting, attitudes towards intoxication, and social learning affect drinking patterns more generally. Her early thinking about social norms and alcohol consumption had taken shape in the context of a gendered analysis of social response to intoxication.

Social disapproval of women's behaviour while intoxicated was central to Gomberg's analysis. In a talk on how most people feel about female drunks and male drunks, she cited the 'almost universal disapproval of women manifesting intoxicated behaviour', and 'a very real double standard in how people view drunkenness' that led to women alcoholics being viewed as 'disgusting' and 'disgraceful'. Society's 'objections center largely around [drinking] being inconsistent with 'a woman's role' for one thing and her vulnerability to rape and seduction for another'. Then appears Gomberg's handwritten response to University of Texas Attitudes Toward Women Scale: 'I am inclined to believe that the roots of this double standard go deeper than this scale suggests. I believe it goes back to some very primitive anxieties about caretaking and responsibility [and] housework'.[16] Gomberg was onto an issue that we have drawn attention to, the normative expectation that women are (over) responsible for social reproduction (Campbell, 2000; Ettorre, 2010), an assumption upon which is predicated the 'double standards' for how women were to behave within the contours of gendered social roles, and an assumption that we scrutinize carefully in Chapter 5. While Gomberg and Blume represented figures who bridged the proto-feminist and feminist approaches to acknowledge and treat women alcoholics and drugs users, their writings make evident just how restrictive the early responses were conceptually and analytically. Value judgements are embedded in constructs of women as 'poor patients' and as performing in deficient and deviant ways relative to 'respectable' women. The problem of the moral discourse of 'respectability' – and the 'immorality' and a pervasive lack of respectability accorded to women's drugs and alcohol use – was a problem not only within families or clinics, but within the women's movement itself in which women were characterized as 'shrill, humourless, unappealing, forbidding ... silly cows. Angry' (Sebestyen, 1985). These pioneers also worked within the larger landscape of health care provision in the US, in which there is a division between public and private systems.

Health as a social right: Pioneers in women's drug treatment in the United Kingdom

Since 1948 in Britain, the state has financed an organized system of medical care, the National Health Service (NHS), which is based on the idea that direct investment in health care enhances national prosperity and public health. Through the development of the NHS, wellbeing became established as a social right; however, over the years, there have been criticisms of the ways in which women are treated within the NHS (Doyal, 1979: 215–38). The medical profession's emphasis on women as informal caregivers has been criticized for reinforcing gender divisions (Annandale, 1998: 21). These issues matter as women are consistently the major consumers of health care in the NHS.[17]

Alcohol and drug treatment for women has occurred and continues to occur beyond NHS boundaries, through the non-statutory sector (i.e., the voluntary sector, which consists of non-governmental organizations or NGOs) in the form of residential care, advice and self-help groups such as Narcotics Anonymous and AA, as well as the private sector (Mold and Berridge, 2010; Dally, 1990). It is our view that the NHS has been instrumental as a powerful regulatory regime, protecting and reinforcing a 'drugs orthodoxy' while helping to implement overall government policies and socio-medical responses to alcohol and drug use and misuse. Indeed, the NHS through the National Treatment Agency for Substance Misuse (NTA), which was formed in 2001,[18] attempts to reduce the physical and social harm caused by drugs. In December 2009, the NTA (2009b: 6) published a document entitled, *The story of drug treatment* in which it was noted that

> Most drug misusers contact treatment services directly. Others are referred by their GP or the NHS, and about a quarter get picked up through the criminal justice system. Treatment services are commissioned by 149 local partnerships, often called drug action teams [DATs]. Half the funding for drug treatment comes from the Department of Health. A quarter comes from other Government

> departments *via* the criminal justice system, and the rest is supplemented locally by [NHS] Primary Care Trusts and local authorities. The NTA monitors national standards and assures the quantity and quality of all this treatment, in accordance with clinical guidelines set by NICE [National Institute of Clinical Excellence]. A mixture of NHS and voluntary sector providers supply the actual treatment.

The marriage between social welfare and public health under the NHS umbrella has had an important social consequence in Britain – the right of each individual to his/her own health and wellbeing is seen to be managed and safeguarded by the state. While most drug users will be provided with state-funded care, they are unpopular as a social group and perceived consistently as undeserving of the care they do receive (MacGregor, 1989). Women drug users and alcoholics continue to experience resistance to perspectives that are sensitive to their needs as women (Ettorre, 1989). Over 20 years ago, MacGregor and Ettorre (1987: 143) argued that 'sensitivity to social groups, cultures and special needs should be a starting point in providing services for *all* drug takers' (143).

In Britain, the feminist response to alcohol and drugs did not emerge until the Women's Liberation Movement (WLM) of the late 1970s, with a well-known British feminist activist who was part of the Spare Rib collective,[19] Sue O'Sullivan (1987: 318), noting that there was much more feminist discussion and action directed towards women and addiction in the US than in the UK. This time lag in Britain was not surprising, as addiction tended to be invisible within British society. Ignorance as well as antipathy were usual responses to drug users who were seen by some psychiatrists as 'weak people … prevented from breeding (by drug use) – to the benefit of the human race' (Laurie, 1967:16). Leading 'alcohol' psychiatrists in the field, Neil Kessel and Henry Walton (1965: 85) viewed women as 'solitary drinkers' who often make 'a pathetic attempt each evening to hide evidence of their drinking' and 'neglect their homes' – again reinforcing dangerous stereotypes.

It was within this type of prejudicial treatment environment, Dr. Dorothy Black, an advocate of drug treatment services for drug using and alcohol using women in the UK, began to treat drug users. She described her career into medicine, her initiation into the drug field and her subsequent encounter with the negativity of her psychiatric colleagues towards drug users:

> I started off in paediatrics first in [University of] Liverpool where I graduated. Then at Great Ormond Street [Children's Hospital in

> London]. Thereafter I got married and it was exceedingly difficult finding posts in the same area as my husband's [who was] also a paediatrician. We also started our family. We have four children and so I spent most of the sixties working part time in a variety of clinics ... – welfare, child health, school welfare, antenatal clinics ... Also during this time, I became involved with the Family Planning Association working in contraceptive advice. In the early 1970s, we moved from London up to Sheffield where I and two colleagues began a clinic for people – first of all with psychological problems, psychosexual problems and also for young people who couldn't be seen at the then family planning clinics. [They] ... were seeking termination and the result of [working in] these two areas meant that I decided that I needed to go back to sharpen up my psychiatry and psychological knowledge... As a result I approached the then professor of psychiatry in [University of] Sheffield ... who agreed to take me on originally as a research fellow.

While working part-time in psychiatry and as a Lecturer in Psychiatry at the University of Sheffield from 1973 to 1981, Black was the consultant psychiatrist of the Students Health Service. It was at that time she first became interested in drug use and drug misusers.

> I think mainly because ... I found them interesting people rather than that I had any burning desire to treat them. But, I then discovered, of course, that most of my colleagues didn't want to see them at all.[20]

While Black did not refer to herself as a feminist, she was influenced by her grandmother, a Suffragette active in the Labour party:

> As I say, particularly my grandmother was a huge influence on me because she was very concerned about inequalities in society and her gardener for example was a member of Sinn Fein who eventually blew up the post office in [town in Lake District] and she went to court on his behalf. She was prepared to stick her neck out. I remember her with huge affection. I think she probably had more influence on me than anybody else I have ever met. And as I say, she was all for women's liberation in politics.[21]

Black was able to translate her liberalism into action while working in Sheffield with women sex workers who were also drug users. A young male probation officer introduced her to this group, which she enjoyed treating despite the overall lack of treatment for drug users at that time.

> Of all the colleagues I worked with during that time, he in fact was the most useful and indeed helpful and also very good to work with ... We particularly were interested in a group of sex workers who worked in the middle of Sheffield in what was then the red light district – many of whom had drug problems ... I wouldn't say they were a majority of my patients but they were a fairly large minority of my patients.... The Regional Health Authority at the time, having initially denied there was any drug problem at all in the Sheffield region, finally agreed that maybe there should be a special unit [so] I was sent off romping round the country looking at various drug [and] alcohol units with the intention that I would draw up a blue print that they might then fund in Sheffield. Unfortunately by the time I had done this ... there were the beginnings of the cut backs in financing and this never happened. But I did have an interesting time going to Newcastle, the Maudsley and St Bernards in London, and Winchester, which at that time were some of the very few places in the country. This is late 70s ... where there were[n't] any specific certainly hospital based drug units ... when I saw drug users, it was within the context of a general psychiatric clinic. It wasn't a specific drug service and I must say I was so frustrated by this.[22]

During this time 'masculinist' perspectives in the addiction field (Ettorre, 1986a and b) flourished and took firm hold of the public's imagination (Bean, 1974; Deedes, 1970; Glatt, 1972; Larner and Tefferteller, 1966; McClelland et al., 1972; Neill and Hymer, 1972; Plant, 1975; Stimson, 1973; Young, 1971). In these contexts, it was almost as if women drug users and alcoholics did not exist. With this injustice in mind, Ettorre argued forcefully that there was a need for a theoretical framework challenging methodologies which 'ignore sexual divisions and do not see the experiences of women'. Additionally, Ettorre contended that a feminist perspective on women and drugs and alcohol should not be colonized within a male perspective or de-valued by patriarchal practices. Black continued to work with women drug users, finding that her colleagues did not want to work with them period and achieving some 'insight ... into some of the pressures that perhaps push women into using drugs ... what I call 'dominant-passive relationship' between the woman and the man who might also be her pimp and indeed the pressure of having to work in the prostitution field ... Other ambivalent attitudes some of the women had which they found very stressful ... They hadn't really ever wanted to do that but for various reasons like lack of any other employment or lack of employment that paid as much or the fact that they would lose their boyfriend ... their supporter ... their protector'.[23]

Conclusion

While there were few women's drug and alcohol treatment programmes during the era described in this chapter, it is not the case that there were none (White, 2002; 2004). Iliff et al. (2007) trace the histories of three private treatment systems in the US, noting that Hazelden, the treatment arm of AA, opened its doors for the treatment of 'curable alcoholics of the professional class' in 1948 and inaugurated a special facility for women in 1956 called Dia Linn, which expanded its capacity in 1962 and four years later moved to Hazelden's main campus in Center City, Minnesota. During the 1960s, Dia Linn was revamped and each woman assigned a primary counsellor, a group for therapy, and access to nursing, clergy, and social workers – the kind of multidisciplinary team that became central to the 'Minnesota Model'.[24] Another women's alcoholism treatment programme that began in the 1950s was founded in Wernersville, Pennsylvania by Richard and Catherine Caron. Called Chit Chat Farms, and later Caron Treatment Centers, the facility drew a dozen or so women parolees from the Pennsylvania State Correctional Institution for Women at Muncie, Pennsylvania. In the spring of 1961 Chit Chat Farms created an inpatient addiction treatment programme for women that operated similarly to its men's programme – but Caron did not create gender-specific treatment programmes until 1996.

This chapter has presented a history of representations of drug-using women by those few pioneering women who initially became interested in studying or treating addicted women – often alcoholics. We showed how moral claims were advanced about the immorality of drug use in ways that continue to marginalize drug-using women. Many public health interventions in the drugs field work through the imposition of moral claims that further stigmatize those who cannot measure up. This type of moralizing-through-medicine has shaped the meanings that drug-using women's bodies telegraph in public space. In order for gender-specific treatment and research programmes to become effective, women have had to contest the morality and moral judgementalism of the discourse directed towards women alcoholics and drug addicts. We suggest reliance upon an ethicopolitical language as a means to achieve the 'de-moralization' of drug discourse that we are suggesting. The earliest programmes for women critiqued neither medical nor moral discourse, but came from within these two dominant registers. With the dawning of the Second Wave women's movement in each country, the critical tools necessary for the de-moralization of drug discourse became more readily available.

2

Raising Consciousness or Controlling Women? Women's Drug and Alcohol Treatment Re-Emerges

The first generation of women's treatment programmes in the 1970s and early 1980s were well-intentioned, often isolated from one another, and often maternalist and 'pro-natalist' at base.[1] They were often undertaken by physicians interested in helping drug and or alcohol-dependent women patients towards greater conformity with dominant social norms. By showing their clients how to be 'good mothers' and trying to inculcate normative views on the creation of attachment bonds with infants, these physicians worked within the structured constraints of gender, unintentionally sending messages that drug-using women should not reproduce and were inadequate to meet the demanding expectations of motherhood. Attempts to survey the state of knowledge and to describe the state of treatment at the time revealed a dearth of programmes and an under-developed state of knowledge. Such surveys were done by the University of Michigan Women's Drug Research Project from 1974 to 1979 and the British organization Drugs, Alcohol, and Women Nationally (DAWN) (London) in the 1980s. These surveys were undertaken with the intention of documenting the paucity of knowledge and changing the knowledge base. We address these surveys later in this chapter when we discuss the organizations that administered them.

Early maternalist drug and alcohol treatment programmes

We interpret these early maternalist programmes as providing an interlude between the classical and postclassical paradigms; we do so not in the spirit of criticism but in order to interrogate the assumptions upon which they were based in a spirit of renewed enquiry. These programmes offer a set of historical case studies in how a form of 'strategic essentialism' was used in order to gain a toehold for women's drug treatment within medical institutions even as these were beginning to undergo change as a result of the feminist and women's health movement (which we will address in the next chapter). Some of the earliest comprehensive or 'multivariable' services for pregnant heroin users were pioneered at the Family Center in Philadelphia by neonatologist Loretta P. Finnegan, M. D. at Philadelphia General Hospital and later Jefferson Medical College. She developed the Finnegan Neonatal Abstinence Score, the first instrument designed to assess the severity of withdrawal symptoms in newborns, which has now been used all over the world. According to Finnegan, her patients 'feared being penalized for the fact that they were an addict and pregnant. They feared having their baby taken from them by child protective services. One of the 'carrots', was if she stayed in the clinic, and if she was compliant, our goal was to keep her with her baby. If she wasn't compliant, we were bound to protect the child'.[2] Citing high rates of co-morbidity among her patients (60 per cent had at least one psychiatric diagnosis in addition to opiate addiction), Finnegan emphasized that between 90 and 100 per cent of women coming into her clinic had been 'physically and/or sexually abused as children and/or adults, which made a great impact on them from the standpoint of drug use. They received counselling for their psychiatric illnesses, including PTSD, and participated in groups where we taught them about childcare and how to be a mother'.[3]

While there has been a long history of medical and scientific tutelage on mothering (Apple, 2006), development of curricula aimed specifically at drug-using women was innovative in the 1970s. As a form of expertise, maternalism may coexist within women's movements, and it may or may not be connected to women's rights or feminist analysis. Like child welfare advocacy, maternalism has often been at odds with or even opposed to women's rights but has the potential to be used as a powerful tool within women's movements. For instance, in lesbian struggles for parental rights or in activist attorney Lynn Paltrow's organization, National Advocates for Pregnant Women (NAPW), a feminist discourse is mobilized in ways that open up emancipatory channels for women whose status and rights as mothers are typically foreclosed – like drug-using women. Indeed NAPW explicitly connects women's human rights to a full array of birthing rights and parenting rights because the vast majority of women are or will become mothers by age 40. We will take up NAPW's linkage between women's human rights and reproductive rights in later chapters.

The seeds of a potentially feminist maternalism lay dormant in the early responses to pregnant drug users. When asked how her programme taught women to mother, Finnegan replied:

> Sadly, most of them had not been mothered well or at all, therefore, they had no prior experience of good care to use with their children. We learn to mother from our mothers. If your mother was not nurturing, or if your mother did not attach to you, you don't attach to your baby. Think of the paintings of Modigliani, the artist who painted the women with the long necks. In his paintings, you'll frequently see that the babies are hanging in the arms of the mother like rag dolls. That's the way the mothers would hold their babies. They didn't hold them in a position so that they could look into the baby's eyes. This is called the 'en face' position. There wasn't the warmth that you can see in the paintings of Mary Cassatt or Edna Hibel. We taught the mothers about attachment and how important it was to show love to her baby. We explained to her that when we send the baby home, the baby may appear to be rejecting her, but that is not the case. The babies were having some residual neurological symptoms related to withdrawal and we encouraged her to keep nurturing the baby, and the baby would come about. Many of these babies would avoid the mother, and not gaze at her, because they were shaking from withdrawal and were still a little uncomfortable. The babies could have these symptoms for several months. Providing comprehensive and compassionate treatment was one of our major contributions, and we were amongst just a few individuals in the 1970's doing so for pregnant women. We showed that these services were very important to not only deal with the mothers' drug dependence, but also to influence the health of mother and baby.[4]

While exemplary in many ways, the clinic setting that Finnegan founded poses an important dilemma for thinking about what constitutes feminist or women-centred drug treatment, and for relations between research, clinical practice, and social movements oriented towards changing power relations. On the one hand, Finnegan's writings, as well as the interview from which the above material came, indicate a commitment to what we might call 'normative motherhood'. However, given that the pedagogy was directed towards women who had both their own (widely shared and thus similar) difficulties enacting motherhood and being perceived by cultural authorities as embodying maternity, it may be worth pondering the forms of embodiment encouraged within this historical context. Drug-using women have historically been refused access to their children, their maternal rights often revoked without due process in the decades prior to the 1970s. In the UK, courts would decide if a child was in need of care and control and would make a 'care order', placing the child in the care of the social service department of a local council that would take over responsibilities as a parent. It has been consistent perceived wisdom in the drugs field that drug-using women believe that social workers and other professionals with whom they come into contact saw drug use as an automatic indicator of unfitness as a mother (Taylor, 1993: 116). Early proponents of women's treatment were aware of the injustice of this assumption; while they typically located fault within the individual women, there was growing cognizance of the social structures and gendered expectations within which the performance of 'good' or 'bad' mothering was enacted.

One reason for the emphasis on mothering was that the experience of giving up a child was a commonality shared by many drug-using women. Reflecting on the early days of women's drug treatment in Britain, Annas Dixon, first chair of the management committee of City Roads, London, one of the first non-statutory residential crisis intervention centres for drug users (established in 1978) and a former member of Advisory Council on the Misuse of Drugs (ACMD), recalled:

> We were like social services really – we weren't clued up enough to be asking as many questions we should around histories of abuse. Actually looking back, I think lots of us have said over the years we began to realise [that] sexual or physical abuse was very much part of the experience of many women but what they did have – nearly all of them – was a history of either a child that had been born that they had given away or had been taken into care.[5]

One of us (Campbell, 2000: 176–9) has previously written about the ritual invocation of 'maternal instinct' in relation to drug panics, an invocation that pressures the notion that poor women can shoulder all of the tasks and costs of social reproduction. The comprehensive nature of this early instance of women-centred treatment included not only addiction and health counselling, but also childcare and education in household management, shopping, cooking, nutrition, parenting techniques, and job training.[6] It both reinforced normative expectations of gendered social norms and extended a form of social inclusion to drug-using women in ways that were designed to fit individuals into the norms of the dominant society from which they 'deviated'.

Perhaps even more succinctly, Campbell (2000) argued: 'Treatment is a set of regulatory practices that attempts to bring individuals into conformity with the state's ideal of the productive citizen. Its success is measured by the compliance and social adjustment of its subjects'. Adjustment and maladjustment were attributes assigned to individuals; Finnegan, who had by then left the clinic she founded in Philadelphia to become the associate director of the Office for Treatment Improvement, noted that recidivism resulted from 'low social adjustment' and physical, psychological, or social impairment. High social adjustment was defined in socially conventional terms as being married, heterosexual, older, better educated, better employed, less criminally involved, and better-adjusted psychologically. As articulated by Finnegan, NIDA's profile of the 'causes' of drug dependence included

1. 'Problem behavior proneness or deviance syndrome';
2. Progressive development starting in adolescence and proceeding to hard-core use;
3. Psychopathology;
4. Impaired function, including 'difficulty in emotional regulation, planning, problem solving, perceptual motor function, language and information processing, coping, and difficulty in interpersonal problem solving';
5. Familial or genetic components;
6. Environmental risk factors, including drug availability, family disruption, and 'cultural norms';
7. Factors related specifically to drugs or their 'routes of administration'.

Well into the 1990s, women's drug use was still framed as a form of individual deviance, maladjustment, and psychopathology, just as it had been in the 1950s, although the maladjustment framework was widened to encompass multiple causes. There was no questioning of the racial-ethnic and class codes embedded in such lists, which subscribed to the 'perennial idea that dominant cultural norms do not cause addiction; only 'deviant' cultural norms do' (Campbell, 2000). Older individual maladjustment models allowed for socioeconomic variables, but failed to account for differentials of race, class, sexuality, and, of course, embodied experiences of gender. Thus treatment models were not adapted to encompass different experiences of substance abuse based on gender. According to Beth Reed, who ran the NIDA-funded Women's Drug Research (WDR) project in Ann Arbor, Michigan:

> the basic models of treatment are set up for how substance abuse looks in men, and much of our ideology about substance abuse is about exaggerated coping styles. What we learned from all these

> scales we put in was that people who have substance abuse problems have in fact really stereotyped ideas about masculinity and femininity, more so than average people. They also feel that they're not living up to those ideals and that's partly because those ideals are stereotypes, caricatures, almost. That might be part of why they got in trouble in the first place .... We were able to [...] establish that addicted women look more like other women than they look like addicted men. It allowed us to challenge the notion that addiction is a unitary thing.[7]

We interpret Reed to be describing a time when feminists were pointing to distortions and misinterpretations based in the use of a male standard in many different domains.

Women's drug and alcohol treatment advocates actively pushed for recognition of the 'multivariable' characteristics of substance abuse. For instance, Reed argued that as a consequence of a 'male standard' having been adopted throughout the treatment system, women experienced a 'double deviance': they were judged as neither 'properly female' nor as 'properly alcoholic or addicted' as they expressed behaviours and psychologies that 'did not fit the masculine patterns called alcoholism or addiction' (Reed, 1987: 153). Here the very definitions of the disorders to be treated were assumed to follow the contours of male behaviour and psychology. Because the behaviours of male addicts and alcoholics – including violence, criminality, drunk driving, and poor work performance – were viewed as costly and socially disruptive, there were social controls attempting to reduce the harms associated with male drinking and drugging. Reed's point was that women's behaviours manifested so differently that women did not appear to meet the definitional criteria. Instead women experienced what would today be called 'co-occurring disorders' such as depression, anxiety, inward-directed self-blame, and other behaviours associated with 'learned helplessness' (Reed, 1987: 155). Pointing out the similarities between addicted women and battered women – indeed, noting that 'many drug dependent women have been battered', Reed maintained that there were motivational consequences for women's decisions to enter and remain in treatment if they were feeling depressed and worthless prior to entering treatment. Such feelings might well be translated into behaviour as 'people who feel worthless often behave to convince others that they *are* worthless'. The confrontational tactics used in men's treatment to overcome denial early in the recovery process might cause women who exhibited signs of the 'learned helplessness pattern'.

The point, however, was that there was a gap in the knowledge base – a gap produced not only by an absence of empirical data and conceptual practices designed to produce new knowledge, but by the very 'governing mentalities' through which knowledge about women's patterns and profiles were to be produced. Again, that gap became apparent to a variety of actors in many different domains of women's health.

Changing the knowledge base

We characterize the emerging women's health movement in the terms offered by feminist philosopher Nancy Tuana, who argues that the movement was an 'epistemological resistance movement geared at undermining the production of ignorance about women's health and women's bodies in order to critique and extricate women from oppressive systems often based on this ignorance, as well as creating liberatory knowledges. While one aspect of the women's health movement was to make available to women basic medical knowledge at the accessible only to healthcare professionals, an equally important goal of the women's health movement was to reexamine traditional medicine not simply in order to 'get it right', but rather to transform our knowledge of women's bodies in order to remove oppression, to augment women's lives, and to transform society' (2006: 2). An explicit emphasis on knowledge production was central to how the women's health movement organized to respond to women's alcohol and drug problems, making the first task an assessment of the current state of knowledge in the newly formed field.

From the School of Social Work and the Institute for Social Research (ISR) at the University of Michigan in Ann Arbor, Reed ran the NIDA-funded WDR Coordinating Project from the mid-to-late 1970s. The WDR created data collection tools, most notably the WDR Admission and Termination Forms, used by four demonstration programmes funded in 1973 to 'contribute new knowledge about the woman addict, her needs for service, and the types of programmes necessary to help her'.[8] The original programmes were residential therapeutic communities (TCs) and outpatient methadone maintenance programmes. The WDR was NIDA's first foray into understanding gender or sex differences, and ultimately data was collected from 26 programmes operational at the time. Through the WDR sub-studies, NIDA was able to gain a more realistic characterization of women enrolled in different treatment modalities. The sub-studies deploy the language of conventional social science, and were designed specifically to compare female to male addicts. The ultimate goal of many of the sub-studies was to characterize the 'modal female addict', to show that women drug users were more similar to other *women* than to male addicts, to pay attention to differences among women, and to suggest that the substance abuse literature produced to date had 'grossly overstated the differences in the family dynamics of heroin users and non-users' (WDR, 1979: 5, 10).

The move to contest the pathologization of drug-using women often deployed a feminist empiricism (Harding, 1986) to dispel 'old untested myths' (WDR, 1979: 6). 'Feminist empiricism' was used as an initial stage, somewhat 'old-fashioned' way of designating that 'the woman problem' lay simply in incomplete scientific approaches or flawed moralistic discourses that could be made right by simply 'adding women' and 'stirring' up the old mix.

But this sort of empiricism contained the germs of an emerging epistemology that reached beyond the 'status quo' towards a more complex feminist epistemological project to produce new knowledges specific to the health needs of drug-using women. The WDR sub-studies directed attention towards drug-dependent women's specific needs, while confirming they had more health problems subsequent to treatment than their male counterparts, and that these problems tended to *worsen* over the length of time in treatment due partly to the fact that 'very few of the programmes had the capacity to treat more complex needs than a cold or the flu' (Andersen, 1979: 13). There was an attempt to broaden understandings of women's health status beyond treatment for addictions, as the study found that few physicians were willing to treat eye disorders, gynaecological problems or provide dental care due to their 'unwillingness to treat known drug addicts' (Andersen, 1979: 13). This problem contrasted to another problem documented by a WDR sub-study by Virginia S. Ryan, which concerned hospitals' inability to identify which women used drugs, and the lack of knowledge and sympathy displayed by most physicians in hospital settings towards pregnant addicts in particular once they were identified. Addicted women were reticent to approach hospitals; pregnant women in particular tended not to seek medical care until post-partum. Ryan's sub-study found that only one of the six hospitals used morphine to 'manage drug maintenance needs, and this hospital was unique in reporting their patients respond positively, do not demand premature discharge, and there is not drug trafficking in the wards' (WDR, 1979: 15). Finally, the WDR study showed that addicted and alcoholic women's opportunity structures, psychological profiles, and behavioural patterns differed from men's patterns: women were more socially isolated, more often primary caretakers of children, and more commonly suffered depression, anxiety and low self-esteem *before* entering treatment (Reed, 1987: 155). Adopting the profiles and patterns of young, white males as an implicit masculine standard forced women into the category of a 'special population', which presented women's treatment advocates with a version of the equality/difference dilemma. Strategically, they could either embrace the benefits that accrue on the basis of claiming women's difference from men, or argue for gender specificity, parity and equity. In this way, women's treatment advocates refused to oppose their calls for equal treatment and gender equity to their continual insistence on difference. They did exactly what feminist historian Joan W. Scott urged feminists to do: 'to refuse to oppose equality to difference and to insist continually on differences – differences as the condition of individual and collective identities, differences to the constant challenge to the fixing of those identities ... differences as the very meaning of equality itself' (Scott, 1990: 142).

The epistemological break between the 'classical' and 'postclassical' knowledge paradigms lies in their very different responses to these kinds of embodied and socially enacted differences. Since the 1970s there have been many gender-specific treatment and research programmes; as Stephen Kandall, M. D. wrote, 'By the late 1970s, the treatment 'glass' for addicted women could be considered both half-full and half-empty' (1996: 232). While a knowledge paradigm based on individual pathology still exercised its grip over the imaginations of most experts in this emerging field, change was in the offing as over time the women's health movement was able to expand the range of differences thought to be central to engaging and rehabilitating women. Insisting on difference – whether that insistence was called 'gender sensitivity', 'gender awareness', or 'gender responsiveness' – was an anti-essentialist recognition that women embody and enact their social shaping as 'problematic consumers' of addictive substances or alcohol in different ways – depending not only upon their social location but also upon the knowledges that frame their experiences and the narratives through which they understand these experiences.

Psychotherapy and psychoanalysis in the women's health movement

Myriad forms of medical paternalism came under criticism from the women's health movement, but special opprobrium was reserved for psychotherapy, which was viewed by many as a site for the oppression of women (Chesler, 1972). In the UK, the well-known socialist feminist Juliet Mitchell developed interests in psychotherapy and psychoanalysis. Her interests were rooted in the radical psychiatry movement, the New Left of the Sixties, and the women's health movement (Wilson, 1980: 200). Feminist historian Elizabeth Wilson (1980: 201) contends that another well-known socialist feminist, Sheila Rowbotham, built her feminist thinking on similar political and cultural traditions (such as radical psychiatry, the drug culture and the underground) which placed a high value on experience, the expression of emotions, the irrational and the individual. Rowbotham (1973) argued that women's oppression was 'internalised and penetrates the very psyche of our being' (33), 'forc[ing] a redefinition of what is personal and political' (xxi), and that as a result of this oppression, 'women must break their silence' (30). Whether deliberately or not, women's consciousness-raising (CR) groups drew on this tradition (Wilson, 1981: 201) to define consciousness-raising as happening when 'women translated their personal feelings into political awareness' (Coote and Campbell, 1982: 6). As women's sexuality, love, relationships with men, health, and well-being were scrutinized under the collective microscope of women's CR groups, women became critical of Freud's overwhelming influence on women's 'psycho-sexual natures, an influence seen as disastrous' (Faulder, Jackson and Lewis, 1976: 50). Psychologist and activist, Naomi Weisstein (1973) wrote a thoroughgoing critique of psychology and socio-biology that brought to the surface similar discontents for feminists active in the women's health movement 'on the other side of the pond'.

Thus, it was not surprising that neither the first Boston Women's Health Book Collective (BWHBC) publication, *Women and Their Bodies* (1970) nor the second, *Our Bodies, Ourselves* (*OBOS*) (1971), contained a chapter on psychotherapy. The British edition of *OBOS* was by Angela Phillips and Jill Rakusen, two journalists described as 'actively involved in the Women's Liberation Movement (WLM) for many years'. It was published in 1978 and based mainly on the 1971 American edition. The original American text was adapted to a British audience with a special chapter on 'Women and Health Care' within the context of the British NHS and related chapters on birth control, abortion, pregnancy, childbirth, and menopause care. There was also a chapter on lesbian perspectives by a group of London socialist lesbians. The British edition had one reference to psychotherapy which referred to how 'some women' who may have 'conflicts about sex' may need 'help to unlock and resolve these conflicts through some kind of psychotherapy, (1978: 62). While at that time feminist criticism of psychotherapy focused on its predilection for the pathological, Mitchell published in 1974 *Psychoanalysis and Feminism,* in which she attempted to reconcile feminism with Freud's ideas about women. Also, in Britain in the early 1970s, there was a women and psychology group as part of the autonomous WLM exploring the work of Mitchell along with other feminist theorists (Coote and Campbell, 1982: 44). In 1976, the Women's Therapy Centre was established by Suzie Orbach and Luise Eichenbaum. While there was some resistance to psychotherapy in Britain at the time, the practice was becoming 'feminised' and beginning to gain ground among well-known feminists in the UK.

During the collective preparation of the American 1984 edition, chroniclers of the collective recall an epic conflict between those who believed psychotherapy could be liberatory and those who felt it contributed to the over-medicalization of women's lives (Wells, 2010: 52). Opposition to including a chapter on psychotherapy can be read as a microcosm of the contestation between medical expertise and women who called for 'a world in which every woman is the presiding genius of her own body' (Rich, 1976). In the initial stages of the feminist movement, consciousness-raising was seen as a feminist practice, but psychotherapy was not (Echols, 1989: 87–91).[9] As a movement practice, CR urged every woman to analyse dominant structures, institutions, and patterns of privilege, whereas psychotherapy was the province of a professional elite enfranchised specifically through the very establishment at which CR took aim. This dilemma can be seen in the ambivalent response of the BWHBC to medicine itself.

Critical of the medical establishment as one of the political-economic forces shaping women's lives, Lucy Candib (then a student at Harvard Medical School) opened her entry on 'Women, Medicine, and Capitalism' for the first mimeographed edition with a quotation from Herbert Marcuse: 'Health is a state defined by an elite' (Wells, 2010: 50). Taking on the dominant medical establishment and a pharmaceutical industry that had been the darling of consumer capitalism since the mid-twentieth century, the collective sharpened its critique of the medicalization of women's health in the 1984 edition. However, the collective also decided to include a chapter on psychotherapy in that edition. As Susan Wells points out in her rhetorical analysis of this chapter, the collective presented the chapter as a 'compromise we could live with', despite 'laminating' together two competing frameworks: one in which psychotherapy can provide women a feminist and liberatory path to emotional well-being, and one in which psychotherapy stands as abusive and oppressive (Wells, 2010: 53, 189). These seemingly irreconcilable frameworks created an ambivalence integral to constituting the very publics about whose bodies and selves the members of the collective saw themselves writing into being. Later in her analysis of the collective's commitment to the critique of medicine, Wells attributes the remarkable textual capacity of *OBOS* to appeal both to the 'body of lived experience' and to the body as constructed and inscribed by medicine without reconciling or synthesizing the two. She wrote:

> For the writers of *Our Bodies, Ourselves,* synthesis was never a question: they needed both approaches to the body, and they fully trusted neither of them. If the body was a surface inscribed by medicine ... then they wanted to be able to read the inscription. The 'lived interiority' of the body, alternately, offered access to the dynamics of subordination, to their own formation as female subjects. Both these processes were politically consequential.
>
> (Wells, 2010: 186)

Keeping in play these multiple layers of meaning meant that theories of embodiment and inscription emerging from the women's health movement were sophisticated epistemologies positioned against the dominant epistemologies of ignorance prevailing at the time. Yet they were pitched in the often playful and irreverent lexicon of the 'body politics' of radical feminism which upheld the idea that because of the 'myth of the vaginal orgasm', 'women have been defined sexually in terms of what pleases men; our own biology has not been properly analysed' (Koedt, 1973: 199; Echols, 1989). Yet the response of many medical professionals to *OBOS* was unexpectedly and ironically enthusiastic, partly because a demographic transition in the number of women going to medical school was then underway. Indeed a rapid growth in the numbers of women physicians can be discerned since the 1970s (Riska, 2001: 48).

The emergence of feminist activism around drugs and alcohol took place in the context of this crucible. The unexpected success of *OBOS* can be measured by its embrace by the very medical establishment of which the collective was so critical. As more and more 'doctor stories' in which physicians had responded disdainfully or hurtfully towards women began to circulate, a reform movement gathered in medicine itself and in the federal research apparatus (Epstein, 2009). In the words of one of the feminist 'founders' of the BWHBC, 'we went from being this sort of marginal, underground group to being the darlings of the press and the medical establishment' (Davis, 2007: 97). The movement is credited with changing doctor-patient relations and drawing attention to power relations within the medical establishment and how these impacted the quality of care that women and girls received. However, like any social movement, this one was built on a series of inclusions and exclusions that validated the experiences of some women at the expense of others.

Side by side with the development of the women's health movement in the UK were the 'six demands' of the women's liberation movement which were a major unifying force for activist women. These six demands included

1. Free 24-hour nurseries
2. Equal pay
3. Equal education and job opportunities
4. Free contraception and abortion on demand
5. Financial and legal independence
6. An end to discrimination against lesbians and the right to a self-defined sexuality.

Health and reproductive rights were covered by the fourth demand, which signalled much broader concerns than contraception and abortion. From the early 1970s on, women's groups were involved in questioning how men usurped women's health. Some feminist activists took up gynaecological self-examination; others joined campaigns for Well-Women clinics in towns and cities throughout Britain; still others joined the National Abortion Campaign (NAC) (Coote and Campbell, 1982: 38–40). The Women's Health Information Centre (WHIC) was founded in London in 1982 with funding from the Equal Opportunities Commission, War on Want and the World Health Organization.[10] The following year the Women's Reproductive Rights Information Centre (WRRIC) was set up in London to focus on reproductive rights; WRRIC was funded by the Greater London Council's Women's Committee (Coote and Campbell, 1982: 41).

In her work on the women's health movement in Britain, Lesley Doyal (1983) saw this movement as divided into three main stages: (1) developing outside of the NHS with the emphasis on 'women as consumers of medical care'; (2) developing within the NHS 'defending it against reductions and privatisation'; and (3) the development of a 'socialist feminist epidemiology' with the goal of eliminating those aspects of contemporary society that 'make women sick' (see also Doyal, 1979, 1995). In both the US and UK, critical attention to key issues constructed as 'feminist' – such as patriarchal medical discourse, gynaecological control of women's bodies, inadequate prenatal and antenatal care for pregnant women, and the 'pure' sexism of sex role stereotypes in medical literature (Scully and Bart, 1973; Oakley, 1979, 1984) – along with emergent reproductive technologies led women's health activists to single out sexuality, gynaecology, and reproductive issues for major emphasis. Most central to our argument in this book, Kathy Davis argues that *OBOS* was an 'epistemological project' contributing not only critique of dominant clinical practices and questioning what counted as authoritative knowledge of women's bodies, but constructing new knowledges and practices.

Knowledge and practice in the addiction and alcoholism arena was one such emergent site; however, one reason that there has been little attention to the history of women's drug and alcohol treatment is because women's health activism has been treated as 'theoretically naïve and methodologically flawed' within feminist theory of the body (Davis, 2007: 124). We agree with Davis that the women's health movement should be regarded as a knowledge project that brought into being new practices – among them feminist psychotherapy and a new attention to women's drug and alcohol use both in the women's movement and in healthcare contexts beyond it. This in turn helped bring about governmental or official attention to women's issues, the effects of which are still seen today in the US and UK.

The *OBOS* 1984 psychotherapy chapter was written by Nancy Miriam Hawley, a University of Michigan-trained social worker who moved from Ann Arbor to the Boston area in the early 1970s, and Wendy Coppedge Sanford, with assistance from two members of the collective who were distinctly anti-psychotherapy (Davis, 2007: 31; Wells, 2010: 52). Unlike most other founders of the BWHBC, Hawley played a role in fostering drug and alcohol treatment for women in the Cambridge-Somerville area and the state of Massachusetts. One of Hawley's friends from Ann Arbor, Norma Finkelstein, who had also been active in the New Left and the women's health movement, had moved to Cambridge, Massachusetts, and wanted to share a full-time social work job with Hawley. In late 1971, Hawley and Finkelstein were hired by the newly opened Cambridge-Somerville Program for Alcoholism Rehabilitation (CASPAR), which was run by Helma Unterberger, then associate director of the Cambridge-Somerville Mental Health Center, and Lena DiCicco, the founder of CASPAR, both of whom worked for the state division of alcoholism. CASPAR was not seeking a traditional mental health social worker. When they entered the field, neither

Hawley nor Finkelstein had any particular knowledge of or interest in alcoholism or drug addiction; neither had entered the field with personal interest or a known family history. Both were parents of young children and activists in the women's health movement. Hawley's involvement in the making of *OBOS* is well-documented by Davis and Wells; Finkelstein worked at the Somerville Women's Health Project, which ran a clinic, where she started a small women's alcohol education project along with a colleague named Louise Rice.[11] Finkelstein became increasingly involved with both the public health apparatus in the state of Massachusetts and in grass-roots health organizing; indeed she was contemplating retirement but still working in the field as this book went to press. In CASPAR Hawley and Finkelstein encountered a group of reform-minded health professionals, including Bill Clark and George Vaillant,[12] and the palpable excitement that came with entering a new field that was in the process of pressuring old frameworks and producing new ones.

Given their involvement in women's issues and new institutions arising out of the movement such as women's centres and clinics, Hawley and Finkelstein were primed to notice how few women came through the doors of CASPAR. Looking back on a career spent trying to gain drug and alcohol treatment for women not only in Massachusetts, but at the national level, Finkelstein said, 'At the time I was still working with the women's health centre and doing a lot of political work. The thing that struck me and Nancy was that we saw very few women, mostly older women, but very few women. If women came into intake at the detox unit – if a woman even appeared at the detox unit, it was like everybody went ballistic. They didn't know what to do. They had nothing for her, no grooming materials, etcetera, if she got her period. It was so rare that they didn't know what to do. They always thought she was enticing the men, and they always got very angry so that she didn't stay long. It was very disturbing, so I started a women's [drop-in] group there, back in '72, '73'.[13] Finkelstein became increasingly vocal about women as an under-served population of alcoholics, and became involved in starting programmes designed to raise the visibility of the issue and change how alcoholism was viewed within the women's community in and around Cambridge. She recalled that alcoholism was not viewed as a disease or illness at the time, noting,

> We've almost come full circle in terms of the disease concept. We had been being schooled every week by Helma Unterberger that the worst thing that had happened to the alcoholism field was that alcoholism

> was viewed as a symptom of an underlying problem, a mental health problem or a social problem, and in order to treat alcoholism, you couldn't allow those 'excuses', you had to go directly to the issue of alcohol use. You couldn't talk to people about why they drink, or what the problems are, because they'll just use that to get the focus off their alcohol use. You had to put the focus back on their alcoholism. So I had been steeped in this. The women's community, of course, thought ... that people drink because they're poor, that people drink because they're oppressed, that people drink because they have been raped.... [B]ack then, we were saying to the women's community, what you need to pay equal attention to is the disease of alcoholism, and to talk about drinking and drunkenness, and definitions of alcoholism and recovery'.[14]

In the mid-1970s, Finkelstein helped found the Massachusetts Coalition for Women's Alcoholism Services and joined in the National Council on Alcoholism women's task force initiative.

In the 1970s, the emerging focus on women's alcoholism and addictions clearly felt new to those involved. The state of knowledge within the field was considered to be under-developed and there was a sense that programmes were learning what worked as they grew. Until policy forced mergers in the 1980s and 1990s, most states separated alcohol from drug treatment programmes. In the state of Massachusetts, alcohol programmes were in the Division of Public Health, while drug programmes were administered by the Division of Mental Health. Two separate cultures had arisen from this institutional division of labour, which held true in many states as late as the 1990s. Until activists interested in women's issues gained a foothold in the federal research and treatment infrastructure, formal and informal barriers to sharing knowledge or practice across the drug and alcohol divide were high. Those activists sought to undo the dominance of mental health in the drug and alcohol field, and they received help from both the states and the federal government during the 1970s. Indeed, CASPAR emphasized 'de-programming' the clinical staff in weekly 'Drinking, Drunkenness, and Alcoholism' (DD and A) supervision sessions designed to reorient those who considered alcoholism a symptom of mental illness to thinking instead about the 'disease of alcoholism'.[15] However, the alcoholic towards whom the state of Massachusetts directed funds at the time was typically an older white male who fit the category 'public inebriate'. Women who were problem drinkers neither fit the typical demographic nor manifested the same behaviours. Women simply did not fit into theory or practice within the field. As she built women's treatment programmes and created coalitions, Finkelstein drew on psychologist Jean Baker Miller's 'relational model', advanced at The Stone Center at Wellesley College, for a conceptual framework. We address the relational model further in the next chapter, as it represents an important feminist contribution to women's treatment advocacy in the US. The relational model provided a way out of the strategic essentialism of the maternalist programmes, and laid groundwork for another important conceptual move that we discuss later – the turn to trauma as a way to understand women's addictions.

The women's health movement was a heterogeneous set of social movement actors interacting at local, state, and federal levels in the US (Epstein, 2007: 55–7). For instance, the BWHBC defined itself as different from the health care delivery system created by the new infrastructure of women's clinics and the women's self-help culture. Indeed the BWHBC defined itself as an explicitly political and implicitly epistemological project. In 1973, Ruth Bell Alexander described the project as 'demonstrat[ing] the process of how we arrive at thoughts and discoveries' (Wells, 2010: 184). During this process, the body was viewed as a source of knowledge and experiences that were inseparable from the mind. At the same time, women's ideas about their bodies had clearly been inscribed by the dominant discourse of medicine. The women's health movement held together this very layered, nuanced and heterogeneous set of ideas about 'our bodies, ourselves'. These sometimes inchoate but often pointedly critical ideas found their way into the construction of women's drug and alcohol use as women's health issues.

The 'DAWNING' of a visible public feminist response – the emergence of DAWN

As discussed above, the British women's health movement emerged from the autonomous WLM, which was rooted in twentieth-century British socialism, as well as cultural and radical feminism which became visible in the UK during the early 1970s. About the same time, the Camberwell Council of Alcoholism (CCA), which had been set up in 1962 in South London, began to mount in the early 1970s a response to concerns over female alcoholism. The CCA was set up 'to obtain the range of services necessary to help people with drinking problems or those affected by the drinking of others' as well as to 'campaign for services and finding ways of educating lay and professional people about the nature and consequence of alcohol abuse' (CCA, 1980: xiii). The CCA noted in the Introduction to its now classic text, *Women and Alcohol* (1980), that

> Members of the council were worried that so little was understood about how to best to meet the needs of these women. As a result a series of seminars for local lay and professional people were arranged and were so successful that an action group was set up ... This group met, almost every week for four years from 1974 to 1978 ... [and was] ultimately ... responsible, with others, for setting up Drugs, Alcohol and Women Nationally (DAWN) whose purpose is to co-ordinate and channel efforts to obtain for women who are alcohol and drug abusers services to assist them and which are their right.
>
> (CCA, 1980: xiii)

Some of the women involved had strong links with the Addiction Research Unit, Institute of Psychiatry, University of London and the Maudsley Hospital, both of which were located in South London. A key player at the time and another member of the CCA sub-group was the clinical psychologist, Dr. Gloria Litman, who was one of the first UK researchers to point out that the double standard operating in the addiction field of disadvantaged women (Litman, 1978). After already making her academic mark in the area with a now classic article on women and alcohol (Litman, 1975), she and Clare Wilson (1978) undertook a survey under the sponsorship of the CCA in 1978 that revealed that while female alcoholics differ from male alcoholics, these differences are not reflected in treatment programmes (Page, 1980).

The CCA sub-group spawned a 'network of activists' (Thom, 1997: 54) that established the UK's most important development for women's drug treatment, DAWN. While a steering committee met in 1979, the first DAWN symposium, 'A Campaign for Women with Alcohol and Drug Problems' was held on 28 November 1980 (DAWN, 1980). The DAWN report revealed that between 1969 and 1974 there was a significant increase in the consumption of alcohol in Britain, especially among women and female drunkenness had been increasing at a greater rate than male drunkenness. These were important times for feminist practitioners and researchers working in this area and raising feminist awareness engendered a time of hope. When a key drugs worker at Release, London, Lyn Perry, published in 1979 the first feminist article on women and drugs and 'the female junkie' in the UK, *Women and Drug Use: An Unfeminine Dependency*, there was much excitement among the feminists in the addiction community.

Perry's article as well as other research produced by Release was a 'way for voluntary groups to justify their own existence by pointing to a clear need not being met by statutory services and therefore, the importance of their own work' (Mold and Berridge, 2010: 71). That the article was published under the auspices of Institute for the Study of Drug Dependence (ISDD), an independent drugs charity and 'dedicated voluntary drugs organisation' (Mold and Berridge, 2010: 72) established in 1968, encouraged activists as it meant that women's voices could begin to be heard in the official drugs community.

In November 1981 when the first DAWN annual conference was held, there was discussion among participants about ensuring that DAWN truly reflect its name, Drugs Alcohol and Women Nationally, and widening the initial focus from alcohol to drugs. It was clear that DAWN was gaining visibility as a feminist-oriented pressure group, although it did at times get 'bad press' because it had a distinct women-only focus and according to allegations by Betsy Thom (1997: 59), a distinct separatist stance,[16] in that DAWN members, when negotiating funds, would only meet female members of the Department of Health. The year 1984 was a watershed year for DAWN as it was one of the local London women's organizations to gain funding for three years for two workers and operational costs from the Greater London Council Women's Committee in April of that year.[17] One stipulation for funding was that DAWN alter its name slightly to Drugs Alcohol Women Nationally (London).

During the next few years, DAWN workers were instrumental in generating a substantial amount of campaigning material in the area. There was a clear mandate from the DAWN management committee,[18] which included women practitioners, women researchers, and women users, for the organization to include all substances and be sensitive to BME groups and sexual minorities such as lesbians (See DAWN, 1984a, 1985a, 1985b, 1986; Nolan and Day, 1988). A turning point in terms of DAWN's credibility was its testimony before the House of Commons Social Services Committee in January 1985, which provides a brief description of its work:

> DAWN is a federation of local groups with the intention of improving the lot of women with drug or alcohol problems. Over the past 6 years we have been active campaigners in the twin fields of prevention and treatment arguing the case for a better deal for women and thus for all. It is our strong contention that most services for drug users in this country are at present under-financed, misdirected, inadequately planned and often ineffective. Frequently, their foundation and working seem to make more account of the views of bureaucrats,

> politicians and academic researchers than of the population they purport to serve – drug users and their families and friends – to their detriment.
>
> (DAWN, 1985c)

The appearance of DAWN at a 'prestigious' House of Commons Select Committee was most likely the result of the publication a year earlier of the results of the DAWN Survey of Facilities for women using drugs including alcohol in London (see DAWN, 1984b). This report was widely publicized and presented clear policy implications for developing services for women. It included seven major findings:

1. Of the 254 agencies surveyed less than half (n=100) offered no services to women.
2. Only one in five projects made any particular effort to help mothers with drug/alcohol problems.
3. Although all of the 100 agencies offering services to women were thought to be aware of the specific needs of women clients, 83 agencies responded that women clients had needs or problems different from men. Of the 83 agencies responding that women had special needs, 18 agencies were unable to actually state any needs or problems specific to women.
4. Only about one in four agencies recognized women's particular problems with childcare and housing, while less than one in five accepted that women face discrimination in treatment.
5. Only 51 agencies were able to specify what, if any, further facilities they felt were needed for women.
6. Despite the fact that London is a multiracial city many agencies responded as if cultures other than white European ones did not exist. Only one in 20 agencies saw more than 10% black women or women of colour clients. None of the specialized drug/alcohol co-ordinating agencies offered any analysis of institutionalized racism and of the problems faced by people from different cultures.
7. Statutory facilities (Drug Dependence Units and Alcoholism Treatment Units) showed the least understanding of women's needs and were most difficult to obtain responses from.

'We must do something about women': The Central Funding Initiative

But the bleak outlook detailed in the DAWN report was about to be overcome. By this time Dorothy Black had become established as a Senior Medical Officer with special responsibility for drug misuse policy at the then Department of Health and Social Security (DHSS) in London. She described it as a 'post which included drugs policy' in the DHSS. Although she accepted the post in 1981, it was not until the following year that

> The then Secretary of State, Norman Fowler, was persuaded, having been to the States, that there was an increasing drug problem and with the advent of HIV and AIDS late in the eighties, he became convinced that more should be done. In fact, it was during the early eighties that most of the funding, Central Funding Initiative (CFI) was set up to begin with ... Then increasing amounts of money went into drug services. So that by the time I left the department in 1991, there was a fairly sizable commitment to services for drug users.[19]

As a government initiative, the CFI was the Conservative government's main response to the Advisory Council on the Misuse of Drugs (ACMD) 1982 *Treatment and Rehabilitation* report (ACMD, 1982).[20] The CFI was responsible for pump priming almost one-third of the 364 dedicated drug services in England through 188 funding grants (MacGregor, et al., 1991). Before the CFI, Black noted that government policy makers found it difficult to talk about drugs:

> They weren't saying anything about policy. I mean drugs had almost fallen off the map. Alcohol at the time was the big drug ... I remember we used to have joint policy meetings – alcohol and drugs – because they both fell under the same Under Secretary [and] drugs always came last on the agenda ... I eventually had a hissy fit and said I wasn't going to come if I had to sit until half past five before they discussed my area. ... I remember colleagues who were what I call proper civil servants who had been in the Department for the whole of their working careers used to say, 'You know, nothing's happened on the drugs front since the sixties' and it hadn't.[21]

While Black was at the department, she was known among feminists working in the field as someone who was sympathetic to women's issues. For example, she was one of 81 participants at a conference, *Women's Problems with Alcohol and Other Drugs: Improving Our Response*, organized by the Alcohol Interventions Training Unit, University of Kent and the Addiction Research Unit, Institute of Psychiatry University of London on 5 July 1986 (See Ettorre et al., 1987). She was involved in agreeing to fund women's services (including DAWN) under the CFI from 1983 until 1989. She recalls how some of these women's services were funded and how she was instrumental in helping organizations such as DAWN and Phoenix House, to get funding:

> I mean in a way, it was more a demand-led initiative if you like. Rather than that I sat [around] and said, 'We must do something about women'... We – all the people in the drug policy group – i.e., nurse, social work, medical, and administrator had to comment on the projects submitted. The nurse wasn't particularly interested, the social worker was very supportive but busy in other areas and the administrator became enthusiastic and would often discuss projects with me. So if you like I seemed to have a major input.[22]

By 'doing something about women' Black helped to provide for a gap in services, which was recognized already some years back by CCA. Her determination and perseverance as a Senior Medical Officer was instructive and exemplary, and she began to realize:

> There was a need for specific projects developed for women.... I remember talking to some of the women who were living there and ... a minority didn't want separate sessions but the majority did because many of them obviously had been exposed to not only adult abuse but sexual abuse in childhood which as you know is very common among women drug users ... They said that they weren't prepared to talk about that in front of men which seemed to be reasonable. I mean they didn't have to go to them. They didn't have to go to the women's session if they didn't want to. But ... I found it very interesting there were a small minority of women who said they preferred having the joint session ... Phoenix ... let them ... which they preferred, whereas in some of the other houses, they didn't have separate sessions [for] women.[23]

Conclusion

This chapter has looked at how the public response to women drugs and alcohol users arose out of new social movements such as the civil rights movements, the human rights movement, and the women's rights movement, with a particular emphasis on women's health movements. The next chapter examines the kinds of programmes that were created as the result of the recognition that the treatment infrastructure these movements encountered was structured in ways that made it difficult, if not impossible, for women to identify with its process and goals. We see how modernist drug rehabilitation was a practice of moulding women drug users to conform to dominant social norms – and also a practice that led them to see themselves as abject, deviant, and at risk.

3
Undue Burdens: The Emergence of Feminist Treatment Advocacy in a Masculinist System

This chapter maps out the history of feminist attempts to carve out the space in which to create and sustain feminist and gender-sensitive treatment programmes during the 1980s and 1990s. We examine those factors that made for sustainable programmes and those that led to non-sustainability and ultimate dissolution or demise. We trace the history of programmes targeted to 'special populations' and women with 'special needs', including sexuality, disability, multi-racial, and ethnic communities, and a history of sexual abuse or trauma.

Special consideration: Working women into the emerging drug and alcohol treatment infrastructure in the United States

During the 1970s and 1980s, feminists participated in a women's health movement that led to the creation of a clinic infrastructure and community-based women's centres throughout the country. As illustrated in the previous chapter, many members of this generational cohort who entered alcohol and drug treatment in the early 1970s were members of the New Left. Radicalized in the 1960s, they were part of the anti-war movement that marched on Washington, D.C.; had connections to the Weather Underground, Students for a Democratic Society (SDS), the Student Nonviolent Coordinating Committee (SNCC), or the Boston Women's Health Book Collective (BWHBC); and had participated in early women's consciousness-raising (CR) groups. They defined themselves as feminists and entered the workforce with an analysis of the gendered social constraints operating in their societies that they had crafted in the course of participating in the new, pro-democratic social movements. They experienced working the telephones for some of the earliest drug hotlines and street-front outreach programmes. The importance of feminist CR as a precursor to the active listening techniques they brought with them into group therapy sessions, and for the woman-centred approaches such as 'learning from the client' that they still espouse today, cannot be underestimated.

The organized women's movement in the US – and, specifically, the women's health movement – was an important backdrop to these activities. Yet the movement was at times an obstacle against which these then-young activists asserted the need for women's drug and alcohol treatment. They came into a treatment field that was itself undergoing a formative expansion and a knowledge explosion quite separate from the women's health movement. Up until this time drug treatment had been a federal responsibility in the US. Alcohol treatment was separate from drug treatment, which was highly centralized and delivered by a relatively small number of clinicians associated with the US Public Health Service Hospitals from the mid-1930s to the mid-1960s (Campbell, 2007; Campbell, Olsen and Walden, 2008). The so-called narcotic farms were massive residential facilities at which myriad treatment modalities were practiced under one roof. They were criticized for their lack of supervised aftercare, follow-up, or even outcomes studies – and their relapse rate was considered dismally high. The ratio of male to female addicts at the Lexington Hospital fell over time from 5:1 to 4:1 to 3:1. Despite these seeming failures, the federal system was the locus of knowledge production about drug addiction and dependence in the US.

The 1966 Narcotic Addict Rehabilitation Act (NARA) paved the way for a substantial shift towards community-based treatment in the 1970s. The complex implementation of NARA, a federal civil commitment law, laid the foundation for a new, local clinical infrastructure by providing service contracts for local treatment agencies *anywhere* an addicted person needed treatment.[1] NARA can best be thought of as an experiment that enabled the federal government to transition away from treating addicts directly in a centralized facility and move towards community-based treatment. The decentralized approach embodied in NARA also demonstrated that persons other than physicians could administer drug treatment. Agency contracts helped bring social workers, vocational rehabilitation counsellors, and other para-professionals into the field, contributing to the decentralized treatment infrastructure that still exists today in the US. The law required services be delivered even where they were not yet available, so field offices supervised and trained social workers to treat addicts. Field office personnel convinced often reluctant Community Mental Health Centers (CMHCs) to include addicts in the populations served. Despite expense and difficulty, the National Institute of Mental Health's (NIMH) Division of Narcotics and Drug Addiction (DNADA) negotiated contracts throughout the country. Where there was a substantial contingent of clients, treatment within NARA settings was oriented towards the Therapeutic Community (TC) modality – and based on confrontational tactics that many women clients and feminist treatment providers found offensive, hierarchical, and more damaging than helpful for women who had suffered previous violence at the hands of partners or spouses. Not until a decade or two later would the 'trauma-informed' treatment services we address in Chapter 5 come into being. However, the germ of the 'trauma-informed' orientation surely lay in women's encounter with some of the very arbitrary uses of authority that they were trying to get away from by growing a treatment infrastructure responsive to women's needs.

It became clear to the women who would become women's treatment advocates in both the alcoholism and drug abuse fields that they were working within an 'androcentric' or male-centred and at times masculinist system in which they would have to carve out the space to create and sustain women's alcohol and drug treatment programmes. Central to these efforts was Beth Reed, who worked on the Women's Drug Research Coordinating Project, which ran from 1974 to 1982:

> When we got funded to do the Women's Drug Research Project in 1974, we did a literature search. In terms of the knowledge base, there were maybe 15 or 20 studies I could find. Most of the studies we found were Lexington studies. There were a couple community-based studies of women and pain medications [and …] the women's health movement took on the issue of the over-prescription of tranquilizers. The Women's Health Initiative, which started here in Ann Arbor at a clinic, they started doing advocacy work around physician over-prescribing. Then the people involved went off to Washington because they wanted to do advocacy work. It was tied to the whole movement of women taking control of their bodies.[2]

Feminists were sensitive to the characterization of women addicts and alcoholics, but they were also seeing what Reed has called a 'gendered treatment paradigm':

> [T]he basic models of treatment are set up for how substance abuse looks in men, and much of our ideology about substance abuse is about exaggerated coping styles. What we learned from all these

> scales we put in was that people who have substance abuse problems have in fact really stereotyped ideas about masculinity and femininity, more so than average people. They also feel that they're not living up to those ideals and that's partly because those ideals are stereotypes, caricatures, almost. That might be part of why they got in trouble in the first place.[3]

Indeed, notions about gender norms and roles pervaded the literature of this time – were women alcoholics more or less 'feminine' than their male counterparts? Were they 'hypersexual' or 'frigid'? Were they too 'liberated' or not 'liberated' enough? What was the role of gendered social expectations in producing and sustaining addiction or alcoholism in women?

It soon became clear to these young activists that if they were to create a national treatment infrastructure focused on women, they would have to work within the federal and state governments, and join some of the more venerable efforts underway in the alcohol field. Women's organizations pushed the US Congress to fund 'holistic' women's treatment programmes through the 1970s and 1980s.[4] Sustained women's treatment advocacy – by a relatively small set of feminist advocates who worked for decades at the national, state, and local levels – has been the most important element in the creation of a women's treatment infrastructure in the US. Then newly constituted from the Nixon White House response to drug abuse, the NIDA hosted three national conferences on women and drugs in 1974, including one on 'perinatal addiction'. The next year NIDA sponsored a National Forum on Drugs, Alcohol and Women, and in 1976, a conference on Women and Drug Concerns.

Held at the Fontainebleau Hotel in Miami, Florida, the 1975 National Forum was a watershed moment for many of those working on the issue. This memorable meeting became an important touchstone for many women's treatment advocates, who described it as the first attempt of which they were aware to bridge the prevailing split between the 'alcohol side' and the 'drug side' (see below). This national meeting brought some of the key women's advocates from both sides together for the first time. Produced by a small company founded by Muriel Nellis, who also directed the National Alliance of Regional Coalitions: Drugs, Alcohol and Women's Health and wrote *The Female Fix* (1980), the National Forum was structured as an 'inclusive discussion, irrespective of existing enmity between the separate bureaucracies and specialists' she encountered even then (Nellis, 1980: 137). Writing about this period, Nellis found the US government's response to women's treatment needs very slow. Attributing this to a 'historic disinclination to tamper with society's expectations of perfection in womanhood' but even more importantly the nation's 'preoccup[ation] with alcoholism and drug abuse as issues signifying violence, crime, and danger to persons and property' (1980: 129), Nellis drew the attention of policy makers, treatment providers, and women themselves to what she called the 'simple and deadly' assumption that structured drug and alcohol treatment: 'that drug addiction in our culture is primarily a male phenomenon' (1980: 128). Thus 'most publicly funded treatment models – among them substitute-drug therapies and lifestyle modification techniques – have been designed to affect desirable change in the male body and male behavior' (Nellis, 1980: 128).

Over the decades the claim that there was something 'male' or 'masculinist' about treatment programmes has been made by many of the women most active in pressuring the US government to expand treatment capacity, increase women's access to it, and improve its quality. Federal support for interchange between women's treatment providers was significant for programme-building during the late 1970s. NIDA's first programmes recognizing women as a 'special population' occurred in 1973–4 (Beschner, Reed, and Mondanaro, 1981). The Drugs, Alcohol, and Women's Health Project, an alliance of five regional coalitions funded by NIDA through its Program for Women's Concerns, was started in October 1975. Among the first successes resulting from these activities issued from the US Senate Subcommittee on Alcoholism and Narcotics hearings on 'Special Problems Among Women' in 1976, which led to a funding stream for flexible programmes specifically tailored to women's needs. US Public Law 94-371, the 'Comprehensive Alcohol Abuse and Alcoholism Prevention, Treatment, and Rehabilitation Act Amendments of 1976', the legislation that came out of these hearings, stabilized the policy framework within which women's treatment programmes first developed. The law directed the Secretary of the Department of Health, Education, and Welfare (HEW) to give special consideration to drug abuse prevention and treatment projects for women and youth. At the time, the Alcohol, Drug Abuse and Mental Health Administration (ADAMHA) was composed of three institutes with responsibility for treatment services and research on substance abuse, alcoholism, and mental health: NIDA, NIAAA, and NIMH.[5]

Efforts to direct special consideration towards women's treatment programmes involved an alliance between women's treatment advocates and the National Council on Alcoholism, which created a national network of women's task forces coordinated by a special office on women that opened in 1975 under the direction of Jan DuPlain. The National Congress of State Task Forces on Women and Alcoholism met for the first time at the annual NCA forum in May 1976, and on 29 September 1976, representatives of these organizations testified before the Senate Committee on Labor and Public Welfare's Subcommittee on Alcoholism and Narcotics in a hearing on 'Alcohol Abuse Among Women: Special Problems and Unmet Needs'. The previous summer, DuPlain had offered the first course on women and alcoholism at the prestigious Rutgers Summer School of Alcohol Studies – the first such course in the entire 34 years of its existence. Details of the congressional efforts of Senators Harold Hughes, Pete Williams, and William Hathaway leading to the formation of the NIAAA can be found in a book by congressional aide Nancy Olson, *With a Lot of Help from Our Friends: The Politics of Alcoholism* (2003).

Within the context of the 1976 hearings, recommendations for funding of older women's residential treatment for those who have 'special problems which relate to a feeling of uselessness': 'If women see themselves as whole people only when they are administering to the needs of others, they stop functioning when they are no longer needed by others. Therefore, both prevention and treatment of alcoholism in women must concentrate on improving women's self-image and ego'.[6] A focus on low self-esteem was also prominent in Jean Kirkpatrick's organization, Women For Sobriety, a women's mutual aid society formed in response to the lack of focus on gender in AA. Coming on the heels of a movement for women's 'assertiveness training', this effort says much about how treatment advocates viewed the implications of social change for addicted and alcoholic women.

When former First Lady Betty Ford disclosed her alcoholism and her 'accidental', 'medical' addiction to pain pills prescribed in the aftermath of an accident in the early 1960s, she propelled the issue to national prominence. Ford's disclosure was unsettling to many, raising questions about the extent to which 'stressful demands made on the lives of many millions of other nurturing, hard-working women' had rendered them 'chemical cripples' (Nellis, 1980: 4–5). For *The Female Fix* (1980) resulted not simply from women's medical access to prescription pain medications, legal psychotropics, and the 'big mood-altering business', but because *both* legal and illegal drugs were associated with addiction (Nellis, 1980: 129). This pressured any easy distinction between legal and illegal drugs, or medical and non-medical use, and made it difficult for therapeutic innovation to take place because the spectre of 'political, legal and economic trouble' discouraged both activists and physicians from translating their concerns into action and pushed efforts into the private sector and into 'mutual aid' or 'self help' societies (Nellis, 1980: 129). Government efforts took place at a distance from these due to their close association with the women's movement and organizations that had religious ties.

Pregnancy and parenting also became prominent sites for women's treatment during the 1970s. In 1975 NIDA funded three-year demonstration projects in six major US cities with a focus on treating pregnant women addicts, and in 1973 NIAAA had funded 14 women's programmes across the country (and 574 for men). The National Coalition for Women's Alcoholism Programs (NCWAP), led by Norma Finkelstein, then director of the Women's Alcoholism Program at CASPAR and Brenda Weathers, who directed the Alcoholism Center for Women in Los Angeles, California, coordinated the 14 NIAAA-funded women's programmes. Yet Finkelstein recalls that even that tiny amount of funding directed specifically towards women inspired charges of 'anti-male bias'. The Coalition was successful in opposing budget cutbacks, including a matching policy proposed by NIAAA for the 1978 fiscal year, that would have reduced the budgets of these fledgling programmes by 20 per cent unless they were directed towards American Indians. Noting that cuts proposed in 1977 posed a 'particular disadvantage' for the newly-funded women's programmes, the Coalition compared the situation to a discriminatory attitude of 'last hired, first fired'.[7] As Finkelstein put it in a retrospective interview, cuts were proposed 'just after the women's programmes had barely gotten off the ground. They were only a few years old, and we decided that they couldn't survive if they had to make up the difference, so we formed what looked like a national coalition of women's alcoholism programmes. It was essentially myself in Cambridge and Brenda Weathers at the Alcoholism Program for Women, which was a very big centre at the time. We got stationery and went to Washington to testify. We did get women's programmes exempted ... There was a lot of federal push, a lot of focus on women in alcoholism, and also on women and drugs'.[8]

This productive ferment of the 1970s ended, however, in the early 1980s due to the Reagan administration's philosophy of devolution and consequent expansion of the block-grant funding model. So-called block grants had two negative effects on women's drug and alcohol programmes. First, the role of the NIAAA was reduced to funding research rather than direct services (Roth, 1991b: xi), a move soon to be replicated on the drug side. Secondly, the block-grant approach effectively merged funding for alcohol and drug treatment with funding for mental health services, and relied upon states to administer funds. Block grants achieve their reputation for effectiveness mainly in situations where there are already existing administrative capacities[9] – and in the case of women's drug and alcohol treatment programmes, capacity varied from state to state. Over time, the value of block-grant funding declines – and in the case of federal alcohol and drug treatment, the decline was abrupt and precipitous as activists had concentrated on the federal level due to the successes of the 1970s. In states such as California, Massachusetts, and New York, where there had historically been state-level funding and awareness-raising activities, coalitions, and other communicative mechanisms, women's programmes were able to hold on through the lean years of the early to mid-1980s. As should be apparent, this geopolitical unevenness was exacerbated by the shift to the New Federalism.

Although the initial women's treatment programmes started up as a result of the 1976 Act were accessible to women and demonstrated their value, this effort was undone by the Reagan administration. The categorical funding awarded as a result of the legislative strategy was replaced by block grants to each state in the early 1980s as part of the 'Reagan revolution', which relied on a strategy of devolution of responsibility for services to state and local governments. Responsibility for research remained with the US federal government. Unlike the high degree of centralization witnessed in Thatcherite Britain (Mold and Berridge, 2010: 97), in the US the 'new federalism' worked through the decentralization of service provision, particularly in mental health-related fields, that set states adrift in the 1980s. This resulted in an uneven terrain due to the presence or absence of women's treatment advocates or availability of private treatment programmes within any given state.[10] Like Britain's Central Funding Initiative, however, which Mold and Berridge (2010: 97) argue 'cast the government in the role of initiator of new services rather than their long-term funder' as part of a strategy for 'rolling back the state' through a 'command and control model,' the US federal government played the role of initiator or 'provider' but left allocation of block grant funds and implementation of programmes to the states. In 1984 the US Congress enacted a very important piece of legislation from the point of view of women's treatment advocacy, for the Alcohol Abuse, Drug Abuse and Mental Health Amendments (Public Law 98–509) contained a specific Women's Set-Aside that mandated states to devote at least five per cent of their total block grants to women's prevention and treatment programmes

(Brown, 1995: 321). The percentage to be set-aside was doubled to 10 per cent in 1988, with priority granted to pregnant and parenting women. During the 1980s, there was also continuing NIAAA and NIDA research on biomedical issues such as pregnancy and FAS after 1977, when the NIAAA sponsored the first research conference on the topic. There was also a nascent national women's 'training culture' in NIDA, described by Reed, who helped shape the national women's treatment agenda:

> What happened in 1985 back when Josette [Mondanaro] and I were doing all this training, we thought it would just be a matter of reading all these books and putting something together. Just as we were finishing those two volumes,[11] we realized that people didn't really know about this literature. It turns out that if I re-read those books now, there's only 40 per cent that I'd have to update – crack wasn't there yet and of course AIDS didn't exist then. But all the seeds of [what we see today] were there.[12]

This cyclic pattern of revisiting and rediscovering the existence of knowledge about women's drug and alcohol treatment has been repeated more than once. We write this book in part to document the many years of simultaneous efforts occurring in the last decades of the twentieth century.

The transition to block grants was viewed as placing women's programmes at risk – or at least in a situation of competing priorities within states, which were experiencing an overall reduction in funding for mental health services, including drug and alcohol treatment. The transition to block grants, however, stimulated organizing attempts to gain a mechanism for supporting gender-specific alcohol and drug treatment programmes. In 1984 the NCA and key members of Congress succeeded in passing Public Law 98–509, the 'Alcohol Abuse, Drug Abuse, and Mental Health Amendments of 1984', which amended the Public Health Service Act (1944) and became known as 'the women's set-aside'. The women's set-aside represented a victory for women's treatment proponents who targeted the federal level, because it required the states to set aside five per cent (and in 1988 the Anti-Drug Abuse Act raised this to ten per cent; Chavkin et al., 1998) of their block-grant funding to new women's prevention and treatment initiatives.[13] While the set-aside propelled states to develop women's programmes, its potent conjunction with the crack-cocaine crisis heightened concerns about pregnancy and parenting. The Offices of Treatment Improvement (OTI) and the Office for Substance Abuse Prevention (OSAP) were formed in 1986 as NIDA underwent a disaggregation of prevention, treatment, and research similar to NIAAA. Beny Primm, an influential African-American physician and civil rights activist with experience taking over buildings in Harlem to start up drug programmes, was chosen to head the OTI. A champion of women's involvement, Primm saw the division of research from treatment and prevention as creating an unwanted elitism between researchers and treatment providers. Of the bureaucratic split, he noted, 'I had problems with that break of research and treatment. I did not want to get involved in an intramural kind of war like what went on. I think there was some resentment on the part of NIDA that some of their funds were taken away to form OTI'.[14] NIDA was increasingly compelled to leave treatment behind except when it could be funded as some form of research. Yet state-level funding, or funding from the non-profit sector, was unpredictable, as the next section illustrates.

Against the odds: *Alcohol and Drugs are Women's Issues*

Formed in 1981, the Women's Action Alliance (WAA) could point to several successes at the national level, including launching the National Association of Women's Centers in 1986 and the still-celebrated National Women's History Month. As the Historical Note to the Sophia Smith collection at Smith College, which holds the archives of the WAA, observes: 'The WAA's main modus operandi was to identify a problem, question, or population with specific needs; formulate and distribute a questionnaire exploring the activities and needs of groups or individuals concerned with the issue in question; and summarize the results in a directory, guide, or manual'. In 1987, the WAA took just this approach in launching the Women's Alcohol and Drug Education Project (WADEP), which sought to reduce alcohol, tobacco and other drug use (ATOD) among women and adolescent girls. Two volumes of *Alcohol and Drugs are Women's Issues*, edited by Paula Roth, were published in 1991 by the Women's Action Alliance and Scarecrow Press.

Alcohol and Drugs are Women's Issues began with a list of facts demonstrating the need for the women's movement to understand that alcohol and drugs are also women's issues – each making the point that alcoholism and drug abuse were either more prevalent or more consequential for women not only in terms of biological vulnerabilities such as morbidity and co-occurring disorders, but also in terms of social disempowerment. Although Roth credited the women's movement with focusing national attention on other women's issues – reproductive rights, violence against women, and 'equal pay for equal work' – she clearly felt that the movement had given short shrift to alcohol and drugs, failing to see them within the broader context of women's issues and not attending to 'multicultural and economic issues' (1991a: *x*). Women's centres – which were promoted by the WAA – were seen as a locus for women's empowerment. Although their number, focus, and force had already begun to decline by the time Roth published *Drugs and Alcohol are Women's Issues* (1991a and b), she saw women's centres as ideal settings for reaching under-served groups of women and children because 'women trust the services and the staff providing the services', and the holistic approaches on offer were 'culturally relevant to the populations served' and delivered in 'non-stigmatizing environments' (1991a: *x*).

Alcohol and Drugs are Women's Issues (1991a and b) was published in two volumes, the first a collection of articles written by two dozen 'women committed to helping women', and the second a nuts-and-bolts programme guide that described the steps by which women's centres could move towards offering drug and alcohol prevention and treatment. This represents the WAA strategy of helping local women's centres by coordinating the production of resources and 'stimulat[ing] and assist[ing] women at the local level to organize around specific action projects aimed at eliminating concrete manifestations of economic and social discrimination'.[15] As the 1980s had worn on, the WAA placed more emphasis on women's health issues, including teen pregnancy prevention and HIV/AIDS. WADEP was part of this turn to health, reaching at its peak more than 400 Latina, African-American and Caribbean women and girls each year.[16] However, the WAA depended on New York City and state budgets for funding and was thus extremely vulnerable to budget cuts that came summarily in 1995, when funding was cut by 65 per cent with just 30 days' notice. Although WADEP was by then considered 'one of the WAA's most successful programs', the $350,000 funding shortfall affected the 20 WADEP training sites throughout New York State. The fiscal crisis in the state of New York affected not only WADEP; the WAA itself dissolved over this financial crisis in June 1997.

Throughout much of the 1990s, WADEP had been one of the WAA's largest and most successful programmes. Working with service organizations, WADEP, under the leadership of Project Director Chris Kirk, offered skill-based training to staff, teaching them how to identify, assess, and intervene with substance users. It then provided technical assistance to establish comprehensive prevention programmes. By 1995, WADEP had worked with more than 50 organizations, creating prevention programmes that linked ATOD use with other issues in women's lives, including domestic violence, pregnancy, and unemployment. Records of the WADEP are mainly related to funding, including lists of funders, correspondence with funding organizations, and funding proposals. It is clear that WAA/WADEP was adept at obtaining funding and creating bridges between programmes. However, WADEP's difficulties securing state funding illustrate how the gains of the 1970s and 1980s were eroded once they were translated into institutional structures that could only be sustained until the late 1990s.

Political opportunity structures: Feminists pressure to change the climate at the federal level

Changes in health care delivery systems towards managed care in the US created opportunities as well as closing down some of the former centres. The opportunity structure conditions or shapes the form that gendered treatment takes in both the US and the UK. Ironically, the crack-cocaine crisis of the late 1980s and early 1990s, which produced a wave of prosecutions with tragic results for individual women, many of whom were unable to access treatment, spurred new federal efforts to get more women into treatment. By the early 1990s NIDA's gender-specific efforts were channeled towards pregnant and parenting women through NIDA's 'Perinatal 20' initiative, which funded 20 demonstration projects, and an epidemiological survey called the National Pregnancy and Health Survey designed to establish prevalence of drug and alcohol use at the time of delivery. In 1994 NIDA held a conference on 'Drug Addiction Research and the Health of Women', having fully subscribed to the health status argument. In 1988 ADAMHA funded a demonstration grant programme called the Pregnant and Postpartum Women and Infants programme, or PPWI, which led to almost 200 centres by the end of 1991. While these policy affordances at the federal level did not address the variability of state responses, and they remained problematic due to the separation of research from service delivery, they did provide a basis for expanding women's access to treatment in the US. At the same time, NIDA's admission to NIH in 1992 drove an even deeper wedge between research and treatment.

During the 1990s ADAMHA was reorganized to become SAMHSA, which comprises three main centres, including the Center for Substance Abuse Prevention (CSAP) and the Center for Substance Abuse Treatment

(CSAT). Primm directed CSAT during the transition from OTI, recounting, '[W]hen the OTI became CSAT, I made the changes that I always wanted to make. I was able to talk about comprehensiveness and [t]hat was implemented. I'm just ecstatic about that. It revolutionized drug treatment. I was able to get representation from Native Americans, Hispanics, and blacks on all committees involved in choosing grantees'.[17] Indeed there was more attention to multiculturalism or 'cultural competence' emerging in the treatment system; this is reflected in CSAT's second entry into its Treatment Improvement Protocol (TIP) series, which was for Pregnant, Substance-Using Women.[18] The CSAT publications from this period emphasize women's need for 'comprehensive care' and use the language of gender specificity. The consensus panel argued that the 'continuum of care should reflect the complexity of [the pregnant, substance-using woman's] multiple roles as a person in recovery, parent, partner, and, frequently, single head of household' (CSAT, 1993: 9). The case management system advocated considerably more coordination between prenatal and drug treatment providers than most women in publicly funded treatment programmes could expect at the time. The consensus panel was clearly aware of this, noting that the 'consortium of service providers may change over time' and that some of the philosophies and practices of these providers might contradict one another, as behaviours viewed as helpful support by social service providers might be viewed as 'codependent' or 'enabling' by drug and alcohol treatment providers. But the TIPs were written as statements of ideal care, long-term support, and coordination between social and health service agencies, and thus they serve as markers of what was considered ideal when they were written.

There were a few key states in which women's advocates were well-positioned to influence state-level policy in ways that encouraged the establishment and expansion of women-specific treatment programmes.[19] However, the heightened visibility of women's involvement in crack-cocaine use had also induced the US Congress to take services for women more seriously by the early 1990s (Campbell, 1999, 2000; Mahan, 1996; Maher, 1992; Sterk, 1999). Again this took the form of short-term research and demonstration grants, rather than a long-term commitment to building a sustainable treatment infrastructure. For instance, Medicaid (the US public healthcare system) expanded demonstration grants for pre- and perinatal care within the Office of Maternal and Child Health (MCH). In the early 1990s NIDA created the 'Perinatal-20' initiative, funding 20 demonstration programmes throughout the US in an effort to improve treatment for 'perinatal and neonatal addiction'. Almost all federal funding took the form of demonstration grants, evaluation, or epidemiological research designed to assess the scope and extent of the 'epidemic'. However, in 1992 the block-grant programme to the states was reorganized; it was divided into one grant for alcohol and drug abuse services, and another grant for community mental health services. The 1992 passage of the ADAMHA Reorganization Act (Public Law 102–321) effectively reduced the funding set aside for women's treatment services to five per cent, and targeted it to pregnant and parenting women, thus narrowing the scope of women's drug treatment once more.

That year the US Department of Health and Human Services created the SAMHSA. The new agency's charge was to reduce the impact of substance abuse and mental health disorders by rapidly 'translating' research findings into improved services for individuals suffering from 'behavioural health' issues, who are typically treated in publicly-funded settings in the US. Carved into three centres, the Center for Mental Health Services (CMHS), the CSAP, and the CSAT, SAMHSA set about improving the quality of services delivered. While much of the US managed-care healthcare system has been set up to reduce the costs of hospitalization, CSAT supported long-term, publicly funded residential substance abuse treatment programmes for pregnant and parenting women through two demonstration grants: the Residential Women and Children's (RWC) programme and the Pregnant and Postpartum Women and Children's (PPW) programme. Most importantly, CSAT was to become and remain a bureaucratic structure accessible to women's treatment advocates, many of whom had created ties to one another dating from the mid-1970s when they first became involved at the federal level. Maggie Wilmore, who in 1976 headed NIAAA's women's alcohol programmes and went on to become head of the CSAT Women and Children's Branch, recalled that the pioneering leadership of the women's treatment programmes funded in the 1970s were 'tuned into the need for a holistic recovery philosophy' and had paved the way for gender specific treatment (Brown, 1995: 322). However, Wilmore's tale shows how discontinuous the advances were. She described the funding cut-offs that hit the 45 newly established NIAAA women's programmes hard in the wake of Reagan's signing of the Economic Recovery Act of 1981, one of the largest tax cuts ever enacted. Few of the fledgling women's programmes recovered, and most quietly went out of existence before there was time to evaluate their effectiveness. Women's treatment advocates learnt the important lesson of building in early evaluation, and used this as a strategy to continue to do treatment and services-related research.

A few years after its inception, CSAT published a 'Comprehensive Treatment Model for Alcohol and Other Drug-Abusing Women and Their Children' (1994), which was meant to direct programmes towards addressing the 'full range of women's needs', beyond the focus on women's drug and alcohol abuse. The model was based on the metaphor of a Navajo Nation basket consisting of interwoven, concentric circles of care considered necessary to support women's recovery. The metaphor was thoroughly described in loving detail:

> In the Navajo Nation, the woven basket is actually a series of concentric rings, one lying within the other, expanding outward and upward until the entire basket is shaped. By itself, one ring can hold nothing and bear no load. When bound together, the circles join, gain strength, and what before could hold nothing now holds stones for building nations and water for building bodies. The concept of interdependence is critical to understanding the model. Each circle requires the existence of the other two and yet they are depicted as dotted lines to illustrate their permeability. The three circles together comprise comprehensive treatment, and any provider seeking to emulate the model must also ensure that there is an interdependent relationship among the three systems ... the circles are also three-dimensional as a basket must be and, as such, have binders that interweave and hold the circles together. Likewise, in treatment, there are activities that weave through each circle, helping to bind the service continuum together.

Our discussion of this metaphor would be incomplete without addressing the two 'handles' that make the basket functional, which were said to be 'cultural competence and gender competence [which] mean more than knowledge about culture or gender'. These competencies are not theoretical considerations but a sense of *practical* awareness and responsiveness to everything that women bring with them into treatment. Women are said to come to treatment bearing the 'baggage' of their socio-economic milieu and their past histories, including 'sexual identity; the sources of potential anger, hurt, and fear; and disconnection from family, friends, and community' (CSAT, 1994). While the 1994 version did not mention the history of trauma and the co-occurring disorders that will later be layered into the relational-cultural model, the metaphor is clearly capacious. CSAT asked treatment programmes to carry a great deal as they seek to stimulate 'services that will be characterized as holistic, wraparound, and/or comprehensive' (1994). Such ideal levels of comprehensiveness and specificity could not be achieved by the wholesale, nationwide adoption of a universal 'best practices' model – as CSAT points out in closing, the model was not universal but must be 'adapted to its community and its consumers'. By 1995 Wilmore could claim that she and her colleagues in leadership positions had finally made gender-specific women's treatment and women's health, including mental health, part of the national treatment agenda (322). Additionally, criminal justice settings, traditionally considered a conduit to treatment for men, have increased women's treatment programmes as women's incarceration rates rose in the 1990s and early 2000s (Grella, 2008: 329).

Despite such improvements making a difference for some women, the adaptations that programmes were expected to make for communities and consumers have become ever more complex over the past two decades of SAMHSA's existence – yet accessible, gender-responsive women's treatment remains unavailable to the vast majority of women who need it in the US. This chapter tells the story of that increasing complexity at the federal level, the emergence of a technocratic services regime, and the emergence of a professional class of women's treatment advocates who have worked both within their home states and at the national level to develop visibility for women's drug and alcohol abuse since the 1970s and 1980s. Has the conceptual and organizational complexity served the goal of sustainability?

'Level of burden': Changing conceptual practices in women's drug treatment

Many of the developments discussed in this chapter occurred at the programmatic level, but also represent a new set of conceptual practices that constituted new categories through which the governance of drug-using women took place. One clear example was the widening of the category of what was to be 'treated' beyond drug or alcohol abuse or dependence and towards the more integrated and comprehensive category of 'substance abuse'. In the 1970s and 1980s, Reed described a 'world ... divided into alcohol and drugs':

> I was on the drug side. There were real hierarchies between mental health, alcohol, and drugs, with drugs on the bottom as the most stigmatized. You'd go to meetings and the mental health people wouldn't know anything about substance abuse. The alcohol people did not know much out about drugs. The drug people tended

> to know the most. It's like this hierarchy of status where the lower you are, the more you have to know about the people at the top. The Institute of Medicine had a thing in the 1980s where they were trying to synthesize all of the knowledge about women. Connie Wiseman was there as the alcohol person and I was there as the drug person. Everybody else was mental health, and the mental health people were just clueless about anything having to do with substance abuse. We were very amused.[20]

During the 1980s, cross-fertilization began to occur between the fields of mental health and drug and alcohol treatment. A new set of ideas was generated around the concept of 'co-occurring disorders', also referred to as 'dual diagnoses'.[21] An early advocate for integrating treatment of co-occurring disorders with treatment for substance abuse, Vivian Brown recalled initially confronting resistance from the recovery community: 'For one thing, I think there is one track about abstinence in substance use treatment. In this track, there are those providers who really believe that if you also focus on anything else, including co-occurring mental health issues, it takes away from the focus on the substance abuse'.[22] Those who drew attention to 'co-occurring disorders' went far beyond asking treatment providers to take responsibility for a broader set of disorders than those to which they felt competent to respond. They situated women's substance abuse within a constellation of responses to 'trauma', including sexual abuse in childhood, rape, domestic violence, the witnessing of trauma in others, and what would ultimately come to be called 'structural violence'.

Well aware that the issues many women faced went far beyond substance abuse, Brown argued that when women tried to confront the effects of persistent, long-term violence in their lives, the 'client burden' would increase – the burden of integrating treatment for such a large range of co-occurring disorders would mean that clients had to carry a heavier load if they were going to get well. According to Brown, 'What I was trying to communicate was that (1) most of our clients didn't just have one problem; (2) this level of burden affected retention and outcomes; and (3) those clients (many women) with multiple problems (drug abuse, mental health disorders, trauma experiences, HIV/AIDS and other health problems) were ... deserving of more effective and integrated interventions that could help them recover from such heavy burdens'. Higher levels of burden translated into higher levels of anxiety and fear and ultimately to less time in treatment, as Brown acknowledged in a research paper on women's retention in the PROTOTYPES programme (Brown, Huba and Melchior, 1995: 345). In trying to understand why women left before completing the programme, Brown and colleagues speculated that women with more severe mental or physical illnesses may find themselves 'overwhelmed by the need to participate with others, to behave in a structured community way, and to comply with programme rules and procedures' (Brown, Huba and Melchior, 1995: 345). These speculations arose out of a holistic notion of what kinds of social demands and expectations drug-using women were facing when entering treatment – and they were a far cry from notions of women's biological vulnerability (CASA, 1996) or the constructions of them as depraved or indifferent mothers that circulated in the crack-cocaine scare of the late 1980s and early 1990s (Campbell, 2000). Such cultural representations could only contribute to the individual levels of burden borne by these women by further stigmatizing them.

According to Brown and her contemporaries, women were also subjected to another undue burden – the stigma and blame directed towards them by the larger communities of which they were a part.

> Those women were hated. I had colleagues [in mental health] say to me, 'How can you treat those women?' ... Those women were seen as the lowest of the low. [People thought] 'How dare you have children, and have a substance abuse problem?' When AIDS came, it was, 'How dare you think about having a child when you're infected?' The reason I tied that to 'level of burden' is that it gave me a forum to say to everybody, 'You don't understand the complexity of these issues, that these women not only have a substance abuse problem, but they have anxiety, depression, trauma histories, they're homeless, they've been beaten by their partners, and all of this may have occurred before they even started using drugs.' Drugs became their way of coping. Then people would listen. It began to shift the consciousness in the country'.[23]

Brown, a clinical psychologist by training who describes herself as becoming a 'community psychologist on my own because they didn't even talk about community when I was in graduate school,' was struck by the power of Synanon and the other therapeutic communities she encountered in the 1960s. However, she noticed that women:

> were not getting enough in treatment, and they were not getting in, and they were being abused. That really pushed me over to the women's side. We developed a Southern California Women's

> Coalition – and I was chairperson of that for a number of years – and a Northern California Women's Coalition. Each year we came together and had a statewide woman's conference. At the time, 1970–1971, Dr. Josette Mondanaro was the head of drug abuse services for the state of California. She became a very good friend and she realized that of course we needed to fund some special programs for women. She found the money to fund four residential programs for women only, and their children. Mine [Via Avanta, means 'the way forward'] was one of them.[24]

With the exception of NIAAA funding for women's alcohol programmes and NIDA funding for research and conferences that brought women working on drug issues together in the mid-1970s, there was no federal funding for women's drug treatment. Even when Reagan was governor of California, key women such as Josette Mondanaro and Rita Sainz occupied leadership positions that enabled the state to be a bellwether in funding women's treatment. Within the statewide coalitions, conversations began about the 'connection for women of substance abuse and trauma', and the state made funds available for domestic violence shelters that were addressing substance abuse. For Brown, who was paying attention to the women's movement, it was clear that many women did not want to enter the TCs and methadone programmes set up to meet men's needs.

> [T]he few women again related the stories of abuse in treatment programs. The reason that they did finally go on methadone was that nothing else worked for them. So they were hoping that in this program they wouldn't find the abuse and the use of them sexually. The same things kept coming over and over to me. That's the last piece: women kept telling us they couldn't bring their children into residential treatment, they had to give up their children, and they didn't want to give up their children. That last piece was what brought us to call the residential program a program for 'women and women with children' so women would have a place that would take their children in with them and also that women didn't feel that they had to have a child in order to come into the program.[25]

Brown is one of the few women's treatment advocates who wrote affirmatively about a TC model adapted for women in a special issue of the *Journal of Psychoactive Drugs* that she co-edited with Joan Ellen Zweben. Called the 'modified therapeutic community', Brown reduced the emphasis on confrontation and punitive strategies and enhanced attention to mental health and trauma, as well as services for children. Ideally, TCs supplied a supportive community lacking elsewhere (although much potential of the community mental health movement went unrealized in the US, according to David Musto (1975), Brown spent 22 years working at the Didi Hirsch Community Mental Health Center in Los Angeles). Brown said, 'I really delved into the TC model and delved into 12-step. I really see those two tracks as quite different and both quite important. The TC touched a couple of things for me. One is that, in my mind and from my clinical perspective the therapeutic community was not only a drug programme, but was also a mental health model [that supplied] ... the support, the community, the de-stigmatization within the community'.[26] Brown described a close working relationship between herself and program director, Suzan Sanchez (now deceased), a recovering addict with little formal education. They evolved a highly interactive, relational method by which 'the two of us developed one of the first modified TCs for women and women and children'. In the process Brown recalled bringing the concept of the integration of mental health and trauma into gender-responsive treatment to Sanchez: 'I never saw substance abuse without looking at mental health, and health, and trauma. Sue would say, 'No one in all the time I was in treatment – and she had come through TCs and was also very positive about TCs – no one ever mentioned trauma, no one ever allowed us to talk about it.' She was able to share about her experiences with trauma and violence in her relationships. It was that kind of testing back and forth'.[27]

Brown et al. (1996) described the treatment environment prevailing in traditional TCs in decidedly masculine terms: 'the emphasis was on toughness and the emotional range was restricted to some form of anger. The more tender emotions and feelings of sadness, pain, grief, warmth, nurturance, and protectiveness were rarely seen or they were labelled pathological. Baring one's soul was highly valued (Deitch and Zweben, 1981). *This was not a climate to promote women's healing*' (Emphasis ours; Brown, et al., 1996: 41). Confrontation was so deeply woven into the fabric of the TC model that women's advocates felt it was not only unproductive for women who had been traumatized or victimized, often multiple times by a variety of 'trusted' others, but downright damaging because it promoted forms of obeisance that reinforced a sense of powerlessness within an unsafe environment. The 'modified TC model' or 'women and children's TC model' was based on a set of major adaptations in structural design, treatment, staffing, and training in dual diagnosis/co-occurring disorders (described in Brown et al., 1996: 41–6).

> Although on the vanguard of 'gender responsive treatment', Brown recalled meeting resistance from traditional TCs when introducing gender-specific issues when she told them: 'One, that they need to do different treatment for women, that they needed women's groups, and that one of the groups was parenting skills. Some of the responses back then would be that we don't need that, women are just denying that they're drug addicts and they need to focus on their drug addiction, not their children. They didn't even want to do parenting groups. We've had the same battle within the mental health system. We would try to convince the mental health programs to do parenting skills training, and they wouldn't do it. Some still don't. We're still not there on the mental health side.'[28]

This emphasis on parenting skills has been carefully maintained by the handful of curriculum 'developers' who created a market for 'gender sensitivity' training designed to make existing treatment programmes more 'gender responsive'. As the US treatment infrastructure expanded and diversified – particularly in response to HIV/AIDS and in recognition of the differential impact of the disease on different communities – this expansion enabled a niche market to come about that effectively diffused ideas about trauma and co-occurring mental health disorders throughout the substance abuse treatment community.

Out of these unmet needs, combined with the realization that many drug-using women had experienced multiple forms of violence and abuse within intimate relationships, Brown evolved the concept that there were different levels of 'client burden'. Working against the further pathologization of 'clients', Brown viewed them as carrying greater burdens if they had been traumatized as children or had witnessed abuse; if they had been diagnosed with 'co-occurring disorders' or medical conditions; if they had been homeless or poor; if they had suffered institutional or individual racism. In this way the cumulative effects of mistreatment and ill health could be taken on in the context of treatment – the focus was shifted away from drugs and alcohol and towards the structural contexts and relationships in which they were used. One of our points in *Gendering Addiction* is that drug use has often been understood to subsume all other meaningful aspects of identity, as if the only thing that mattered in women's lives was the drug. This idea of a hierarchy of needs in which the 'drug of choice' dominates contradicts all available evidence – pregnant and parenting drug users resemble other women in that for the most part they remain focused on other aspects of their lives, including their children and their aspirations to be 'good enough' mothers to them. At the same time, feminist treatment advocates recognized that certain aspects of drug-using women's identities as mothers were compromised or damaged in ways that negatively affected their relationships with partners and children.

The Nurturing Program for Families in Substance Abuse Treatment and Recovery

The insight that substance use negatively affected women's capacities to relate to significant others, including but not exclusively their children or partners, became important for women's treatment advocates. Based on the principles of relational-cultural theory of development, a behavioural/cognitive approach to therapy, and Stephen J. Bavolek's Nurturing Program, an NIMH-funded parenting skill-building curriculum designed to prevent and treat child abuse and neglect, the Nurturing Program for Families in Substance Abuse Treatment and Recovery was selected as an evidence-based model programme by SAMHSA and CSAP in the early 1990s.[29] The perceived needs of drug-addicted women can be inferred from this text, which was pitched in an affirmative register emphasizing a restorative process designed to discover and celebrate the 'assets' each participant brings to the table. This construction is exceedingly important as it avoids an attribution that participants were lacking or deficient, but instead posits 'neglect' as the polar opposite of 'nurture'. Emphasizing that women need to build up their 'self-nurturing skills', their capacity for self-disclosure, and their sense of self-awareness, particularly when parenting, the Nurturing Program (NP) is a collaborative curriculum. It is essentially a manualized protocol written to group facilitators who will usher women in recovery into nurturing themselves and/or others. During the 1990s, such manuals became common ways of importing recovery-oriented psychological tenets into 'behavioural health care' settings. They contain practical advice for group facilitators, a theoretical underpinning, as well as detailed activities such as ice-breakers, role plays and meditation sessions designed to heighten self-awareness about being engaged in a collaborative process.

The NP begins by affirming the principles upon which it was based. 'The principle of collaboration enhances the operation of the principle of **nurturing the parent**, while expanding the parents' [*sic*] ability to transmit this nurturance to their children' (NP, 1995: *xi*). This statement suggests that a process of inter-generational *transmission* has broken down, resulting in a sense of loss. In the first edition there was an explicit focus on investigating the sense of 'loss or damage' to a person's sense of heritage, and a recognition that substance abuse is often 'experienced in families also experiencing racism, sexism, homophobia, poverty and discrimination' (NP, 1995: *xii*). By the time the second edition was released, the category 'parents in recovery' had been invented, and the need for such individuals to re-establish strong connections with their children was assumed. Both editions owed their conceptual framework to the 'relational-cultural theory of women's development' advanced by Jean Baker Miller and espoused by the Stone Center for Developmental Studies at Wellesley College.

Becoming aware of what would later be called the 'relational-cultural model' with the publication of Miller's 1974 book, *Toward a New Psychology of Women,* Finkelstein embraced the model and has applied it throughout her work to women who were struggling with addictions, noting that the relational model enabled a fuller taking into account of the 'reality that women are highly affected by their relationships, past and present; women develop a sense of self through these relationships; and women strive to maintain a sense of connectedness to others' (NP, 2006: 1). The impact of substance abuse is chiefly understood as an impact on relationship connections that results from the erosion of the parent's self-image. Thus the argument throughout the NP is that 'success in recovery and success in parenting are inextricably woven together' (NP, 2006: 2). There is careful avoidance of the terms 'mother' and 'motherhood', with the gender-neutral term 'parenting' appearing instead. Despite the resort to gender neutrality, the relational model is primarily a theory of *women's* development. Miller, writing the second edition of *Toward a New Psychology of Women* (1986), explored the basic features of women's 'psychic structuring' as the 'context of connections with others': 'Indeed, women's sense of self becomes very much organized around being able to make and then to maintain affiliations and relationships. Eventually, for many women the threat of disruption of connections is perceived not as just a loss of a relationship but as something closer to a total loss of self' (Miller, 1986: 83). Miller notes that she used the word 'affiliations' throughout the 1976 first edition, but that she adopted Carol Gilligan's use of the word 'connections' from *In a Different Voice* (1982). Similarly, the term 'relational model' or 'relational theory' does not appear in Miller's early work, although the conceptual spirit of the relational basis of women's development certainly does and by the second edition, she had begun to think of herself as working on the 'relational contexts' and 'relational modes' that foster or impede psychological development (Miller, 1986: *xxiii*). Relational theory was itself developed within a 'relational' context unfolding in the Boston area within the broader context of the women's movement.[30]

The second edition of the NP portrayed on the cover the 'Developmental Rainbow', mapped onto Erik and Joan Erickson's eight stages of human growth across the life course. From Gilligan, the authors of the NP drew the two tasks of development, the development of autonomy and the growth of attachment and connection. Emphasizing each as a growth process, the curriculum then maps them onto recovery, which is figured as a dynamic conversion experience whereby individuals 'rework' the eight stages of human growth through the development of a sense of trust in self and others as a basis for redefining an identity that is no longer centred on 'drinking or drugging' (NP, 2006: 15). The eight stages of growth are redefined as 'struggles', involving a series of binary oppositions such as 'identity versus role confusion' or 'autonomy versus shame and doubt', and assigned a colour. The goal is, of course, to achieve the qualities encapsulated in the first term. One of the major tenets of the NP is to show that substance abuse has a wider range of effects than those upon the drug-using individual. Many of the activities are designed to show that 'substance abuse NEVER affects only one person. It affects everyone who is in a relationship with that person: child, parent, partner, boss, friend, and teacher' (NP, 2006: 26). In particular, substance abuse is understood to affect families – and the notion of 'family' is both very wide and very pluralistic within the curriculum itself, including families headed by women who are parenting alone. But how does substance abuse have these effects?

The NP adopts that idea that substance abuse distorts feelings and enables the repression of emotion and communications with emotive content. Here, the dominant trope is one of the 'management' of emotions that may seem overwhelming or disproportionate to the events precipitating them, the management of feelings, none of which are 'negotiable' and all of which require 'skill' to manage effectively and constructively (NP, 2006: 30–1). Group facilitators are taught to view those used to 'substance abusing lifestyle[s]' as isolated and often unskilled at 'appropriately' displaying emotion themselves or responding to that of others. Sessions are designed to broaden the range of appropriate emotional responses with which participants feel comfortable, and facilitators are to at all times model how to 'manag[e] emotions that may seem mystifying or frightening' (NP, 2006: 28). Again, the gender-neutral language masks the direct connection to women's reputations for greater emotionality and emotional ability. While the progenitors of the relational-cultural model have often been mistaken to be 'essentialist', we read them as having been quite clear about the social contexts and differential power relationships that hinder men's development of more 'affiliative mode(s) of living' and render loss of connection dangerous to women: 'For women to derive strength from relationships, then, clearly requires transformation and restructuring of the nature of relationships', wrote Miller (1986: 96). The NP locates one of the most important transformations in the relative clarity of emotive communication.

Distorted communications are one of the specific effects that substance abuse is said to have on relationships within this way of thinking, which grew to importance within SAMHSA in the early decades of the twenty-first century. The effects of distorted communication are denial, remorse, and blame, each an unhealthy way of handling substance abuse that distorts relationships among family members and contributes to the problem of 'our baggage' (NP, 2006: 44). Distortions make family members unable to engage in clear confrontation with the substance abuser – they become 'fearful of telling the truth, and sometimes are not sure what the truth is' (NP, 2006: 44). As this situation becomes 'normal', children develop similar uncertainties about what is true and 'do not learn to verify reality, because that reality is denied' (NP, 2006: 44). The heavy weight of 'our baggage' drags down productive communication and muddies clear communication. The result is a kind of chaotic confusion and a life organized around drugs and alcohol – rather than the clarity of identity and ordinary schedules and routines sought as the desired outcome.

Calming and consoling techniques were viewed as essential 'acquired skills' for participants to learn because of the assumption that 'many addicts and alcoholics learned to use drugs and alcohol in order to calm physical or emotional agitation' (NP, 2006: 64). Having used drugs and alcohol and endured the discomforts of withdrawal, they were left without coping skills. Guided visualization and meditation were offered as compensatory skills – ways to calm oneself or cope with anxiety and uncertainty. This section, quite interestingly, is part of the topic, 'What Babies Teach Us'. The underlying idea is that infants have instinctive 'jobs' central to their development; these jobs are integral to the infant's 'basic drive to stay alive and form attachments' (NP, 2006: 59). Extensive charts trace 'the baby's job' from birth to four or five months, because these jobs are to be 'reworked' in adulthood. Adults in recovery have to rework each of these developmental milestones: 'many of the concerns of early recovery reflect issues of infancy: the need to build trust, the importance of being effective in stating and getting needs met; the importance of building routines and dependability' (NP, 2006: 69). The 'massive learning project' that is infancy is compared to what adults in early recovery must go through as a result of their disrupted relationships and the 'shattering effects of violence within the family or in the community' (NP, 2006: 69).

Trauma can have several different kinds of distorting effects, and trauma became the linchpin of the relational therapy movement as well as now permeating the women's treatment infrastructure in the US by the early 2000s. For women who have been subjected to sexual abuse, especially during childhood, 'body language' is often distorted or misinterpreted (NP, 2006: 54). Such women experience unclear bodily boundaries and different 'tolerances' for touch (NP, 2006: 79). In addition trauma was reconceptualized within the women's movement as an injury to relationships (Herman, 1992; Robb, 2006: 273). Drugs and alcohol were reconceptualized as (dis)organizing principles that displace ordinary satisfactions and 'nurturing routines' such as mealtimes (NP, 2006: 86). Routine is an issue partly because many participants in the NP experienced a palpable 'loss of excitement' when they entered sobriety (NP, 2006: 88). If participants formerly experienced only partying as 'fun,' they needed to evolve a new sense of play and new ways to celebrate (NP, 2006: 133). They need to see early sobriety as a form of experimentation that can open the door to a shift in identity formation (NP, 2006: 117). While this problem does not seem to connect to trauma, the 'nurturing routines' cannot be built up without resolving the sense of safety. A 'nurturing routine' involve the following tenets:

- Consistent, but allows for negotiation among family members.
- Allows for participation by children; everyone has a part to play.
- Is 'built up' in steps, not imposed by force.
- Contains some gentle, loving touch.
- Can contain some activity aimed at calming or focusing attention.

However, some disruptions of family structure that result from substance abuse may have been subjected to irretrievable losses; these must be grieved 'safely', and in a timely way but not too early in the recovery process. The risk perceived is that those who are too traumatized might return to drugs and alcohol as a way of soothing grief (NP, 2006: 125).

'Building recovery' is seen as a developmental process that requires re-working or re-experiencing of the development of identity, role, and self-image through a 'rethinking of the consequences of their actions' in taking a drink or using a drug (NP, 2006: 117). 'Think things through' is one of the mantras of recovery-based programmes. The idea is to build up a sense of purpose as an adult in recovery – an adult whose identity is shifting from one of denial – 'being a person without a problem with alcohol or drugs' – to being a 'person with a problem' (NP, 2006: 120). The sense of purpose is seen as essential to moral and cognitive development theory because it is intertwined with the work of 'internalizing values' that consciously or unconsciously inform decisions, behaviour, relationships, lifestyles, and careers (NP, 2006: 117). The sense of purpose is also shared with 12-Step recovery programmes based in AA. Participants in the NP are compelled to accept their 'identity as an alcoholic or addict' (NP, 2006: 117), illustrating the consonance between the 12-Step recovery orientation and the N.P.. They are also asked to accept the impact of their relationship to drugs and alcohol upon their relationships with important others, especially their children. It is easy to see consonance between the NP and relational-cultural theory. Both were to become important for the federal women's treatment guidelines published in 2009.

'Repairing the Fractured Parent-Child Relationship':[31] Treatment Improvement Protocol (TIP) 51

Federal treatment guidelines in the US appear as Treatment Improvement Protocols, or TIPS. In 2009 the relational-cultural model was translated into the TIP 51, the 'best practices' federal treatment guidelines for women. The appearance of the discourse of the relational-cultural model in the federal guidelines represents a lifetime of work on the part of the women involved, and from their perspective represents a crowning achievement. Brown co-chaired the SAMHSA Advisory Council with former SAMHSA administrator, Charles Curie, and served two terms on the SAMHSA Women's Advisory Committee. Based in California, she campaigned for a two-pronged national women's drug treatment agenda emphasizing co-occurring mental health disorders and trauma.

> We knew in the Seventies that one of the differences between women's treatment and men's was the trauma histories and the trauma pattern. It took all this time to really push that agenda. It should have happened in the Seventies because that's where the women's treatment community was at in California. But the history of trauma work has always had an up and down pattern ... It's hard for me to

> believe that it has taken almost 25 years to even get to the point where we are now in terms of the co-occurring disorders work, and trauma took just as long to become a focal point.[32]

Hampered by a federal organizational restructuring that divided 'social services' from 'research' that occurred in the early 1990s,[33] the women's treatment advocates continued to emphasize the need for further research despite the restructured relationship between research and treatment and prevention services. Brown said,

> One of the good things was that SAMHSA and OTI before it [was that they] they really allowed R and D kind of funding to blossom in the beginning. In the early years, you really could go for research and development. That's part of what PROTOTYPES stood for, the idea that we needed new models and more research. That's when I started to increase my publications because we needed to show outcome data. At that time, I was still under the belief that policy is made on data, which is not really true, as you know, but I did believe at one point that if we could do the research, we could try out different models and really refine the models and then train other people. That's the idea that PROTOTYPES was built on.[34]

While Brown's work at the Didi Hirsch CMHC had centred on integrating treatment of women's substance abuse and co-occurring disorders, this was unusual within the context of the CMHCs. While SAMHSA initially funded research demonstration projects on women's issues, Brown recalled that 'over the years it became more difficult for some of the clinical researchers and the field researchers to get funding from NIH and NIDA. Then what happened was the separation of research from practice, which I believe was a bad mistake. I think the R and D should have been kept by SAMHSA, but SAMHSA did not have the mandate or the funding to do research anymore'.[35] Then in 1999 SAMHSA was able to fund a massive national study that ran for five years and involved multiple sites. The Women, Co-occurring Disorders, and Violence Study (WCDVS) enabled women's advocates to meet and craft a national agenda that was infused with the tenets of the relational-cultural model, as well as assumptions drawn from the parenting skills and safety curricula developed by prominent women's treatment advocates (Noether, et al., 2005). Just as the NIDA women's conferences from the mid-1970s on had supported advocates' ongoing relationships with one another, the WCDVS provided a platform from which to organize. The contours of the women's treatment agenda are easily glimpsed in the TIP 51 – in fact, the NP can be said to be enjoying a second life in the wake of the WCDVS.

A revision of the 'Nurturing Families Affected by Substance Abuse, Mental Illness, and Trauma', based on the original NP, was one of the WCDVS deliverables for Women Embracing Life and Living (WELL), the Cambridge, Massachusetts project that was one of the nine SAMHSA-funded sites that comprised the WCDVS. 'The WELL project has found that mothers may experience a myriad of emotions and issues that influence their ability to parent effectively', including 'loss of self-image as a capable and affective parent', 'trauma memories' triggered by the child's behaviour, diminished trust, empathy, and intimacy, and denial of their own problems. Their own needs to 'seek out safety' might leave them paying less attention to their children, who then might be asked to 'take on significant life management responsibilities' in ways that placed them in adult situations before they are fully mature' (Finkelstein and Markoff, 2004). The last item concurred with Judith Herman's understanding that safety is a first stage of recovery from trauma because 'survivors feel unsafe in their bodies. Their emotions and their thinking feel out of control. They also feel unsafe in relation to other people' (Herman, 1992: 160).

Safety is the central priority within the emerging trauma-informed treatment assemblage. Central to this assemblage has been the rise of a new class of professionals, often with backgrounds in social work or clinical psychology, who deploy a technocratic vocabulary and a set of shared assumptions about trauma and its connection to women's substance abuse, including alcoholism. The programmes, 'tools' or 'manualized protocols' that circulate within this assemblage tend towards cognitive behavioural therapies and 'motivational interviewing',[36] which is based on training TC staff to use the tools of 'motivational enhancement' rather than confrontation that may be felt as bullying or threatening in ways that may feel to the 'client' like a revisitation of abuse. One of the other cognitive/behavioural manuals often referenced is *Seeking Safety* by Boston-area clinical psychologist Lisa M. Najavits (2001, 2002, 2007). This curriculum, widely used throughout the Veterans Administration with both male and female veterans, aims to treat PTSD co-occurring with substance abuse. Najavits is one of a new breed of curricula 'developers' that create curricula that have been repeatedly evaluated so as to join those curricula that count as 'evidence-based' protocols (Brown, et al., 2007). Brown described her current effort to work bottom up from the county level in California to create a trauma-informed treatment infrastructure. Her 'gender-responsive' trainings sometimes involve Najavits and other developers such as Stephanie Covington, an alcohol researcher whose research uncovered the role played by sexual abuse in women's substance abuse disorders. Brown described one of her training workshops titled 'Looking through the Trauma Lens', which presented both Najavits' 'Seeking Safety' curriculum and Covington's 'Beyond Trauma' and 'Helping Women to Recover' curricula.

Gender in an evidence-based world

The context within which the above-noted R and D took place was a top-down attempt to infuse Evidence-Based Medicine and Evidence-Based practices (EBPs) throughout the state-level treatment infrastructure. Within the substance-abuse treatment field, federally convened consensus panels sometimes had difficulty determining what the 'best practices' were in areas where research and evaluation had not yet validated particular practices or protocols to the extent considered necessary to promote them to the status of EBPs. 'While each TIP strives to include an evidence base for the practices it recommends, SAMHSA/CSAT recognizes that the field of substance abuse treatment is continually evolving, and research frequently lags behind the innovations pioneered in the field. A major goal of each TIP is to convey 'front-line' information quickly but responsibly'. This meant that there was room for a process of consensus-building in the interpretation of what counted as a 'best practice'.

In 2009, SAMHSA, the federal agency charged with overseeing treatment and prevention services in the US, released a TIP titled *Substance Abuse Treatment: Addressing the Specific Needs of Women*, Series 51.[37] This TIP employs a 'biopsychosocial framework' and illustrates that many principle tenets of the NP and the relational-cultural model have crept into the federal framework. This is not surprising, as Finkelstein chaired the TIP consensus panel and long-time feminist activists such as Reed and Brown served on it. By this time a core group of feminist advocates, whose work had long been inspired by the women's movement and 'community psychology', were able to create criteria for programmes to be considered 'gender-responsive': such criteria included acknowledging that 'women's unique developmental milestones' take place within a complex interplay of 'physiology' and 'sociocultural influence' that determines their 'treatment needs'. The executive summary emphasizes that 'substance abuse treatment for women be approached from a perspective that encompasses the contexts or "ecology" of women's lives', including the 'impact of gender and culture'.

Women's substance abuse is constructed as so complex in the TIP 51 that treatment requires various modes of 'cultural competence specific to women' that are adapted to 'differences among women'. The core principles of gender-responsive treatment emphasize women's uniqueness in terms of development and health, while also acknowledging that there is no singular category of 'women'.

Core Principles for Gender Responsive Treatment for Women from the TIP 51

- Acknowledging the importance as well as the role of the socioeconomic issues and differences among women.
- Promoting cultural competence specific to women.
- Recognizing the role, as well as the significance of relationships in women's lives.
- Addressing women's unique health concerns.
- Endorsing a developmental perspective.
- Attending to the relevance and influence of various caregiver roles that women often assume throughout the course of their lives.
- Recognizing that ascribed roles and gender expectations across cultures affect societal attitudes towards women who abuse substances.
- Adopting a trauma-informed perspective.
- Using a strengths-based model for women's treatment.
- Incorporating an integrated and multidisciplinary approach to women's treatment.
- Maintaining a gender-responsive treatment environment across settings.
- Supporting the development of gender competency specific to women's issues.

The NP's emphasis on calming and consoling within the family also appears in the TIP 51's executive summary on the characteristics of the family of origin: 'Exposure to chaotic, argumentative, and violent households, or being expected to take on adult responsibilities as a child, are other factors associated with initiation and prevalence of substance use disorders among the female population'. Women appear significantly more sensitive than men to changes in 'relationships, relationship status, and the effects of a partner's substance abuse'. In clear and almost clinical prose, the TIP 51 lays out the exact ways in which women are more vulnerable to, more susceptible to, and ultimately more influenced by relationships, particularly substance abuse disorders in their male partners.

Not only are women constructed as more easily influenced than men, they are diagnosed as more biologically vulnerable despite the acknowledgement that research on physiological effects has been inconclusive. Despite this, the emphasis in the TIP 51 lands on the 'significant differences' in metabolism of alcohol. 'Telescoping' is explained as women having 'more complications and more severe problems from alcohol use than do men, and these complications and problems develop more rapidly'. Despite this acknowledgement of women's greater *biological* vulnerability, the primary emphasis is on gender as a form of *social* complexity; that substance abuse disorders and co-occurring mental health disorders, including those arising from a history of trauma, are interconnected; and that, given this, treatment and prevention programmes cannot centre solely on substance abuse. The TIP 51 executive summary puts it thus:

> Gender specific factors that influence the treatment process and recovery evolve around the importance of relationships, the influence of family, the role of substance use in sexuality, the prevalence and history of trauma and violence, and common patterns of co-occurring disorders. Among women with substance use and co-occurring mental disorders, diagnoses of posttraumatic stress and other anxiety disorders, postpartum depression and other mood disorders, and eating disorders are more prevalent than among men who are in treatment for substance use disorders. Consequently, clinical strategies, treatment programming, and administrative treatment policies must address these issues to adequately treat women. Likewise, women often need clinical and treatment services tailored to effectively address pregnancy, child care, children services, and parenting skills.

Prior to the rise of the gender complexity paradigm, the prevailing North American recovery community insisted that individuals overcome their denial and identify themselves as addicts or alcoholics as a necessary precondition for entering treatment. Abstinence was the linchpin, not only of US drug policy, but also of the recovery movement – despite 'backsliding' or relapse being a common event. Brown refers to this attitude as the 'Old Guard … insistence that abstinence is the only way' to recovery. The New Guard – which Brown saw encompassing both the feminist treatment advocacy community and harm reduction advocates – emphasizes multiple pathways to recovery; relapse as a norm rather than an exception; and 'harm reduction' as the route to recovery.

> I would certainly say the goal, eventually, would be abstinence, but for certain people, we're going to get them there through harm reduction. We know that some people, those with a number of problems or vulnerabilities, may need extra support to get to abstinence. We need wet housing and other programs and steps along the way. That's why I also think that the managed care push to shorten treatment and eliminate residential treatment is very foolish. There are people who need the extra support of 24/7 residential (not inpatient or hospital) programs, but managed care does not recognize that need. If you're really treating women and women with children who have co-occurring problems, including trauma and domestic violence, you need to have a place for them to be safe where there is prevention and treatment for the children. We moved from the position where we said we were doing treatment for the mom and prevention for the children because when we really assessed the children, we knew they also needed treatment.[38]

The emphasis on treating the woman by treating the family is central to the relational-cultural approach. The TIP 51, Chapter 7, 'Women's Treatment Issues and Needs' stated:

Relationships and the need for connection

Relationships are central in women's lives – as part of their identities, as sources of self-esteem, as the context for decision making and choices, and as support for day-to-day living and growth (Covington and Surrey, 1997; Finkelstein and Piedade, 1993; Finkelstein, et al., 1996; Miller, 1976, 1986). Connections are relationships that are healthy and supportive – mutual, empowering, and emotional resources. 'Disconnections' involve relationships that are not mutual and empowering: one member is dominant, there is imbalance in the give and take, or a disparity exists in emotional supportiveness. Disconnections range from feeling 'unheard' or 'unknown' to extreme forms of disconnection, such as sexual abuse and violence. Disconnections create major difficulties for most women, such as lowered self-esteem, feelings of powerlessness, and lack of assertiveness. The experience of relationships as connections and disconnections is a central issue in personality development, with repeated severe disconnections potentially having serious psychological and behavioural consequences.

Drug abuse, alcohol abuse, and co-occurring mental health disorders appear as consequences of unhealthy relationships (also referred to as 'disconnections' as they are in relational-cultural theory). The TIP 51 heralded relational-cultural theory as a major paradigm shift, offering three tenets of the model: (1) the 'powerful effect of the cultural context on women's lives'; (2) relationships are the 'central organizing feature in women's development'; and (3) 'pathways to growth' and recovery open once women's 'relational qualities and activities' are acknowledged. Indeed, treatment appears to be a process of relational development – rather than self-development, as in relational-cultural theory, the 'self' is constituted only 'in relation'.[39] Treatment, according to the TIP 51, 'provide[s] a woman her first opportunity to establish new, healthy relationships – especially relationships with other women'. The strengthening of relational connections cannot occur, of course, with individuals who have been involved in unhealthy relationships of violence and betrayal in the past. Counsellors are urged to 'help women to examine past relationships, including issues of loss, violence, and incest; to validate and build upon [their] relational skills and needs; to learn how to parent successfully; ... to let go of problematic, abusive relationships' (quoted from Finkelstein, 1996: 28). Treatment is thus the successful confrontation of loss – and the loss includes the 'loss of a primary relationship with their drug of abuse' (Cramer, 2002). Within the world of the relational model, 'relationships' extend to those between the person and the drug. This is a profoundly social and cultural account of drug and alcohol addiction – despite the nod to physiological or metabolic 'gender differences' early in the TIP 51, the document dwells largely upon the psychological and cultural differences exerted by women's differential orientation towards relationships.

The current paradigm is also 'non-judgemental' in that it seeks not to moralize women's drug use. Drug-using women are assumed to be unhealthily judgemental towards themselves due to their internalization of pejorative messages from the dominant culture and their ongoing attempt to grapple with shame. This is considered a particular pitfall for pregnant women; counsellors are urged to exercise caution in 'evaluating pregnancy outcomes based on use of alcohol, drugs, or tobacco during pregnancy and their possible effects on the newborn' because 'it is almost impossible to make accurate predictions on neonatal outcomes'. Counsellors are implicitly advised to restrain themselves from any negative judgements and instead to create a 'positive environment' that 'emphasizes the recovering woman's control and self-efficacy; it is another element of empowerment for recovering women' (Covington, 2002). The emphasis on treatment as delivering positive and empowering messages was designed to counter the negative and disempowering messages that pregnant drug users typically encounter from healthcare professionals and other authorities.

Nor does the TIP 51 moralize about motherhood or draw upon idealized notions of what mothers ought to be and do. Instead it draws upon the NP's emphasis on the erosion of parent self-image: 'Mothers who are in substance abuse treatment feel a strong connection with their children and want to be good mothers..... Women who believe they have not cared for their children adequately or who believe that they are perceived as having neglected their children carry enormous guilt' (quoting Sun, 2000). The problem was diagnosed as a lack of adequate role models, information, skills, and resources that would enable them to maintain caring relationships with their children. The language of 'maternal assets' carefully skirts any notion that such women are themselves deficient – as parents they may lack 'assets' and 'skills', but *not* the capacity to gain or regain them. Availability and distribution of such 'assets' and 'skills' varies; many problems seen in drug-using women are said to stem from their unrealistically high expectations of their children's development. Age-appropriate developmental milestones are emphasized so that mothers can adjust their expectations. A middle-class bias pervades the TIP 51 when parenting styles and family configurations are addressed, despite the gender-neutral and non-discriminatory language of a federal policy document. Structures and resources – including discursive resources such as a vocabulary that might widen the repertoire of 'parenting styles' – for so-called attachment parenting are rarely available to single or low-income women. Where attachment parenting is the approved nurturing style, 'anger management' is necessary so parents can learn 'constructive discipline strategies without corporeal punishment' and thus learn to maintain attachment instead of provoking disconnection or its most problematic form, dissociation as a response to abuse or violence. That these parenting styles have class-biased histories and may characterize the implementation of white, middle-class values is left implicit in the text when it acknowledges that 'culturally congruent parenting practices and expectations' must be taken into account. While there is a tension between 'cultural congruence' and the pedagogy of 'parenting styles' being advised here, it is clear that issues of attachment are not simply class-biased but pose real developmental issues for all parents, but especially for trauma survivors who are parents.[40]

Within the community of women's treatment advocates, there is also an implicit critique of 'child protection' and 'child welfare' based on a radical feminist critique of the use of the rhetoric of 'the family' that masks the use of children as a conduit to a mother who is blamed for all of the failures of the social structures within which mothering takes place. The WCDVS confirmed the conviction of women's treatment advocates that children whose mothers are in substance abuse treatment – especially those with co-occurring mental disorders and a history of having been victimized themselves – need much more than the forms of 'treatment' that have been on offer. 'While a woman is learning to parent, her children need assistance to overcome the effects of her substance abuse. It is likely their mother has been emotionally and physically unavailable at times. Counselors can help children realize that their mother's behaviour was unintentional and, as she regains control of her life, she will likely become more available'. Some programmes are structured to integrate treatment of intimate male or female partners and children, as is Brown's California programme PROTOTYPES (discussed below). However, it is important to realize that the feminist inclusion of children in treatment is based on a radical critique of 'the family' that is supportive of women who are pregnant and/or parenting, as well as those who are not. The inclusion of children in treatment does not rely on 'the family' as an idealized construct through which women are 'managed', that is, guilt-tripped into staying away from drugs and alcohol. Substances are seen to impede *all* significant relationships in a woman's life, including but not limited to mother-child relationships.

What is it about substance abuse that gets in the way of relationships? The barriers articulated by women's treatment advocates turned out to be psychological obstacles – shame, guilt, and self-blame about past drug and alcohol use – that can make a woman unavailable to her children and thus an inadequate parent. However, sometimes children *themselves* can become 'triggers' for traumatic memories or relapse. In this case, the TIP 51 reminds readers, the otherwise normal developmental processes through which mother and child are proceeding – breastfeeding, bathing, 'providing sexual education' – can trigger PTSD. While this claim may seem preposterous on initial reading, this is the claim underlying attempts by women's treatment advocates to create a 'trauma-informed treatment infrastructure' in which parents are taught to identify their actions as symptoms of trauma triggered by behaviours and activities integral to the mundane and everyday activities of mothering, rather than those of rape, war, disaster, or other forms of violent attack.

Women's substance abuse treatment enters the domain of trauma

Women who are survivors of intimate partner abuse, 'gender-based' or 'domestic violence' are categorized as 'at risk' for substance abuse disorders. The precise mechanisms by which exposure to trauma or violence as *either* a victim, witness, or perpetrator results in substance abuse are unclear. The very language of women's treatment advocates, who refer to Consumers/Survivors/Recovering Persons (CSRs), reflects the belief that 'surviving' trauma is a central causal mechanism leading to substance abuse, or operating as a 'risk factor' for *either* being abused or abusing others. Survivors are said to be resilient and even adaptive, but at times they may rely on 'unsafe coping mechanism' such as drugs and alcohol to achieve numbness or dissociation (Herman, 1992). Throughout the TIP 51, which promises TIPs tailored to those with co-occurring PTSD and substance abuse, PTSD is characterized as a disorder borne of disconnection and maintained through dissociation (Herman, 1997). Thus the only remedy – once safety has been secured – is reconnection through reinvigorated relationships. The relational model may represent many pathways to recovery, but all lead through the thicket of relationships.

By the mid-1990s, it was increasingly common for publications to associate PTSD with substance abuse, and to make the case that PTSD is associated with relapse. Herman (1992) offered three stages of the recovery process, starting with the establishment of safety; moving through a second stage of remembrance and mourning that involves the survivor's reconstruction of the 'trauma story'; and a third stage of reconnection and reconciliation with the traumatic past. One of the important contributions made by the pro-democratic social movements from which all of the US women's treatment advocates came was the capacity to support and sustain legitimacy for the survivor's voice. An unlikely partnership between Vietnam veterans and women's health and treatment advocates, social movements like the women's movement, the women's health movement, and the antiwar movement supported and legitimated the experience of women and soldiers who had been traumatized, or who had witnessed traumatic events. 'Mass movements for human rights were at least able to budge the conventional resistance to seeing the diseases of subordination' (Robb, 2006: 296). These insights were then extended to drug and alcohol dependence – which was cast as yet another 'disease of subordination'.

Listening to their women 'clients', treatment advocates had long suspected that a high proportion of drug-dependent women had suffered physical and sexual abuse, as well as growing up in structurally violent contexts. They set about documenting their intuitions and advocating for attention to the fact that 'women remain targets of physical and sexual abuse for a greater part of their lives' (Gil-Rivas, Fiorentine, and Anglin, 1995: 100). Here was a social gender difference that clearly had implications for treatment and that helped women's treatment advocates to make the case for research funding:

> Because the experiences, treatment needs and treatment outcomes of women and men are disparate, future research in virtually all aspects of drug use and treatment should attend to possible effects of gender. Researchers should design studies and conduct analyses that regularly assess possible differences between women and men. It may be a wise policy to assume that research findings (and treatment plans) typically cannot be generalized across gender unless otherwise determined.
>
> (Gil-Rivas, Fiorentine, and Anglin, 1995: 101)

Advocates realized that the settings in which research was conducted would be important. We next consider two innovative US women's treatment programmes, one on the west coast and the other on the east coast, that evolved to respond to the research imperative as well as changes in the macro-structure of healthcare delivery in the US. Both emphasized recovery from trauma as part of recovery from drug dependence. Both were run by chief executive officers (CEOs) who participated in the women's and anti-war movements, and entered the drug treatment field as a result of political commitments to social change and community psychology.

PROTOTYPES and SSTAR: Model women's treatment programmes in the US

PROTOTYPES[41] originated as a hybrid response to an environment demanding research, constant programme evaluation and validation of EBPs, and the realization that the CMHCs 'were no longer responding to emerging community needs', as co-founder Brown put it.[42] Brown and executive vice president and co-founder Maryann Fraser 'wanted to develop new programmes and models, get research funding to test and then refine them, and then train other organizations and help them if they were interested in taking up/adapting these programmes/models. Hence the name 'PROTOTYPES: Centers for Innovation in Mental Health, Social Services'.[43] The first PROTOTYPES Women's Center opened in late 1987, with grants from Los Angeles county. Coming out of Brown's realization that many of the women with whom she had been working on recovery might be diagnosed with HIV/AIDS, PROTOTYPES was one of the first programmes in California to integrate substance abuse treatment with attention to HIV/AIDS. Brown was bothered by the focus on women as 'vectors of infection' to others, while their own risk of infection was being ignored. Beginning in 1988, NIDA funded PROTOTYPES as one of three participating sites in the Women's and AIDS Risk Network, for which Mondanaro was the Principal Investigator, and which provided outreach to women at high risk for HIV/AIDS in three US cities. AIDS outreach continues to this day at PROTOTYPES. Because of her work in both women's substance abuse treatment and HIV/AIDS, PROTOTYPES named one of their programmes 'The Josette Mondanaro Women's Resource Center'. In 2008, after 22 years at PROTOTYPES, Brown retired from her post as CEO. Under her leadership, the non-profit agency had expanded from 20 to more than 200 beds, 24 service delivery sites, and several campuses, including a large housing project distinctive for architectural and environmental innovation, and a $20 million budget.

Because PROTOTYPES went where the need was perceived to be, the programmes are diverse and tailored to serve multiple populations (including men and boys), and housed in some of the most economically depressed neighbourhoods such as South Central and East Los Angeles. In a recent programme for youths involved in the juvenile justice system, PROTOTYPES worked collaboratively with Homeboy Industries to develop employment opportunities for youths, including a restaurant, bakery, and silk-screening studio. There are multiple divisions within the non-profit corporation, including a Mental Health Division that grew from a $700,000 programme to a $4 million programme, an HIV/AIDS Division, and a Training and T.A. Division. PROTOTYPES evolved to serve men, women, and children from a wide range of racial-ethnic and class backgrounds. Staff meetings were designed as learning collaboratives, and PROTOTYPES hired and continues to hire staff who were themselves 'recovering, who had diagnoses of mental illness, who had trauma histories, who were sex workers, who were living with HIV/AIDS', as well as youth leaders. Staff were representative of the communities in which PROTOTYPES was situated – typically one third African-American, one third Chicana/o, and one third white. Fully half were, according to Brown:

> what we call consumer/survivor/recovering people. I think the communities recognized that we were serious, that we hired from the community, that we trained people who came in perhaps as outreach workers, and they were trained and moved up and became program directors. I think that, plus sitting with people – and I truly do believe in the wisdom of the people – in community groups was what built the trust. My first community groups were in Venice in the Sixties, and half the people in the room were nodding out. We just hung in there until we figured out together what drug treatment programs were best for the community. I think it's that participatory structure that got people to really understand that we were serious about our commitment to community representation.[44]

Due to the efforts of women's treatment advocates at the national level, women's drug treatment is now linked to many other conditions, and some programmes have moved it into primary care settings. Stanley Street Treatment and Resources (SSTAR) began as the Center for Alcohol Problems, incorporated as a non-profit in 1977. It operates out of Fall River, Massachusetts, just across the border from Rhode Island. SSTAR's current executive director, Nancy Paull began working in this programme in the 1980s. Active in both the feminist and antiwar movements, Paull felt that alcohol problems comprised an 'equal opportunity illness', but noticed few women attending the alcohol treatment programme. Assuming that childcare was the issue, she obtained funding in 1979 for a pilot day treatment programme for alcoholic women with children and partnered with a day care centre to create a programme called DAWN (Day Alternatives for Women's Needs). Although the programme served between eight and ten women and had great results, it was considered 'too expensive' by the commonwealth of Massachusetts. When Paull assumed the directorship in 1985, DAWN was gone but the experience shaped the direction in which she took the organization.

> One of the things we had learned from the women in the day treatment program was that a lot of them were using benzo[diazepine]s as well as alcohol. The majority of them had had histories of trauma.

> In our detox, we couldn't treat drug addiction. One of the first things I did when I came back was to get a license to become a drug and alcohol facility. In those days, alcohol was run by the Department of Public Health and drugs was run by the Department of Mental Health, and the two didn't talk to each other. It really took an act of the legislature to get . . . my alcohol detox [to] become a drug detox. We got eight drug beds – it was tiny. My nursing staff was all up in arms and many quit because they didn't want to deal with those people. We had nice little alcoholic men who were very grateful for whatever you did and all of a sudden, we were bringing in this younger population of drug addicts, both male and female, who were much more lively and difficult to handle.[45]

The structure of state social services sectors presented problems for programmes moving towards integrated substance abuse and mental health services. Such problems were compounded when domestic violence funding was sought. The fledgling SSTAR programme

Figure 3.1 SSTAR parade float. Photo courtesy of Nancy Paull

(see Figure 3.1) sought 'trauma money' then under the control of the Department of Social Services, which was responsible for domestic violence programmes. Such programmes had arisen out of a grass-roots women's movement mainly geared towards funding shelters, rather than treatment, that 'did not appreciate that we were medicalizing trauma issues'.[46]

The need to navigate multiple state structures in order to survive shaped SSTAR, which became a licensed mental health centre with contracts with the Department of Social Services, the Department of Public Health, and the Department of Mental Health in order to meet the needs of its mainly women clients. As the organization grew and differentiated, the drug problems to which it replied also multiplied as southeastern Massachusetts and Rhode Island were hit with high levels of opiate use. The 'medicalization' continued, according to Paull, as a result:

> During this evolution, we saw that more and more people, including women, were now using opiates so we started the first opiate detox using clonidine versus methadone. We saw this as a women's issue because methadone commits someone to coming in every day of their lives, and if you have kids, it's really difficult. In the early days, we were drug-free and we used a clonidine protocol. Our medical director, Dr. Frank Lepreau, is the one who researched that and came up with that protocol. We were so lucky to get that doctor, who was a radical in his own way ... He came every day of his life to SSTAR.[47]

In the very early stages of the HIV epidemic, Paull encountered a client who described a virus with which he had been diagnosed at a VA clinic. 'We knew we had such a high rate of opiate injection use, and I thought it was going to be huge. That's when we started, as fast as we could, learning about it. We formed a collaboration with the Brown [University] infectious disease programme and they helped us start our community health centre. They sent over free doctors and started counselling and testing. No one in Fall River wanted to deal with HIV. We had no big public clinic, and none of the private docs wanted to deal with HIV'.[48] SSTAR became the first programme in the state of Massachusetts to offer HIV testing and counselling in a drug treatment setting. The programme hired two female Infectious Disease specialists and gradually evolved towards primary healthcare.

'Women', according to Paull, 'are in the forefront of everything we think about and everything we do'.[49] However, she described a volatile funding environment in which there has been an attempt to shorten lengths of stay and cut costs. 'We had the only female detox in the state and the state wouldn't support it, so we had to close it because it was more costly to run it. Now we're back to this mixed-gender detox with all this specialized programming for women. The numbers for women are changeable – women don't necessarily want to come in because of children ... Less beds are more expensive beds because you needed the same amount of nursing staff and physician staff'.[50] She also described a programme in which there has been an ongoing commitment to therapeutic innovation.

In the late 1980s SSTAR pioneered a clonidine detox protocol for pregnant women; as word got around that the programme would admit pregnant women, women from both Massachusetts and neighbouring Rhode Island sought it out. According to Paull, 'Once the word got out that you could be pregnant and come in here, every pregnant woman from all over the state started coming here. Drug addicts and the underground movement were talking to each other. It also turned out that we were getting a lot of women who were pregnant and older, and had lost their other children at birth because once they were found to be using drugs, the kids were taken away. So it really then became a political issue as well as a women's rights issue'.[51] SSTAR continued to operate with state contracts until the programme was granted federal PPWI money and was able to build a facility designed for women with children, which opened in 1992. The layout was flexible in accommodating several mothers with infants as well as children, with a common laundry room, playroom, and a living room with kitchenette so bottles could be heated right on the wing in the middle of the night,. Day care, work rooms, group rooms, and a computer room for vocational training were included.

SSTAR relies on 'Seeking Safety', one of the curricula described above, to deliver conjoint treatment for substance abuse and PTSD. Paull recalls, 'We didn't call it PTSD in the beginning. We just knew that the woman had been traumatized and that had psychological consequences that needed to be dealt with. We also felt that women would run from treatment when they weren't medicated anymore and when they were starting to face these flashbacks. They would run and get medicated. So we just felt early on that it had to be dealt with. A lot of people talk about it today, but very few people do conjoint treatment for women ... Our clinicians have been trained in trauma-informed treatment ... All our staff has been trauma-informed. We also offer services for men who batter, because we feel that's critical'.[52] SSTAR has also become involved in an international, United Nations-led effort to help under-resourced nations create treatment systems. 'In terms of treatment, I really feel that the United States has done addiction treatment wrong from the beginning in terms of the specialization of it. We haven't alerted primary care and had primary care work with it from day one. It's so stigmatizing and the stigmatization has hurt women far more than it has hurt men. The way we treat addiction in this country has hurt women far more than it has hurt men'.[53] Asked if she ever envisioned herself as a CEO of a large healthcare system, Paull answered, 'No. I started out wanting to make a difference in the lives of people with addiction issues; and then became concerned about how women specifically were not getting the help they needed. To impact that you need to be involved in policy and research. The international work has brought a whole new dimension to how I look at things, and I love to be able to work with different cultures to see what have we done – what pieces do we have that might make a difference in their world. And I have definitely seen what pieces other places have that could benefit my clients'.[54]

Conclusion

Despite flourishing programmes such as the two documented above, federal and state support for women's substance abuse treatment continued to suffer, and in the US they remain the most likely 'special population' to be underserved (Parra, 2002). Citing 'additional barriers' such as 'stigma and shame associated with a woman's substance abuse, the lack of early identification by professionals, lack of child care, lack of residential treatment programmes that can accommodate mothers with children, and lack of transportation' (Amaro, 1999: 657–9), women's treatment advocates continued to produce data showing that the cost to society of women not enrolling in treatment exceeds the cost of funding programmes. Yet comprehensive women's programmes continue to be considered 'too expensive' to fund for long. As the twenty-first century began, a chorus of voices arose once more to attest to the continuing need – and the continual lack of access and resources to sustain treatment.

Secondly, data from the Nordic countries and North American data from both Canada and the US shows that, contrary to twentieth century claims that women are more difficult to treat than men or more stubbornly addicted, women fare as well or better than men in treatment.[55] While 'women with strong ties to drug subcultures are at higher risk of relapse', according to Irmgard Vogt's 1998 survey of western European and North American data, women are also able to maintain social networks and make use of them for 'natural recovery' when they are ready to do so. While the proliferation of treatment options for women is heartening, the problem remains that most women who wish to access treatment are not in a position to do so. The prevailing drug policy framework is not conducive to the kind of programmes that we argue for in this book, and are in fact either hostile toward or irrelevant to most women's lives. The next part of this book lays out the conceptual frameworks of the governing mentalities in each of the countries in order to illustrate the dominant drug policy continuum that has co-constituted both criminalization and medicalization through much of the last century. The point is that the 'governing mentalities' (Campbell, 2000) of criminalization and medicalization overlap and co-construct each other, rather than working in opposition to one another as many assume. This can be clearly seen in light of recent trends to criminalize women drug users, particularly during pregnancy; the increased use of incarceration as a form of drug policy in the US; and in foetal and child 'protection' and removal policies. While harm reduction appears to offer a 'third way' alternative to the dominant governing mentalities, it is increasingly assimilated to them. 'Sadly, in the context of so much research, knowledge, and experience [with harm reduction], there is very little known about the unique trajectory and circumstances of female drug users throughout the world' (Sherman, Kamarulzaman, and Spittal, 2008). That this statement should continue to be valid after the four decades of feminist advocacy that we have described in Part I stands as a testament to the need for a more sustained and systematic approach than what has prevailed thus far.

Part II
Gendering the Governing Mentalities

Drug policy provides the larger framework within which women's drug and alcohol treatment programmes take shape. In the following chapter, we turn to policy design theory as a way of looking simultaneously at how the social construction of drug-using women as 'target populations' for drug policy interacts with the social construction of knowledge and ignorance that we charted in Part I. 'The choice of [policy] design elements reflects political and social values, historical precedent, national trends in ideas about "good" policy, as well as a host of "local" knowledge that leads to enormous variability in policy designs across time and space. These choices produce policy experiences for those people who are directly affected, and the choices influence policy learning that stretches far into the future' (Schneider and Sidney, 2009: n.p.). Anne Larason Schneider and Helen Ingram argue in their book *Policy Design for Democracy* that policy designs have consequences for the quality of democracy (1997: 66). Based on Schneider and Ingram (1993), their fifth chapter, 'Social Constructions of Target Populations: Degenerative Policy Designs' tracks how divisive and stigmatizing social constructions interact with political power in what they call 'degenerative policy-making systems'. We see 'degenerative policy-making systems' as particularly apt for characterizing the attributes of drug policy:

- Unequal distribution of social and political power.
- Social constructions that separate the 'deserving' from the 'undeserving'.
- Institutional cultures that legitimize strategic, manipulative, and deceptive communication and uses of political power.

(1997: 102)

We contend that drug policy making takes place in such 'degenerative' contexts, and thus teaches lessons about citizenship, democracy, and social justice that are 'closely tied to the type of target population' chosen to bear the burdens or receive the benefits of a particular policy design.

Policy makers choose target populations – often before choosing the exact problems to be resolved – in terms of relative distribution of benefits and burdens; 'deviant' target populations are highly substitutable especially in degenerative situations (Schneider and Ingram, 1997: 113). Advantaged populations are selected whenever possible for benefits-only distributive policies such as tax incentives and business subsidies; disadvantaged groups become targets for more punitive polices even in so-called therapeutic settings. The concept of 'target populations' has been taken up widely as a contribution to postpositivist policy analysis. Schneider and Ingram (1997) divide 'target populations' into the following four groups: (1) politically advantaged groups, who learn quite different lessons than those treated as (2) deviants, who have little power and are negatively constructed; (3) contenders, whose power may be increasing but who are typically still negatively constructed; or (4) dependants, who are politically weak but positively constructed. These four types of target groups receive distinctive messages about citizenship that in turn influence their orientation toward government and political participation, and ultimately shape their distinctive experiences with the political process (Schneider and Ingram, 1997: 104).

Previously writing about the 'governing mentalities' that structure drug policy discourse, Nancy D. Campbell noted that

> Governing mentalities animate the conceptual practices and material institutions of power; they guide prevailing interpretations of events and evidence. Although figurative in nature, they are materialized in institutions, policymaking cultures, and bureaucratic-administrative programs and procedures. Governing mentalities derive their power to compel from both symbolic and material registers. They are the cultural processes of formation and figuration that shape public policy debates and outcomes. By attending to material and discursive practices and their consequences for women's lives, the governing mentalities model expands the possibilities for feminist cultural studies and policy analysis.
>
> (2000: 50)

The consequences of considering drug-using women to be largely 'unworthy' subjects of drug policy are clear. We have in both the US and the UK a situation in which what exists as 'gender-sensitive treatment' or 'women's treatment' is simply not good enough to attract, retain, and deliver adequate treatment for most women who need it. This is the effect of a combination of epistemological and political factors ranging from the 'epistemologies of ignorance' – that structured forms of knowledge production that initially refused to admit women's drug use might differ from men's – to logistical barriers, such as lack of childcare and transportation that affect women's capacities to carry out their assigned roles in social reproduction. As feminists began to create programmes and write about these differences within feminist conceptual frameworks, they brought new factors to the surface, including relational and cultural gender differences that are not well-encompassed by the dominant forms of knowledge concerning 'addiction', which have recently migrated almost entirely towards neurochemistry and neurogenetics. These 'contending mentalities' provide compelling alternatives to the 'governing mentalities' that structure drug policy.

We argue that the drug research and treatment arena has been resistant to approaches sensitive to the gendered, classed, sexualized, and racialized power differentials that structure the lives of drug-using women. There has been a refusal to consider 'gender' in fully social terms – and as something that can in fact *shape* biological vulnerability and biosocial reproduction – and a wilful mishearing of the feminist analysis of 'gender' as meaning simply 'women' rather than requiring attention to the entire social system by which gender is produced and the 'epistemologies of ignorance' through which gender is continually not known – or not seen to be salient. This wilful ignorance has both contributed to and been shaped by drug policy, which has tended for many decades towards law enforcement and supply reduction, rather than 'demand reduction'. But when demand reduction is considered, it is always couched within the classical mode of intervention targeted towards the brain and behaviour of a sick, maladjusted, and misbehaving *individual* – who is not understood to be gendered and located within a set of *relationships* contributing either to her addiction or to her recovery or to an ongoing, 'chronic' round of relapse. We argue that drug policy should shift the target of intervention to the set of relationships between persons, drugs, and social contexts that position individual brains and bodies within cultural geographies where illicit drugs are often the healthiest economic sector to which they have access. Our sense is that neuroscience is inadequate to visualize the traces of the cultural repository of ideas and images that underlie our assumptions about addiction, which have a great deal to with ideas about governability and perceived lack of governability that are central to the governing mentalities of drug policy discourse – and with gender, race, class, sexuality, and other social differences.

Reconstructing addiction as a 'chronic, relapsing brain disorder' is highly unlikely to de-stigmatize it and may run the risk of even further stigmatizing addicts as deranged or damaged individuals – addicts are those whose 'neurobiology [has] gone awry' (Volkow, 2004). The concept of 'brain disease'/'brain disorder' accomplishes cultural work within the scientific communities producing knowledge about addiction in helping to shift research on drug addiction towards 'brain science' in an attempt to transcend the stigma that has long dogged not only drug-addicted persons but those who treat and study them (Campbell, 2007). However, the price of localizing addiction to 'the brain' is reduced recognition that the activities and practices comprising drug problems take place in particular social, economic, political, and cultural contexts – and that addictions are lived out by people, not by their brains. People are gendered, racialized, classed, and located along multiple axes of difference; policies that do not recognize this run a great risk of missing the point. We continue with this book by looking more closely at drug policies in the US and the UK in hopes of determining where gender resides within drug policy.

4

'Unearthing Women' in Drug Policy: Where Do Women Fit – Or Do They?

Across the phases of British drug treatment policy

In Britain the policy framework within which treatment responses to women drug users and alcoholics developed can be situated within political changes reflecting distinct phases or periods. For Susanne MacGregor and Lynne Smith (1998: 70) these phases are characterized by treatment and care as well as control and punishment – all shaped within a pragmatic system whose treatment objectives have varied from abstinence, stabilization, risk reduction, and harm minimization. These authors argue that the British system has developed by trial and error, step-by-step experimentation, and avoidance of extremes. While how women have fared within this system is affected by these developments, objectives and characteristics, women's involvement with this system has been marked by their invisibility and/or extreme moralizing. Citing Virginia Berridge's (1984) work, MacGregor and Smith (1998: 70) outline how British drug policy has gone through five phases, with a sixth now underway. We argue that the sixth phase is completed and a seventh is on its way. When we look at these phases with special reference to women and ask how women fit into drug treatment policy in Britain, the question arises, 'Where do women fit – or do they'?

Treating women 'degenerates' (1800s–1920s)

Medical experts during the latter half of the nineteenth century established the view that inebriety or morphinism was a mental disease: a functional neurosis as well as a moral vice. Furthermore, inebriates or morphinists were seen to be 'morally bankrupt' individuals as well as vicious and deprived sinners, suffering from moral insanity (Berridge and Edwards, 1981: *xxix*). For medical experts, inebriates and morphinists needed treatment to be cleansed of their vice and to be cured of their disease which were classified in a biologically determined way. Berridge (1999) has outlined how various Acts of Parliament, including the *1868 Pharmacy Act*, the *1879 Habitual Drunkards Act*, the *1888 Inebriates Act*, the *1890 Lunacy Act*, and the *1908 Poisons and Pharmacy Act* shaped this first phase of British drugs policy. It is interesting to note that medico-legal discussions of 'female' inebriates and morphinists first appeared after the passage of the *1879 Habitual Drunkenness Act*. The Society for Promoting Legislation for the Control and Cure of Habitual Offenders[1] was founded by a group of doctors in 1876 and was instrumental in pressing for the passage of the 1879 Act. The society's main aims were 'to investigate the causes of inebriety and to educate the professional and public mind on the facts of the physical aspects of habitual intemperance' (Eccles, 1942). Led by its founding president, Dr. Norman Kerr, the Society for the Study of Inebriety (SSI) became the main public debating forum for the development of the disease theory of inebriety. As Berridge (1979: 76) suggests, the SSI gave moral judgements a certain degree of scientific respectability, succeeding in 'uniting alcohol, mental illness and narcotic addiction in a disease conception which rapidly became pervasive'. In July 1903, the SSI established a scientific journal, *The British Journal* of *Inebriety*,[2] that attended to women inebriates in its second issue, of which six out of ten articles focused on how women's inebriety was related to effects on children (Zanetti, 1903); motherhood (Shaw, 1903); racial degeneration (Sullivan, 1903); overlain infants (Westcott, 1903);[3] criminality (Holmes, 1903); and restoration (i.e., rehabilitation) (Waugh, 1903). These articles were based on a discussion 'Inebriety in women, and its influence on Child-Life' held by the SSI on 14 July 1903. A closer look at these articles reveals that these experts were concerned about 'habitual inebriates'[4] particularly women who came within the provision of the *1899 Habitual Inebriates Act*, an act empowering magistrates or judges to commit 'habitual inebriates' to Inebriate Reformatories for a period not exceeding three years. In effect this created a nationwide system of Certified 'Homes' or 'Retreats' for the middle and upper classes and Certified and State Reformatories for the working classes. The anonymous author of an article, 'The Treatment of Inebriety in Institutions' in the *British Medical Journal* in 1900: 1199 stated that by 1898:

> Six reformatories for inebriates were receiving patients; most of these were in receipt of financial contributions from local authorities.

> Two more are in course of construction. By these accommodation is, or will be, provided for 302 criminal inebriates ... There are at present 17 certified retreats licensed for 305 patients, 131 males and 174 females and 4 other institutions, hitherto conducted as private homes, are contemplating applying for licence under the Acts.

At this time, it was obvious that alcohol was seen as an 'evil constantly working in our midst' (Scharlieb, 1907: 59) and that 'no greater problem faces the people of this country than inebriety in women' (Somerset, 1912: 81). In 1911, the wife of Bramwell Booth[5] (1911: 58) offered a clinical analysis of 300 cases of inebriate women received by the Salvation Army and concluded that these inebriate women came from all walks of life including business women, domestic servants, nurses, teachers, barmaids, and no definite occupation. She noted that while the Salvation Army had an already established assistance for 'outcast women' they 'have over fifty homes in Great Britain' and 'no less than eighty three departments of work for the relief of women' with 'homes established at Stamford Hill and Denmark Hill' London (62). It is interesting to note that these Salvation Army establishments treated alcoholic women, as well as women who were opium users. It was striking that 'a permanent restoration' (62) or 'cure' (69) was sought after for these women regardless of their having taken 'the Normyl[6] and other cures' (62) or remedies.

In the run up to the 1920s, a variety of medical experts, including neurologists, pharmacologists, psychiatrists and general practitioners, participated in public debates about inebriates and drug users. Others experts included members of the Salvation Army, the National Temperance League, the United Kingdom Alliance,[7] and those actively involved in other professional societies, such as the National Council for Mental Hygiene, the Royal College of Physicians, the Royal Society of Medicine, the Eugenics Education Society and the British Psychological Society, and civil servants or officials at the Ministry of Health and the Home Office and the Health Organization, the predecessor to the World Health Organization. All these experts contributed to ways of speaking about 'addiction' which represented a substantial part of the overall discourse on public health and morality existing at that time. With special reference to women, these experts' ways of speaking constructed moralistic views detrimental to these women who were seen as 'contributing to racial degeneration' by procreating offspring likely to be 'parasitic of dangerous to the community' (Sullivan, 1903). In reality, these women were 'morbid subjects' and 'science' was called upon to take up 'the most terrible of our social sores – habitual inebriates'

(Holmes, 1903: 72). These females 'degenerates' (Travis-Clegg, 1913) were put into industrial farms, retreats or reformatories, evidencing a well-organized system of management and detention. Control and punishment appeared to trump treatment and care for female inebriates. This was necessary as from the official point of view 'moral defects were passing into physical failings' and women needed to be consigned to places where they will be 'saved from themselves until such time they can stand alone' (Somerset, 1912: 81).

Women in a masculinist system (1920–60)

During Phase 2 (1920s–60s) as MacGregor and Smith (1998: 71) argue, the *1920 Dangerous Drugs Act* became prominent, while *The Rolleston Report*[8] of 1926 reasserted the disease model of addiction. H. B. 'Bing' Spear (2002: 5) contends that the development of British policy during this time must also take account of the provisions of the Hague Conventions which Britain signed and which came into force in 1919. The *1920 Dangerous Drugs Act* and the 1921 *Dangerous Drug Regulations* put into domestic legislation the provisions of the Hague Convention. During this time *The Rolleston Report* of 1926 reasserted doctors' freedom to prescribe doses of opioid drugs as a form of 'legitimate medical treatment' and laid the foundations of what has been referred to as the British system (Spear, 2002: 31). In effect, *The Rolleston Report* of 1926 allowed doctors to interpret the meaning of legitimate medical treatment and to prescribe heroin or morphine to addicts in certain circumstances, a policy which remained unquestioned until the Interdepartmental Committee on Drug Addiction (The Brain Committee) was appointed in 1958 (Stimson, 1973: 25). During this phase, the treatment of women varied and some women found care in private homes, an idea left over from the original inebriates' retreats. In 1929, John Reid (1929: 58) spoke of the treatment of upper and middle class women as female patients who 'cannot be trusted' and had to be treated 'as children' in his home, Ecclesfield Home, in Ashford Middlesex. A few years earlier Margaret Vivian (1927) talked about how 'drug-takers are commonly considered to be outside the pale', looked upon as creatures 'devoid of honour, incurable, untruthful' and are 'almost universally regarded as degenerates, liars, and utterly unreliable persons' (129). Here, Vivian, a female doctor, discusses a female patient who was under her care:

> One of my patients was cured seven times in seven different homes in England and on the Continent. Each time she relapsed owing to

> the ease with which she obtained supplies of heroin from a medical man with a facile conscience. Then suddenly the latter came under the ban of the authorities and was threatened with all the pains and penalties of the D.D.A,[9] should he transgress again. The patient came to me and was cured for the eighth time, more by virtue of the D.D.A. than owing to the efficacy of the treatment. In all these cases time is an important factor. She has remained cured up to the present.
> (131)

During this phase, it was clear that some Inebriates Homes, many functioning since the late 1800s, were treating female drug addicts as well as alcoholics. One director (Member of the Community of St. Mary, 1944: 17) of a former Inebriates Home, Spelthorne St. Mary, spoke in 1944 of how the average number of 'inmates' in her home was 60–70 with an average length of stay about three months (18). She did not differentiate between alcoholics and other drug addicts because 'their backgrounds morally, mentally and physically are very similar'. She notes:

> In the case of morphia and barbiturate addicts there have usually been special opportunities in their professional or home lives for procuring these drugs. Nurses, doctors, dispensers and the wives of medical men are therefore most often among such patients. There are certain groups of women who obtain drugs, chiefly morphia both from doctors and others who apparently obtain and distribute them by questionable means. These patients are usually a dissipated and somewhat degraded type with no desire for a permanent cure. They come to have the drug tapered and frequently leave before withdrawal is complete and return to their habits needing a smaller amount to give the satisfaction they crave. This type of patient has greatly increased during the war.

What is being described above is the phenomenon of 'therapeutic patients' those who had come into contact with drugs through medical treatment and/or their or their spouse's employment. Martin Plant (1975: 39) contends that during and after World War II,[10] returning troops introduced cannabis smoking to Britain, while at the same time there was an increase in non-therapeutic heroin dependence with 'proselytizing drug dependents, people who tried to recruit others to their habit'. What becomes evident during this phase of treatment and policy is that while a system of medical control operating within a penal framework of international controls and national drugs legislation existed until the 1960s (MacGregor and Smith, 1998: 71), drug addicts were viewed as 'sick' people who should be given a regular supply of controlled drugs by medical personnel in order to lead normal lives. Reflecting on this phase in his background chapter for *Drug Problems in Britain* (1981), Griffith Edwards noted that

> in the simplest terms, Britain's drug problem was of interest exactly and only because of its trivial size ... Opium offences had numbered 184 in 1921 but had fallen to 6 in 1938. The first official statistics furnished in 1934 to the League of Nations gave a total of 300 addicts for the whole country ... The breakdown in this long-established equilibrium came in the early 1960s.
>
> (9)

Regardless of the low number of addicts at this time, the developing 'British system' was 'masculinist' to its core. This was evidenced by the use of 'he' and 'his' to refer to all addicts in all policy documents and legislation (see, for example, Ministry of Health, 1926). Even when the terms 'patient/s' or 'addict/s' were used, these signalled men, male patients, and/or male addicts. While women may have been treated for addiction during this phase, the focus of treatment and policy was firmly on men. This is regardless of the fact that Home Office records reveal from 1936–59 the number of known addicts ranged from 613 in 1936 to 454 in 1959 and if these figures were categorized by sex, the numbers of known male and female addicts were relatively comparable. However, when analysing these statistics, one sees clearly that female addicts slightly overtake male addicts in years 1937–8, 1940, 1954–7 and by more than in 15 per cent in years 1945–47 and 1958–9 (Spear, 1969). Thus, it is curious as to why addicts were consistently referred to as 'he'.

Women addicts as expendable (1960–80)

Alex Mold (2008: 21) argues that the British system put in place by the Rolleston Committee's report remained 'unchanged for nearly forty years' because the situation highlighted by the report 'stayed the same'. When the Brain Committee (named after its chairman, Sir Russell, later Lord Brain, a neurologist) or Interdepartmental Committee on Drug Addiction was convened in 1958, it took evidence on a questionnaire from organizations which the committee felt were important, as well as doctors with special experience treating addicts (Spear, 2003: 100). Spear is critical of the certainty with which committee members and the subsequent report denied any real increase in addiction, despite the rise in numbers of known addicts at that time. The Brain Committee attributed this rise to 'intensified activity for its (i.e., addiction's) detection and recognition over the post war period' (Section 24). With regards to doctor's prescribing, the committee noted only two doctors as 'habitual offenders, who were brought to notice during the past 20 years' (Section 37, Ministry of Health, 1961).

With regards to treatment, the Committee's basic findings were that: 'addiction should be regarded as an expression of a mental disorder rather than a form of criminal behavior' (Section 27); 'every addict should be treated energetically as a medical and psychiatric problem' (Section 28); 'the best unit for the initial treatment ... is the psychiatric ward of a general hospital' (Section 31) and 'it is doubtful whether there is scope for establishing specialized institutions in Great Britain exclusively for the treatment of drug addiction' (Section 30). In this context, it is important to note that the report included an Appendix IV '*Summaries of the case histories of known stabilized addicts*'. Out of the six case studies presented in this Appendix, four referred to women addicts, Mrs. A. Mrs B and C – all housewives and Mrs E, a manic depressive. It was clear from statistics available at the time that between 1958 and 1961, the year of the publication of this report that women addicts *outnumbered* men (see Spear, 1969: 247). Nevertheless, there were no major changes in policy. This could lead one to a cynical interpretation – women addicts were believed to be expendable and not as important as men addicts.

In 1964 the Brain Committee was reconvened to consider whether or not 'the advice they gave in 1961 ... needs revising' (Section 4) (Ministry of Health, 1965). Spear, who was working at the Home Office Drugs Branch at that time, recalled that the Brain Committee was reconvened because of a report put in by the Home Office which provided data on heroin prescriptions, revealing the existence of over-prescribing doctors (Spear, 1988). After 'holding eight meetings', 'studying submissions from the Home Office, Ministry of Health and the Scottish Home and Health Department' and 'inviting written and oral evidence' from experts in the field (Section 7), the Committee reported in 1965, making some key recommendations. These included

- All addicts[11] should be formally notified (Section 18).
- The establishment of specialized centres for the treatment of addiction (Section 22) with the proviso that compulsory detention of addicts in crises in these centres would require legislation (Section 24).

- The 'prescribing, supply and administration of restricted dangerous drugs' (i.e., heroin and cocaine) 'to drug addicts to doctors on the staff of the treatment centres' (Section 26).
- The establishment of a standing advisory committee to keep 'dependence on drugs under constant observation' (Section 42).

Special centres were to be set up as soon as possible in London with 'facilities for medical treatment, including laboratory investigation and provision for research' (Section 22). It was also noted that 'a centre might form a part of a psychiatric hospital or of the psychiatric wing of a general hospital' (Section 22).

As a result the Second Report of the Brain Committee[12] the treatment of addiction was meant to be concentrated in new clinics, subsequently called Drug Dependency Units (DDUs) based in hospitals. MacGregor and Smith (1998: 71) contend that on the one hand this eroded the medical professional independence and on the other, it gave the medical profession relative independence to decide on the composition of treatment regimes. They say:

> A short period of competitive prescribing soon gave way to an emphasis on methadone, especially its oral form. Maintenance increasingly gave way to reduction, which meant short term prescribing or no prescribing of methadone. The amount of heroin prescribed fell by 40% from 1971–1978, mostly in the early 1970s. From a fairly early stage the clinics accepted a few patients for long-term prescription of heroin. Those that remained were a few early long term patients who were allowed to remain on maintenance treatment.
>
> (MacGregor and Smith, 1998: 71)

In a study of the early London DDUs,[13] Gerry Stimson (1973: 48) noted that by 1968, the year that the first DDUs opened, there were: 600 doctors licensed to prescribe heroin, 39 clinics providing treatment for heroin users – 15 in London and 24 in other parts of England – and 1,139 patients on the books with 74 per cent (n=904) in London clinics. By using a stratified single stage sample by clinic, sex, and age, Stimson focused on 128 cases drawn from London clinics. He had a higher response rate for males than females: non-respondents in his sample were more likely to be female than male (75). Out of his final sample of 111 addicts, 84 were male and 27 female, which was a ratio of 2.6 to 1. Stimson had difficulties with his analysis concerning the inclusion of his female respondents because, as he related, it was not easy to give these female respondents an 'Employment rating' which was key to inclusion in one of his four designated groups: 10 of his 27 female respondents had been classified as 'housewives'. In his research, he devised a cluster analysis based on four groups of male addicts *only* – the Stables, Junkies, Loners, and Two Worlders. However, in the end he compared the female scores to the male scores 'by eye', put the females in relevant analytic clusters and found that the 'direction of difference' for male and female groups on variables was similar and that patterns of behaviour were comparable to those of males (188). While Stimson's study considered sex an important variable, it is interesting to note that being a housewife appeared as an anomaly in his research design. Surely women addicts were being treated in DDUs but generally 'female drugtakers' were viewed as 'adjuncts' to males when associating with deviant groups' (Plant, 1975: 65) and circulating within the treatment system. Most probably, this adjunct and furthermore abject, deviant status made it more difficult to define women as true addicts in need of treatment or as capable of being normalized.

In this context, a Prison Medical Officer, Dr. P.T. d'Orban carried out a now-classic study of heroin addiction in women at London's Holloway prison. d'Orban confirmed the 'deviant' status of women drug users by reporting that

> The women in this study were a highly disturbed group who showed more evidence of psychiatric abnormality than male heroin addicts (p. 76) ... Disturbed psychosexual development was one of the most striking findings... 35% were currently exclusively homosexual (1970: 70) ... [The respondents had] an official delinquency rate of 60% prior to heroin use.
>
> (1970: 76)

Around the same time, Sister Joan Elizabeth (1974: 81) reveals a strikingly different approach to women addict from d'Orban's[14] when she says:

> What we call our treatment is sometimes very prosaic and ordinary. We just try to provide the right kind of environment with just enough direction for our people to discover that if they are going to get better, it is they who have got to do the work ... Living side by side each other we grow together as a family ... Seen against highly technical approaches to the problems of alcoholism and drug addiction especially in respect to those who have been termed offenders

> our way probably sounds very naïve. However, we believe these problems are brought about when by what the people [*sic*] are as human beings and the circumstances in which they find themselves and their relationships with others.

All of the above treatment and rehabilitation work was framed by *The Dangerous Drugs Act 1967*,[15] which was followed quickly by *The Misuse of Drugs Act 1971*[16] and then the *Misuse of Drugs (Notification and Supply to Addicts) Regulations 1973*.[17] This type of legislation was aimed at making the DDUs 'compete with the illegal market keeping the Mafia out', Stimson's (1987: 37) contention, which places medicine in a 'functional relationship with the illegal market' with medicine's main task 'being the social control of drug distribution'. 'Keeping the mafia out' can be seen to characterize the 'masculinist culture' which was at the heart of the British drugs treatment system.

MacGregor and Smith (1998: 71) argue that during this phase of the drug treatment system the amount of heroin prescribed fell by 40 per cent from 1971 to 1978 and that from a fairly early stage, DDUs accepted few new patients for long-term prescription of heroin. They cited Gerry Stimson and Edna Oppenheimer (1982) showing that addicts who remained attached to DDUs were allowed to remain on maintenance treatment. While the clinics continued to be an important part of the statutory health and welfare response to drug users (albeit to more males than females), DDUs were supplemented by a variety of non-statutory services, such as rehabilitation houses and street agencies.

Prior to the 1980s, drugs policies implied a dichotomy between treatment and rehabilitation as noted by the ACMD (1982). Treatment tended to be restricted to the medical setting of DDUs, while rehabilitation was seen as a non-statutory agency response and regarded as a more active process encouraging self-determination and personal integration as well as the development of social skills and interpersonal relationships. MacGregor and Elizabeth Ettorre (1987: 131) outline two parallel approaches that emerged within the overall treatment system in Britain at that time: (1) an individualized containment-cum-confrontational approach adopted by statutory agencies such as DDUs and (2) a self-help community approach supported by non-statutory agencies. Already by that time, the Standing Conference on Drug Abuse (SCODA), a national coordinating and representative body for drug services and drugs workers had been championing for more social (i.e., community approaches, etc.) than medical models of care since it began its work with Department of Health and Social Security[18] funding in 1972. MacGregor and Smith

(1998: 72) imply that this social model of approaching drug use began to influence thinking in the drugs field and led to the emergence of the notion that 'problem drug users' experienced social, psychological, physical, and legal problems, and should be treated through a social-psychological approach based on social learning theories and models. From the point of view of women, this type of approach hinted at seeing the whole person – with gender included in the mix.

Helping women in crisis? – City Roads

City Roads, an innovative short-stay residential unit for crisis intervention for drug users, opened in London in May 1978. It targeted specifically the 'chaotic drug users' who were often seen as 'multiple drug users in the sense that they used a variety of drugs more or less discriminately depending upon what happened on the illegal market (Jamieson, Glanz and MacGregor, 1984: 14) – at that time barbiturates were becoming widely available. MacGregor, Professor and Leverhulme Emeritus Research Fellow at the London School of Hygiene and Tropical Medicine, recalls how she first got involved in doing research at City Roads and in the drugs field:

> I had been a researcher at the MRC Social Psychiatry Unit with John Wing at the Institute of Psychiatry. We had done a study of Camberwell Reception Centre (for homeless single men) and so I was known to the DHSS ... and there was a woman there ... who was the civil servant responsible for the homeless. They had a homelessness and addictions subcommittee ... When they decided that they were going to fund City Roads as a demonstration project, they ... needed to have an evaluation component. She suggested my name ... I always say, 'I came into drugs through homelessness' ... So I was then asked to be involved in the steering committee and it was a kind of action research project. It was between action research and evaluation ... I was involved from the start – which was quite unusual. I sat on the committee which was the working party which was talking about setting up City Roads before it actually began in 1978 ... Then we did the evaluation of City Roads – we had a three year grant from the DHSS from 1978 to 1981 to set it up as a crisis intervention service. It was the first crisis intervention service for multiple drug misusers, as they termed it then, and the term 'chaotic' began to appear at that time – also 'chaotic drug misusers'. So that was ... how I got ... into the drugs field ... Then I carried on I stayed on the Management

> Committee of City Roads ... So I ... maintained a connection with City Roads ... It was a very interesting project ... it was the first one to bring a ... multidisciplinary approach. It brought in nurses as well as social workers , community psychiatric nurses then ... [The whole thing] was focused on ... the story of people turning up at A and E and nowhere to send them on ... It developed ... the idea of a professional approach.[19]

Although City Roads was described as a 'hybrid service' combining statutory and non-statutory approaches (Mold and Berridge, 2010: 59), the majority of members of the initial Steering Committee were people with a background in the voluntary sector (Jamieson, Glanz and MacGregor, 1984: 31). Perhaps, it would be more accurate to characterize it as a non-statutory project given that at that time most innovation in the drugs field emerged from within the voluntary sector. On the other hand, City Roads demonstrated the need for a holistic approach in whatever sector it was offered (Jamieson, Glanz and MacGregor, 1984: 193). Annas Dixon, the First Chair of the Management Committee of City Roads, a Lead Social Worker at the University College Hospital DDU (UCH DDU) and a former member of Advisory Council on the Misuse of Drugs recalls her experiences at that time:

> Barbiturates use was becoming a major issue which was part of the history of how I got involved with City Roads ... around 1975 ... Bob Searchfield, the first director of SCODA had a brief from the then DHSS to find a building to set up a residential crisis centre for London because they were finally getting very concerned about the number of people who were dying who were overdosing on Barbiturates and dying. It was recognised there was a need for somewhere that needed to be residential to intervene in this pattern of drug use. It was part of my job was to find ways ... of making contact with people who were on the slippery slope who were mainly into Amphetamine use or Barbiturates. Therefore, they wouldn't get a script at the clinic so we also wanted to keep them away from the drug clinic because (you know) the next step would be mixing with all these hard-line junkies that milled around the Camden Islington area ... My job was ... doing one to one work with that client group most of whom were quite young, sort of late teens to mid twenties a lot of whom had come from other parts of the country and were squatting locally ... I ended up as the Chair [of the Management Committee] because there wasn't actually too many other people

> that were that well placed to take this on ... because I worked at UCH Drug Clinic ... just up the road ... In May '78 we opened and it's still going strong. It still has the original philosophy of ... being there to provide a three week crisis intervention stay to detox people or to stabilize them – obviously ... from opiates nowadays.[20]

In reflecting on what it was like to treat women, she recalls:

> I became the social work team leader at UCH Drug Clinic ... It merged my duties with the advisory role when they sorted us out into a proper social work team ... there were ... one or two women on my team – one ... went on to run one of the women's refuges [they] were already into issues around the needs of women much more than I was ... because I ... was aware, but ... interested ...[in] all clients, irrespective of gender ... I ... didn't differentiate. People were aware that the majority of the women were very much at risk ... if they weren't already in prostitution they were on the edge of it and often coming for help it would be at the point where they started down that road or that they'd felt like ... if I don't go [and get treatment] ... get myself a legal supply of drugs that's going to be the trigger.[21]

It is interesting to note here that City Roads was known locally as being responsive to women problem drug users, albeit more women users appeared to attend Accident and Emergency (A and E) Departments in hospitals than at City Roads, implying that crisis intervention was dealt with perhaps more effectively in the statutory sector's hospitals. Ann Jamieson, Alan Glanz and Susanne MacGregor (1984: 69) note that there were twice as many men seen at City Roads between 1978 and 1981 (68 per cent were men and 32 per cent women) and they refer to Hamid Ghodse's (1977) study of A and E departments, which suggests a higher percentage of women attending these hospital departments than City Roads. In Ghodse's study, 53 per cent were men and 47 per cent were women, a high percentage, and 'twice as many male heroin users [as] female, the latter having a greater tendency to use psychotropic drugs (i.e., non barbiturate hypnotics, major and minor tranquillizers, antidepressants and stimulants)' (Ghodse, 1977: 275). He refers to Home Office Statistics for 1974 that show female addicts account for less than '26 per cent of the total addict population' and claims that 'this population of drug-dependent patients attending casualty departments appears to be different from that of the drug treatment clinics' (Ghodse, 1977: 278). What is of interest here is nowhere does he attempt to explain why there was a higher percentage of women drug users attending A and E Departments. Could their reasons be linked to experience of violence, abuse, trauma?

The non-statutory sector or voluntary drugs agencies in Britain – by contrast to the statutory sector – has been consistently more responsive to marginal groups, including women and BME groups (Ettorre, 1987). Whether or not this reflects the perceived wisdom in the addiction field in Britain at that time is not clear. Indeed, Herbert H. Blumberg (1981) in an analysis of medical services, particularly outpatient clinics, reports that more males than females attend services and that especially for 'younger women' there may be a hesitancy to attend clinics. Additionally, Carol Smart (1985) studied 36 DDUs in England and Wales, finding that the ratio of those seen over a four-week period was two men to one woman. It was certainly true that women appeared to get a better deal when approaching voluntary drugs agencies or at least workers in these agencies appeared to be more aware of women's issues at that time. That more women were attending A and E Departments rather than voluntary crisis intervention centres such as City Roads does not necessarily indicate the responsiveness of the statutory service, A and E Department, to their needs. In effect, Ghodse's study tends to reflects the opposite, given that more women (n=24) than men (n= 18) out of total of 42 'left A and E Departments against advice'. Could the assumption be here that they were treated with disdain and/or got fed up with their negative treatment and walked out of A and E? Unfortunately, we may never know.

Women drug users: Grass-root responses in the midst of social disorder (1980s)

As MacGregor (1989: 11) contends the themes that dominated public concern about drugs in the 1980s centred on the question of social order. Fuelled by the Thatcher government, fear was expressed that the fabric of society was being undermined by subversive elements, criminal, and alien imports, and corroded by an unacceptable change in values (11). Thus as MacGregor and Smith (1998: 72) contend, during this phase there was an increasingly punitive approach to drug use as it became closely associated in the public eye with crime and social disorder, and with poorer more working-class population groups. The ACMD had published a series of influential reports (ACMD, 1982, 1984, 1988, 1989) which suggested that service provision should be focused on problems rather than substance-centred; that the full range of statutory services should attend to drug users not only specialist; that there should be multidisciplinary teams set up; that training should be improved and that the issue if HIV/AIDS and drug misuse must be dealt with in a systematic way (see MacGregor and Ettorre, 1987: 137–9). In these documents, it is perhaps striking that women were not singled out as a separate groups of users. Additionally, the assumption remained that drug users were men. For example, the ACMD (1982: 34) Report on *Treatment and Rehabilitation* noted under the Section 5, 'Treatment and Rehabilitation: A Comprehensive Approach' that

> Services designed for problem drug takers would recognize the medical, legal and social problems facing an individual, ***his*** [*sic*] family and the community as a result of drug taking, whether or not the person is considered an addict within the terms of the Misuse of Drugs Act 1971.
>
> (34)

Tackling Drugs Misuse (Home Office, 1986) outlined the Conservative Government's drugs policy, which was aimed at reducing supplies from abroad through Customs and Excise and firm domestic controls, helping police to be more effective and improving treatment and prevention.

Arguing that 'perhaps' the official government strategy at the time was expressed in the ACMD reports, John Strang (1991: 1045)[22] contended these were the 'real strategy documents' that had received both 'covert and overt endorsement from the government' and 'have become the blueprints for subsequent developments of services...providing a framework for the promotion of involvement by general practitioners, backed up by a local drug service or community drug team in every district'.

In light of the increasingly punitive approach highlighted by MacGregor and Smith (1998: 72), 'two sides of policy' – treatment and the criminal justice system – began to converge during this phase.[23] Nevertheless, as these authors contend, the Department of Health made a major effort to develop community-based services through the CFI. We already discussed earlier in Chapter 1 how the bleak outlook detailed in the DAWN report of 1985 was overcome and how Dorothy Black, Chief Medical Officer at Department of Health and Social Security, did 'something about women' when she was deciding to distribute funds for the CFI (MacGregor et al., 1991). What is important to remember is that the issue of women and drug use was beginning to become visible during this phase. However, regardless of visibility, there was little blueprint for change or innovation. Drug misuse orthodoxy, which was linked closely to treatment and research, still favoured men and the field was dominated by a masculinist frame of mind.

Betsy Thom reflected on the field in relation to awareness of women during this time:

> There were very, very few women doing anything at all and some of them were people like yourself who were researchers and had a body of theoretical knowledge. But quite a number were service providers – people who knew it from experiential knowledge and theory, but not from the wider theory. But what was also interesting is that these people [*sic*] were trying to work together I don't know how successfully – obviously – but some ... [were] clearly I think [feminist].[24]

She also highlights the paucity of knowledge on women at that time:

> The body of knowledge was enough to think you knew everything and that's far from the case now. There were obviously things going on that I didn't know that you were aware of because you were more involved with the groups. But I thought, 'Oh, yes, I know most of what's there is or at least I am aware it's there.'[25]

Nevertheless there were some developments in treatment that favoured women users, but these developments tended to be sporadic, short term and dependent upon 'soft' money. For example, a women's group was set up at Phoenix House, a rehabilitation house in London, by the Deputy Director, Diane Goldman in the mid-1980's; a specific service for women was set up in 1985 at the Alcohol Counselling Service (ACS) in Brixton, London organized by Jean White, Senior Counsellor at ACS and Lyn Perry, who worked at Release London in the 1980s, had an interest in helping women drug users. As Thom implies above, the only way to know about these developments for women was to become involved with these grass-roots, feminist 'groups' or initiatives.

In this context, the DAWN Survey (DAWN, 1984b) mentioned earlier in Chapter 2 had already put down an important marker evidencing that women drug and alcohol users were losing out in the field. Here, it is interesting to note that 65 per cent of agencies surveyed by DAWN responded 'Yes' when asked 'Do you see any need for facilities for women drug/alcohol users in your area which do not yet exist? A few years later in 1986, Jan Waterson and Ettorre (1989) surveyed women participants in two conferences, which addressed the issues of women's problems with alcohol and other drugs. Their findings revealed that 56 per cent of respondents reported that their agency offered particular facilities for women. Although these facilities were rudimentary, they included 'women only groups' and 'women workers with a concern for this client group, women'. Key findings were that voluntary or non-statutory agencies were more likely than statutory ones to make provisions for women; there was a glaring lack of childcare facilities for women and the public stigmatization of women with addiction problems was a common occurrence.

MacGregor and Smith (1998: 73) note that this phase supported the development of community based services and in turn, Community Drug Teams (CDTs), which included specialist workers such as community psychiatric nurses (CPNs), who grew in influence. These teams represented an innovative form of service delivery and were modelled on the earlier Community Alcohol Teams (CATs) from the late 1970s (Clement, 1989). While these teams were an effective base from which statutory workers could be drawn, generalist workers such as general practitioners, public health nurses, and health educators began to be drawn into the pool of drugs workers. A division between the advocates of abstinence, championed by the Conservative Party's confrontational 'War on Drugs' (Barton, 2003: 23), and proponents of harm minimization – a 'new name' for the harm reduction practices that emerged in sections of the non-statutory or voluntary sector in the 1970s (MacGregor and Smith, 1998: 73) – appeared.

Initially, the turn towards harm minimization helped to stem the spread of HIV/AIDS and educate the public about the danger of using dirty needles when injecting drugs, but the tension and, at times, compromise between firm enforcement and treatment in the drugs field remained. Importantly, during this time DAWN produced a publication, *HIV and AIDS: Facts for women who use drugs* (1987) that aimed to 'redress the balance' about public information on HIV/AIDS. Given that much of the information on HIV/AIDS was aimed at men and none written specifically for women who used drugs, this was a milestone in the field. The DAWN publication also included sections on lesbian sex, pregnancy, and childcare – all issues that had not been dealt with before in the drugs field.

Criminalization, normalization and masculinization (1990–7)

MacGregor and Smith (1998: 73) note that the rationale underlying community partnership is that drug use is the result of failed socialization and community disorganization. During this phase the young drug user in deprived areas was seen as the principal social problem. By 1990, the UK had been under the Thatcherite regime already for 11 years.[26] Adrian Barton (2003: 23) contends that Thatcher's 'War on Drugs' helped to change the culture of substance misuse as well as the state's reaction to it. During this phase interconnections between drugs, crime, punishment, and treatment became increasingly refined and reinforced within drugs policy (Duke, 2010: 14). At the same time, leading drugs researchers began to claim that recreational drugs use was becoming normalized for many young people (Parker, Aldridge, and Measham, 1998; Measham, Aldridge, and Parker, 2001). Fiona Measham reflects on her first research in the field and what happened when she worked with Howard Parker on *Illegal Leisure* (Parker, Aldridge, and Measham, 1998):

> I was the junior ... the research assistant ... in my late twenties so it's my third research post ... I was bringing the gender and alcohol into it but it was the beginning of the longitudinal study that ended up being the book, *Illegal leisure* ... When we did the first survey, we had these really high rates of drug use. But the focus wasn't [on] drugs, the focus was on alcohol and offending. But we'd asked about drugs as well because we were thinking, 'Wow, something is going on here' ... So we ended up sort of refocusing on drugs and it just happened to be at the beginning of the whole increase in recreational drug use in the early nineties. We just happened to capture that and of course because Russell [Newcombe] and Howard [Parker] were drug researchers anyway. They were ... really excited ... So we ended up sort of focusing more on that [i.e., recreational drug use] and less on alcohol.[27]

In the early 1990s, work at the Lifeline Project in Manchester suggested that the drug culture itself was changing. At that time, their researcher, Mark R. Gilman, identified a new group of potential clients – young, recreational polydrug users who frequented rave dance venues; were knowledgeable about the effects of a range of drugs such as LSD, ecstasy, and amphetamines; and viewed drug selling not as a commercial venture but as a way of subsidizing their social life by providing a service in demand by others in their social group. As Gilman (1991) contends, their problems were mainly legal in that possessing a Class A drug with intent to supply was a charge which carries a maximum penalty of life imprisonment. In effect these users 'suffered from the legal repercussions of courtroom mitigation tactics' when in courts opiate users were presented as 'innocent victims' who are dealt with leniently, while (any kind of drug) dealers were presented as 'evil villains' and punished harshly (17). Unlike the US, prior to the 1990s, the criminal justice system did not have an important role in British drugs policy, as the focus was on service development and harm reduction initiatives, particularly those related to HIV/AIDS (Duke, 2010: 14). However, the pressure to secure a public health response to HIV/AIDS pushed the issue of drugs in the criminal justice system into mainstream drug policy debates. Underlying this pressure was the continuing fiscal austerity of the Thatcher government and the awareness that treatment must become cheaper (MacGregor and Smith, 1998: 73). However, as MacGregor and Smith (1998) point out, cost did not seem to be a consideration with regard to imprisonment. During this phase the ACMD (1988, 1989, 1990, 1991, 1992, 1993) highlighted the special problems around HIV, injecting drug use, and intervention in the criminal justice system, especially in prison (Duke, 2010: 15).

In September 1990, the ACMD Criminal Justice Working Group was appointed 'to examine and report on aspects of the criminal justice system as they affect drug misusers and on measures to improve their effectiveness' (ACMD, 1991). This Working Group produced three reports: ACMD (1991) *Drug Misusers and the Criminal Justice System Part I: Community Resources and the Probation Services*; ACMD (1994) *Drug Misusers and the Criminal Justice System Part II: Police, Drug Misusers and the Community*; and ACMD (1996) *Drug Misusers and the Criminal Justice System Part III: Drug Misusers and the Prison System: An Integrated Approach.*[28] These ACMD reports[29] were the aftermath of the 1991 *Criminal Justice Act* (Home Office, 1991) which provided 'affirmation of the need for probation to coalesce its efforts with those of the substance misuse services and which created, for the first time, a statutory framework whereby conditions of treatment could be attached to probation orders for illicit drug offenders' (Thomson and Young, 1996: 50). Or as Karen Duke (2010: 15) says, the Act represented one of the first attempts at using the criminal justice system as a site for drugs treatment. MacGregor (1995: 11) summarizes aptly the influence of the Act:

> [the Act] impacted on drugs policy by introducing major changes to the supervision and punishment of offenders in the community. It allowed for diverting less serious offenders from custody into community penalties. A specific provision enabled it to be a requirement that the offender should undergo treatment for alcohol or drug dependency. The probation service was to play a larger role.

In May 1995, the Conservative Government published its drug strategy *Tackling Drugs Together: A Strategy for England 1995–1998* outlining its three-year plan. While the strategy focused on crime, youth, and public health, it allowed the criminal justice system to feature more prominently in drugs issues. The strategy recognized the need for increased collaboration between the range of services involved with drug misusers and set up Drug Action Teams (DATs) across the country to implement the strategy. The teams were expected to adapt the national strategies to their local circumstances.

MacGregor described doing research for the Cabinet Office to evaluate the DATs when they were first introduced. She described *'Tackling Drugs Together: A Strategy for England 1995–1998'* as the first real strategy proposed by the Conservative Party and how it proposed to coordinate across health, criminal justice, probation, prison, and police – in 'bring[ing] them all together in drug action teams'.[30] For her that marked the point in British drugs policy 'where health and criminal justice approaches began to come together' and there was definitely 'more contact with the criminal justice system'.[31] She contrasted what she termed the health and criminal justice approaches:

> I have always come at it [drugs] from the health point of view ... but also ... injecting a social perspective but ... that's a very particular perspective. ... The whole criminal justice approach ... is quite different and those two sides are ... completely different pathways.[32]

She continues:

> Traditionally, the health approach [is] ... very broadly ... more humanistic and ... influenced by the ethics of medicine – sees a human being sitting in front of them ... an individual [who has] a problem – and doesn't necessarily locate that individual in a social context. Yes [it] is very strikingly non moralistic ... One of the things that is very striking about psychiatrists and social workers and particularly, the psychiatrists is that they [with] some exceptions ... are genuinely caring.[33]

Treatment and policy remained visibly masculinist during this phase of community partnership in drugs policy. Measham reflected on how the debate over normalization of adolescent recreational drug use had helped to push 'gender off the agenda':

> Gender was well off the agenda [in the 1990s] ... I think part of the original appeal of appointing me was I would sort of keep [gender] a little bit in the lime light. That wasn't possible ... One of the things with the normalisation debate ... [is] it's got totally out of

> hand ... Normalisation was just a little idea to explain a little project ... [At] the Liverpool harm reduction conference they have got a whole panel on normalisation ... It has become this grand unified theory of everything, which it was never meant to be. My concern in relation to the work we were doing in the nineties was it pushed gender off the agenda ... Conceptually we were saying ... that gender doesn't matter ... I was thinking how have we got to this position ... that gender doesn't matter ... and I was thinking, 'No, no, no, hold on' ... The statistics would say there is no statistically significant difference ... I would say, 'That doesn't mean that gender doesn't matter just because there is no statistically significant difference' ... How did this happen [when] the normalisation debate was saying, 'Yes, lots of women were taking drugs – people from all sorts of different ethnic groups and different social groups'.[34]

For Measham the question was, 'How did gender or ethnicity or class operate in terms of people using drugs?' She did not think that just because many people from different ethnic groups and social classes misused drugs, that gender was insignificant or did not need to be explained.

On the one hand, the normalization debate helped take gender off the agenda. On the other hand, this debate allowed researchers to shift the focus towards women and girls who had typically remained outside of the treatment system. At this time, Sheila Henderson's work presented images of women in popular culture and within the drugs rave scene. Measham said:

> [I was] impressed with Sheila Henderson's work because she was ... based at Lifeline [in Manchester] ... She was tackling ... the very gendered image of ... the opiate user in treatment ... It would have been very much ... a white working class man in his thirties and her trying to challenge all of that ... Her work ... was ... a very small project ... but it was enormously influential ... because it was really challenging not just the image of drug users but also what was happening in drug treatment at the time.[35]

During this phase, the emphasis upon the social problem of the young (usually male) drug user in deprived areas was beginning to shift. Measham contends that this phase shaped a different notion of the drug user in which young women could be included:

> The early nineties ... was the big ... shifting from the eighties version of problems to ... pleasures, recreational use and women's weekend

> use ... [It was] not ... this sort of ... poverty ... this idea that [drug use] was associated with social exclusion with ... those issues of daily dependant use and ... that it could be about weekend use. It could be people that are functioning in the week ... We would say now recreational use because it was always about the problem drug use and about addiction and daily dependant chaotic use and so I suppose the big change ... was the work by Sheila Henderson and your work[36] talking about pleasures.[37]

While the policy and treatment discourses appeared to continue in a masculinist vein, a small body of feminist work was beginning to challenge the assumptions behind those discourses. At the same time, the feminist organization DAWN, which had enjoyed its heyday in the 1980s, was on the wane and in danger of closure. DAWN encountered funding difficulties after the Women's Unit of the Greater London Council was replaced by the London Boroughs Grant Unit. DAWN had been housed at GLAAS (Greater London Association of Alcohol Services), whose director was Elspeth Kyle. DAWN's resources had been depleted and there was only a part-time worker, Annie Ryan, who worked at DAWN from 1996–8. Although Kyle wanted to keep DAWN afloat, the decision was made to let it fold in the late 1990s.[38]

When the Labour Party had a landslide general election victory on 1 May 1997, 101 of their female candidates were elected as Members of Parliament. Known popularly as Blair's Babes, their election hinted at a new era in British politics with regards to gender politics. Would this supposed new era have any effect upon the 'de' gendering of addiction and addiction politics?

Opening up policy concerns for women drug users (1997–2010)

MacGregor's (2010) piece on 'Policy responses to the drugs problem' presents an authoritative view on this policy phase. MacGregor (2010: 1) argues that the origins of the New Labour Party approach to illicit drugs lay in the policies of the previous Conservative Government, as exemplified in *Tackling Drugs Together: A Strategy for England 1995–1998,* in which the link between illicit drugs and crime was emphasized. MacGregor (2010: 2–3) also noted that after the Task Force to Review Services for Drug Misusers published its report in 1996, its Chairman Dr. Pilkinghorne spoke of drugs misuse as 'a complex issue', 'a chronic relapsing condition' and used the phrase 'treatment works'. The Labour

Government pursued this work and appointed a National Anti Drugs Unit Co-ordinator (taking a page from the US, this position is referred to as the 'Drugs Czar'). A ten-year strategy detailed the work under the Labour Government and MacGregor (2010: 8) outlined a meticulous overview of key events occurring in the drugs policy arena from 1995 until 2008. While there was a focus on crime, coercion, and public disorder in New Labour's policies (Duke, 2010), policies during this phase were shaped by perceptions of the drugs problem as a public health concern (MacGregor, 2010).

From the point of view of women drug users, the ACMD Report, *Drug Misuse and the Environment* (ACMD, 1998), the establishment of the National Treatment Agency (NTA) in April 2001, and the ACMD reports *Hidden Harm: Responding to the Needs of Children of Problem Drug Users* (2003) and *Hidden Harm Three Years On: Realities, Challenges and Opportunities* (2007a) were key milestones in the New Labour approach. *Drug Misuse and the Environment* (ACMD, 1998) was an important document that facilitated recognition of gender as a key environmental (meaning social) factor in drug use in the official policy response to drugs. This report also noted that female drug users tended to utilize drug services less frequently than men (xiii) and that the assumption that women's drug use is less acceptable than men's needed to be challenged (73). Nevertheless, any emphasis on gender as a key environmental factor was overshadowed by a focus on the family as an influence on drug use, both from the point of view of parents monitoring children and from the perspective of parents as problem users themselves.[39] Consistently this emphasis on the family as a key site of policy concerns was a way of obscuring women.

The establishment of the NTA in April 2001 was set up with the remit of expanding the availability and quality of drug treatment (MacGregor, 2010: 5). In an analysis of 165 documents published by the NTA from August 2002 until January 2010 (including reports, information, provider guidance, DVDs, research reports, leaflets, user guidance, etc.), 12 specifically mentioned women.[40] The June 2005 NTA Research Report *Women in Drug Treatment Services* (Best and Abdulrahim, 2005) along with the April 2006 N.T.A. Research Report *The Impact of Treatment on Female Drug-Using Sex Workers* (Bloor et al., 2006) were important because they opened policy concerns on how treatment impacts the lives of drug using women. Most if not all NTA documents that highlighted the need for an awareness of the needs of women drug users were based on the assumption that better services meant more women involved, regardless of whether or not these services were attentive to women's needs. MacGregor saw associations between drug using women, sex work, and motherhood as two sides of the same problem. She says:

> Women were seen either as having sexual problems by virtue of being women so we thought ... [they] should ... have a bath [as] ... they [are] sex workers, you know ... or they were seen as mothers. [T]hey ... always had to be something else ... it was either sexual ... or they were mothers ... [the] whole issue about women not coming to services because they were afraid the children would be taken into care ... was quite a big thing.[41]

Hidden Harm: Responding to the Needs of Children of Problem Drug Users (ACMD, 2003) and *Hidden Harm Three Years On: Realities, Challenges and Opportunities* (ACMD, 2007a) represented the visible extension of policy concerns from the needs of service users to families and children of drug-using parents, including women. Viv Evans, who joined Adfam, Britain's leading organization working with and for families affected by drugs and alcohol,[42] as Chief Executive in 2002 and who also worked on the ACMD Hidden Harm Working group, discusses her experience:

> I have a huge interest in the kinds of issues we covered in *Hidden Harm* so that obviously touches on women who are drug users and how they parent and what happens to them and pregnant women ... that interests me a lot ... How can we get good outcomes for children if they are born to a mother who has got an addiction problem?[43]

The ACMD felt so strongly about the findings of *Hidden Harm: Responding to the Needs of Children of Problem Drug Users* (ACMD, 2003) that a working group was established to monitor and promote implementation of the recommendations in the UK. This was the first time that the ACMD had set up such a group (ACMD, 2007a). Evans was a member of that group; she became a champion for *Hidden Harm*:

> Being on the *Hidden Harm* committee really was a huge – very important experience for me because I ... learned such a lot ... The reason I was interested in being on the committee was because ... I remember ... speaking at a conference in Kent. It was ... about drug education in schools ... and two women head teachers came up to me afterwards and said, 'We are so exercised by this. What do we do with the parents who are either not sending the kids to school

because we really think they have got a drug problem or ... they pitch up late to pick them up? ... They have obviously had too much to drink.' ... So that's what brought it to my attention ... I suppose through the school system ... I learnt a lot from the process of doing [this sort of thing].[44]

Co-constructing criminalization and medicalization (2011–present)

As this book went to press the current coalition government in the UK was retiring the NTA. On 7 July 2010, the Secretary of State for Health announced on that the NTA would be abolished in April 2012 and its functions transferred to a new Public Health Service.[45] In response to this announcement DrugScope (2010) released a press statement saying:

> DrugScope responded to the government's decision to abolish the National Treatment Agency for Substance Misuse (NTA) as a statutory organisation. The NTA will cease to exist as an organisation in its own right but its functions will be transferred to a new Public Health Service, which will be directly accountable to the Secretary of State. The Public Health Service will also incorporate the functions of the Health Protection Agency. The government's move follows publication of the report of the Department of Health's *Arm's Length Bodies Review*. The report states that moving the NTA's critical functions to the Public Health Service would 'tackle the dependency problems of individuals, and address the entire range of issues which users face.' The government aims to establish the Public Health Service by April 2012.

In this same press release, DrugScope Chief Executive, Martin Barnes said:

> The decision to abolish the NTA as a separate organisation and transfer its functions to the new public health agency is perhaps not surprising given the government's commitment to reduce the number of health bodies. The NTA has overseen an unprecedented expansion in the availability and quality of drug treatment. The progress achieved needs to be preserved and mechanisms and resources put in place to further improve and sustain treatment outcomes and recovery. The announcement that the NTA's functions will be transferred to the new public health agency and not abolished is

> encouraging – it is vital that drug treatment continues to be championed. The transfer is likely to mean a greater and welcome focus on tackling alcohol related harms and on drugs as a public health issue. But recovery from addiction requires the support and engagement of a range of local agencies, including providers of housing, training and employment, and it is crucial that this partnership approach is reflected across departments within government. An effective drug and alcohol treatment system will be a key plank in delivering on many of the government's policy objectives – better public health and a reduction in drug and alcohol related harms, but also reducing crime, reoffending and introducing alternatives to prison for offenders with drug and alcohol problems.

The dissolution of the NTA meant that treatment was once again devolved to health authorities and police as part of a neo-liberal austerity programme to cut public sector jobs. Where the NTA once kept alive the discourse about drugs on public health, in its absence there will be a resurgent discourse on crime. Again the 'governing mentalities' (Campbell, 2000) of criminalization and medicalization co-constitute each other in ways that suggest it will be difficult to stabilize a regime consisting of one without the other.

Across the phases of American drug treatment policy

Unlike British drug policy, US drug policy cannot be characterized by 'avoidance' of the extremes between which it has oscillated for the past century. Rather than seeing the two dominant policy approaches – medicalization and criminalization – as mutually exclusive, we argue that they should be seen as co-constitutive and mutually reinforcing despite the seeming ideological opposition between the two. The US holds the distinction of locking up more men and women on drug charges than any other country in the world, both in terms of proportion and absolute numbers. Yet it also has an elaborate public health and private treatment infrastructure for treating drug and alcohol problems, some part of which has focused on women's needs since the 1970s due to the actions of the women's treatment advocates described earlier. The important question becomes, which women are in positions to access treatment, and which are not? Which women bear the brunt of 'criminalization', and which instead receive 'medicalization'?

The US had a well-established national treatment infrastructure in the nineteenth century, beginning with large congregate care institutions such as 'asylums' and 'poorhouses' that housed addicted or alcoholic women. Specific institutions for 'inebriate' women operated in the nineteenth century, including the Martha Washington Home in Chicago (1869), the Temple Home in Binghampton, New York (1876), and the New England Home for Intemperate Women in Boston (1879) (White, 1998). However, White's history of treatment in the US was written to make the point that the nineteenth century treatment infrastructure was dismantled in the early twentieth century. By the passage of the Harrison Act (1914), which criminalized narcotics, few institutions with the capacity to treat addicted women remained. Enforcement of the Harrison Act was mainly geared towards sending male offenders to prison, and prosecuting physicians who over-prescribed opiates.

Some enterprising municipalities started up narcotic maintenance clinics in the late 1910s and early 1920s after a 1919 US Supreme Court decision upheld the constitutionality of the Harrison Act. Men and women registered at these clinics were typically maintained on morphine; hundreds were served from the working and professional classes. For instance, data from the clinic in Shreveport, Louisiana showed that the 'most recurrent occupation reported were waiter and waitress; one in ten (10.4%) gave that occupation. Professionals (doctors, lawyers, judges, etc.) made up 3 per cent, and 1.8 per cent said they owned their own businesses. Such businesses ranged from a small Chinese restaurant run by a 43-year-old Chinese man who had been addicted for 24 years, to the largest dry goods store in town. Of the 176 women for whom we have data, the majority reported occupations; only a little more than a third (35.2%) said they were housewives' (Waldorf, Orlick and Reinarman, 1974). Almost one-quarter of the patients treated in Shreveport were women; by comparison only one-fifth of those treated at the New York City clinic were women. The morphine maintenance clinics were but short-lived solutions to problems created by zealous enforcement of the Harrison Act. By the late 1920s, fully one-third of male convicts in federal prisons were there on Harrison Act violations, which was not the case in female prisons or reformatories. Concerns about prison over-crowding led Congress to undertake a major treatment innovation known as the federal 'narcotic farms' (Campbell, Olsen, and Walden, 2008).

While the story of these large, centralized institutions designed 'for the confinement and treatment of persons addicted to the use of habit-forming narcotic drugs who have been convicted of offences against the United States' has been told elsewhere (Campbell, 2007; Campbell, Olsen, and Walden, 2008), they represent an attempt to treat addicted men, and after 1941, women, through a public health approach. The US Congress mandated that research take place at the narcotic farms with the goal of finding a cure as soon as possible. Treatment was designed 'to rehabilitate addicts, restore them to health, and where necessary train them to be self-supporting and self-reliant' (US Public Health Service Newsreel, 1937). The emphasis on rehabilitation was also an emphasis on normalization – on returning the addicted person to a state of compliance with non-drug-using social norms. As pointed out in previous chapters, this meant not only restoring their mental and physical health, but also getting them to comply with gender norms. These institutions held upwards of a thousand men, and never more then 300 or so women, despite ongoing concerns about the lack of capacity for women.

The narcotic farms housed the only public treatment programmes available in the US, with the exception of a few state facilities in New York and California. Judges and federal marshals sent all addicts east of the Mississippi and women from all over the country to the farm in Lexington, Kentucky. All addicts west of the Mississippi were sent to the facility in Fort Worth, Texas, which did not accept women. Women could also 'volunteer' for treatment at the farms by obtaining medical certification of their addictions from their doctors, and showing up for admission. If women arrived as primary opiate addicts – and there were empty women's beds – they were admitted for treatment with the variety of vocational and recreational therapies, as well as individual and group psychotherapy, then on offer at the institution. However, women often did not make the trip alone because it would take them far away from friends and family. They sometimes accompanied partners or husbands, hoping for a rehabilitation that rarely came.

A shift away from centralization and towards community-based treatment came in the late 1960s. Changes in mental health policy initiated by the Kennedy administration led to the opening of CMHCs in the mid-1960s. While the CMHCs did not initially address drug addiction, many expanded their programmes to do so. At the same time, as Americans witnessed a wave of popular drug experimentation among students and college-age youth unlike any it had seen before, national drug policy leaned away from lengthy criminal sentences and towards shorter terms of civil commitment. As mentioned above, NARA (1966) required the establishment of treatment capacity wherever addicted persons lived. The shift away from large centralized institutions towards smaller, community-based service providers was gradual but clearly underway even before the Nixon administration, responding to the possibility of large numbers of Vietnam veterans returning opiate-addicted, created a new White House Special Action Office on Drug Abuse Policy (SAODAP). SAODAP eventually morphed into NIDA, which presided over a rapid expansion of methadone maintenance clinics in the 1970s.

Attention to the drug problems of women and the role of gender in exacerbating them began during this era. In the US women's crack-cocaine use was catapulted to national attention in the mid to late 1980s, lasting well into the 1990s. This highly racialized and sexually saturated topic drew negative attention to pregnant and parenting drug-using women. While such attention had the effect of expanding women's programmes, it did so within narrow parameters and only in urban areas where there was a substantial crack-cocaine problem. Coupled with concerns about marijuana smoking by middle-class youth, the crack situation led to the Anti-Drug Abuse Act of 1988, which established the goal of national drug policy as the creation of a 'drug-free America'. The Act created a new White House Office of National Drug Control Policy (ONDCP), which was still in operation at the time this book went to press. During the 1990s, women's incarceration rates increased exponentially. US Bureau of Justice statistics showed that women convicted on felony drug charges rose by nearly 40 per cent between 1990 and 1996. Most women cannot access drug and alcohol treatment in prison, and the circumstances of many drug-using women's lives do not lend themselves to treatment as it is currently configured.

When the federal disaggregation of services and research took place in the early 1990s,[46] research functions were ultimately placed within the NIH, renowned for biomedical research. This consolidation of addiction research in NIH relegated everything other than basic neurobiochemical and behavioural research to 'service delivery' or 'technology transfer', which were defined as arenas in which applied science would be transferred from the site of its production through basic research or clinical trials to the site of consumption in the treatment infrastructure. Treatment providers mediate this movement of the so-called the science-to-service cycle by implementing 'science-based' or 'evidence-based' practices. Various strategies were utilized by state agencies to get providers to buy into science; these were framed as 'blending' or 'bridging' research and practice in the early twenty-first century. Because people experience addictions in terms of social impact, the specialized languages of neurobiology sit uneasily with on-the-ground understandings of frontline practitioners.[47] US treatment professionals occupy an ambivalent position relative to scientific research on addiction; they are expected to embrace its results. Initially comprised of persons who had personally experienced addiction and recovery, the treatment workforce has undergone a gradual social process of professionalization, including the development of specific curricula, licensing, credentialing programmes, and workforce development. This process produced an influx of workers – some two-thirds of whom were white, middle-aged women – who have not themselves experienced addiction and recovery.[48] As credentialed professionals emerged from the previous para-professional era, treatment providers have organized professional associations and work closely with the single state agencies that oversee the disbursement of federal funds to county-level and municipal service agencies. This massive bureaucracy is in turn state-funded and thus under the control of state legislatures. Given this social organization, it is easy to see why best-practice guidelines produced by federally convened consensus panels or new pharmacotherapies prescribed by physicians do not make it all the way to frontline workers or their clients.

Although NIDA created a Medications Development Division in 1990, the effort has borne little fruit due to the disinterest of private sector pharmaceutical companies in problems of substance abuse. Thus all pharmacotherapies on the market for the treatment of alcoholism and drug abuse – except for buprenorphine (marketed by Reckitt Benkhiser under the names Suboxone or Subutex) – were known and used 35 years ago at the inception of NIDA, and it has proven very difficult to get new ones onto the market. However, in 2000 President Bill Clinton signed into law the Drug Abuse Treatment Act (DATA), which allowed physicians to prescribe buprenorphine in the privacy of their offices rather than in the heavily regulated stand-alone methadone clinic system. While NIDA created a nationwide Clinical Trials Network (CTN) in the 1990s and struck an inter-agency agreement to develop a linking mechanism between the CTN and the mechanism developed by SAMHSA/CSAT called 'Addiction Technology Transfer Centers' (ATTCs), which were initiated in 1993, the effort to translate scientific research into treatment technologies has been slow. The mission of the ATTCs was to transmit information 'for the purpose of achieving behavior change' among clinical practitioners (Backer, 1991). The ATTCs sought to translate scientific research into usable form, offer technical assistance, and distribute a range of resources, including the much-vaunted *Change Book: A Blueprint for Technology Transfer* (2000).[49] The ATTCs are federally funded attempts to change grass-roots behaviour by getting treatment providers to redefine themselves as 'change agents'. Change in this case means becoming willing recipients of technology transfer, by replicating the 'best practices' guidelines. But the technology transfer model fails to acknowledge the production of local or 'indigenous' knowledge, rides roughshod over the very cultural specificities and competencies that feminists have striven to bring to attention, and prevents full partnerships. What would it mean for those most affected by addiction research and treatment to have a stake in more deliberate selection of scientific research questions; paradigms or modes of knowledge; increased scrutiny of the political process of priority-setting so central to resource allocation; and a greater degree of responsiveness between researchers, clinicians, administrators, and clients/patients/recovering persons?

US drug policy remains far from questions of political participation. As this book went to press, scientific and service researchers were in the throes of another of the periodic reorganizations we have recounted. NIDA and NIAAA were in the process of merging into one institute. While there was enthusiastic discussion of potential names for this institute, there were also worries by drug and alcohol researchers alike about the potential for loss of resources and visibility. When we consider what the fate of NIDA's research programmes on 'Women and Sex/Gender Differences' or NIAAA's research on women and drinking within this broad restructuring, we must be concerned that women's treatment advocates will have yet another round of reinvention ahead of them. However, NIDA recently created a new women's initiative called 'The Women's International Group', which meets monthly online through NIDA's Virtual Collaboratory, which is part of its international programme. In 2011 the 'Conference on Women, Children and Gender' will be held preceding the annual meeting of the College on Problems of Drug Dependence (CPDD). As this book has shown, women's treatment advocates have long insisted on integrating drug and alcohol treatment and treatment for co-occurring mental health disorders, including those caused by exposure to violence and abuse, with a holistic and thoroughly social understanding of their consequences for women's lives.

Conclusion

To close out this chapter, we repeat our question: Has the increasing conceptual and organizational complexity of treatment served the goal of sustainability? Ultimately, this can be reframed as a policy question: Has the increasing conceptual and organizational complexity of drug policy served the goal of reducing drug-related harm, deflecting from the targeting of vulnerable populations, increasing the effectiveness of treatment, or expanding access to treatment? What do we make of the close ties between treatment, research, and punishment, or between 'medicalization' and 'criminalization'? In an era of 'biomedicalization', will the co-constitutive character of punitive and palliative regimes continue? Most importantly, are women as a class, by comparison to men as a class, once again losing out?

5

Reproducing Bodies and Governing Motherhood: Drug-Using Women and Reproductive Loss

We argue that *gender* and gendered social norms actively define the reproducing body, as well as female bodies with or without reproductive potential, and the pregnant body.[1] This chapter demonstrates how the larger political climate and policy environment shapes responses to illicit drug use by women from diverse backgrounds, limiting the likelihood they will receive treatment and escalating the likelihood they will be punished in some way. We attend to a regulatory regime of reproduction in which a variety of powerful normative disciplinary practices determine what sorts of bodies should reproduce even in this 'post-disciplinary' age. The assumptions of the classical approach to understanding the causes and consequences of substance abuse still structure the disciplinary practices with which pregnant 'addicts' are met in respect to reproduction. We aim to trace the cultural representations of pregnancy and drug use with regards to our 'bodily obsessed' society, examine the regulatory regime of biosocial reproduction with special reference to pregnancy and drugs, and look closely at the 'real' material sites or gendered bodies upon which the classically assumed chaos, contagion, and disorder of drug use are inscribed.

We consider women drug users, who (Campbell, 2000) refers to as 'using women', to experience a form of reproductive loss.[2] The concept of 'reproductive loss' conjures not only a sense of death and dying, but emphasizes the sense of grief and mourning central to the 'reproductive loss' experience by 'using women'. We use the term 'reproductive loss' to emphasize that drug-using women lose or, more precisely, are robbed – sometimes physically, sometimes metaphorically, and sometimes legally – of their capacities for biosocial reproduction. By virtue of the very fact that they use illegal drugs, these women are seen as socially polluted in ways that might be generationally transmissible or contagious, and thus they are not considered worthy of making babies or being reproductive. Reproductive loss for drug-using women is about losing one's reproductive potential in the eyes of society – and as the programmes at which we looked in the previous chapter attest, these losses can be seen as traumatic events having negative effects on women's lives. A powerful exclusionary process targets any woman who uses illegal drugs for devaluation. As a result of the form of social exclusion to which they are subject, women experience a very deep, embodied sense of shame, pollution, and social exclusion.[3] We also suggest conceiving of reproductive loss in biosocial terms, seeing the ways in which women's roles in social reproduction are foreclosed even as their 'core activities' continue to be framed by their feminine and reproductive roles (Anderson, 2005). Taking up questions raised by Elizabeth Ettorre (2007), we ask: 'How are we able to contest effectively popular culture's negative views, perceptions and stereotyping of 'using women' as non-reproductive and basically 'shameful'? and 'How does an embodiment perspective grounded in feminist epistemology allow us to mount this contestation'? Our work challenges the gendered stigmatization of pregnant drug users. We would like to win back for women drug users their right to reproduce 'normally' and counter the deep sense of reproductive loss that marks their lives by challenging the culture's negative views, perceptions, and stereotyping of 'using women' as non-reproductive and basically 'shameful'. In order to do this, we must be sensitive to the sort of reproductive losses that using women currently experience.

Challenging 'poison', 'pollution', and contagion: A trio of traditional assumptions in the drug field

The sorrows and joys in the lives of women drug users have been obscured for many years by long-established assumptions holding men to be the socially dominant and active subjects in the drug-using culture; women have been viewed as socially subordinate, relatively passive, and silent. Yet even as male drug users occupy the cultural space of 'dominant user', and knowledge about drug-using women's lives has been suppressed or simply ignored, female users have become targets of societal rage (Kandall, 1996: 285). These 'masculinist' assumptions have been challenged by scholars working within feminist perspectives that centre women's activities, identities, and subject formations (see, for example, Anderson 1995, 1998, 2005, 2008; Ettorre, 1992, 2007, 2007; Evans, Forsyth, and Gauthier, 2002; Hammersley, Khan, and Ditton, 2002; Henderson, 1996; Measham, 2002; Murphy and Rosenbaum,

1995, 1999; Raine, 2001; Sterk, 1999). For example, Sheila Henderson (1996) suggests that female drug users for whom recreational use is marked by personal agency directed towards the pursuit of pleasure may experience a type of 'feminised' sensual pleasure. 'Feminizing drug use', these women combine fashion seeking, clothes consumption, music, and dance into a cultural space demarcated by 'fun' (Henderson, 1993). However, this more pleasurable form of 'feminization' is the flip side of the demonization and social exclusion that takes place particularly on reproductive grounds.

Drug-using women have been typically constructed as abject[4] – as shameful, disgusting and toxic to themselves and especially to their children. They are depicted as transmitting abjection and toxicity by giving birth to 'addicted babies', babies whose first 'assault' occurs while they are still within the womb. There has been much discussion of the mythical status of so-called 'meth babies' and 'crack babies' among feminist advocates, as well as concern among clinicians about the rush to pass judgement and make unfounded claims about the prospect of such children (Mayes et al., 1992). However, this point has been lost upon much of the public due to the morass of moralism in which it has been mired among child welfare advocates. The relentless focus on babies projects blame onto the women who give birth to them – the production of 'soiled' babies through 'polluted' mothers sullies ideological notions of the 'innocence of babes' and of 'sacred motherhood'. Because these women have been 'poisoned' or 'tainted' through their use of drugs, motherhood is not seen as their right. Their very status as human beings and as political persons is called into question by those who advocate for the rights of the foetus against those of the pregnant woman, often by turning to the intertwined lexicons of 'poison', 'pollution', and contagion.

Some substances are seen as more polluting, both chemically and culturally, than other substances; some are seen as more potent and therefore as more capable of rapid diffusion. In earlier work on popular drug discourse, Ettorre (1992) spoke of a hierarchy of drugs implying strong moralizing features, and drew upon a classic piece by David M. Warburton (1978), which defined internal pollution as a state 'when the security of the internal environment of our bodies is destroyed'. Warburton characterized drug consumers as blamed for conspiring in the internal pollution of their bodies, which were then constructed as vectors with the potential to spread contamination to others. This view on internal pollution is evident in attitudes towards women drug users, who are seen as 'polluted women' who must be controlled through *external forces* because they lack internal controls. Assumptions about women's role in social reproduction place them in the way of discriminatory laws and policies that seek to constrain their potential to 'contaminate' society. Pollutants such as drugs are coded as dirt or symbolic 'matter out of place'; pollution is defined as 'a type of danger which is not likely to occur except where the lines of structure [i.e., cultural boundaries] are clearly defined' (Douglas, 1966: 113). The consequence of crossing such cultural boundaries bearing a polluted or soiled identity is an extraordinary stigmatization. Indeed the social status of the female drug user is often irreversibly low even throughout participation in treatment and recovery processes.

Not until women are able to resume their 'proper place' within social reproduction are they accorded any gains in social status and respect. Because in the private, feminized sphere of domestic life, women, particularly mothers, serve as the primary emotional copers – a reality with long-term effects on women's psychic lives (Ernst and Goodison, 1997) – they are placed in a double bind when they themselves are perceived as the source of 'contamination'. Regardless of when, where, how, and why women take illegal drugs, they are viewed as having polluted their gender identities and their reproductive bodies – as well as contaminating the private space of family life and the public space of communal cleanliness. In a popular sense, women drug users' bodies signify the extremes of internal pollution – and they are 'used' in political discourse to signify the limits of social tolerance of contamination.

Additionally, if a woman who uses drugs is pregnant, her body is characterized as 'doubly polluted' because she consumes illegal drugs that are popularly understood to contaminate not only her own body, but that of the foetus she is carrying. Unlike most non-drug-using women's bodies, pregnant drug users' bodies are viewed as potentially lethal foetal containers and they have sometimes been held accountable even for stillbirths clearly not attributable to drugs. Whether their babies are taken from them after birth or control is sought over their capacity to reproduce through forced contraception or sterilization,[5] their bodies are viewed as unfit to reproduce and 'judgmental attitudes deter women from identifying themselves as substance misusers'.[6] Pregnancy thus represents the paradox of a wilful reproduction that has broken all of the cultural proscriptions against it. The pregnancies of drug-using women are 'pregnancies out of place'; hence calls to police and prosecute are motivated at their deepest level by archaic concerns about how to contain social disorder, pollution, and contagion.

Abjection, ambivalence, and anguish: Viewing social reproduction through the lens of embodied deviance

We return to 'embodied deviance', a concept raised in the introduction to this book, defined as the claim that the bodies of individuals classified as deviant are marked in some systematically recognizable way (Urla and Terry, 1995: 2). Deviant social behaviour is understood to manifest in the very substance of the deviant body – and, increasingly, the deviant brain. Scientific knowledge production processes are often invoked to bring 'hidden' forms of deviance into view – in the case of drug addiction research the search for 'biomarkers' signalling molecular deviance now occurs at the sub-cellular level. Yet deviance is not simply the domain of science, for individuals who deviate from social norms are viewed as socially and morally inferior. As a form of 'embodied deviance', drug use 'marks' the bodies and brains of individuals, determining their low status and lack of moral agency. When factoring gender into the equation, we see dramatic results in that all forms of 'respectable' womanhood or 'responsible' motherhood are withheld from drug-using women, who are seen to have defiled their bodies with polluting substances that may leave permanent and irreversible marks on their bodies and brains, as well as those of their progeny.

Responding to this form of embodied deviance is all about how to respond to wilful feminine self-contamination in the face of gendered social norms and practices that discipline women through relationships to others in relation to their reproductive capacities. Within biomedicine, the reproductive body serves as the symbol of the age of biopower, the force producing and normalizing bodies to serve prevailing relations of dominance and subordination (Shildrick, 1997). Marking female bodies as reproductive has been a crucial means through which biomedicine produces and normalizes female bodies to serve prevailing gender relations. As women's bodies, including drug-using bodies, are pressed into the service of biosocial reproduction, they are assigned value by how well they reproduce. Drug-using women have been consistently stigmatized and devalued as reproducing bodies (Murphy and Rosenbaum, 1999). However, reproduction remains a route to normative femininity for women, who may or may not accord their drug use the same salience as a feature of identity as do cultural authorities who evaluate their fitness to reproduce so negatively. Most studies show drug-using women to have the same or similar aspirations for themselves and their 'pregnancy outcomes' as do non-drug-using women.

Indeed, many women do not experience such radical disconnection between themselves as actors in conventional social worlds and themselves as actors in informal or illegal economies (Anderson, 1998, 2005). Focusing on women's empowerment and agency, Tammy L. Anderson (2005) contends that women perform four core activities fundamental to the social and economic organization of drug-using social worlds, including (1) providing shelter, housing and other basic sustenance; (2) purchasing goods and services; (3) subsidizing or promoting male dependency; and (4) dealing drugs (for fuller discussion, see Ettorre, 2007). Each of these core activities places women in control of households within the informal economy, contributing to what Nancy D. Campbell (2000: 224) called 'social reproduction' in ways that are embodied and 'transferable' to the conventional world. Women carry out each of the core activities despite the projection of the material and symbolic properties of embodied deviance onto them. Paradoxically, women often remain responsible for others and essential to social reproduction – while cast as 'irresponsible' and 'deviant', they continue to perform conventionally gendered social roles and they love their children no less than non-drug-using women. Indeed as Kim Clarke and Juliet Formby (2000: 10) contend, 'There is a worldwide social disapproval of drug users and drug use. Women's drug use is seen as incompatible with their 'traditional role' of mother and homemaker – even though women drug users want to be, and can be, competent mothers (and effective employees)'. Within the core activities through which social and cultural reproduction takes place, the above paradox generates the extraordinary ambivalence with which drug-using women are met wherever they seek help. Even within feminist and women's health-oriented treatment programmes, this ambivalence remains a deeply felt burden for 'patients'/'clients' and 'treaters'/'providers' alike.[7] Far from dismissing this sense of ambivalence and anguish, we see it as a major obstacle for implementing sustainable treatment programmes.

A major assumption supporting addicted women's continued engagement in core activities is that female bodies are normalized as life-giving and generative in the reproductive sense. While this assumption is taken as a biological given, it is enacted within contradictory cultural strictures having negative impacts on individual women. Pregnant drug users are encouraged to seek medical help, particularly drug treatment and prenatal care. On the other hand, they often face coercion and denials of their respect and dignity when they do present for help; many have been subjected to involuntary and sometimes uninformed drug testing; many have had their babies taken from them immediately following birth.[8] As noted in previous chapters, this was common practice in the US even before the attention it received during the maternal crack-cocaine scare of the late 1980s and early 1990s. One of the most moving testimonials was produced in the late 1950s by Marilyn Bishop, also known by her pseudonym 'Janet Clark', who was Howard S. Becker's informant for *The Fantastic Lodge: The Autobiography of a Girl Drug Addict* (1961).[9] An opiate addict at the time, Bishop had given birth to a daughter, who had, she said, 'absorbed' her 'toxic condition', and who had thus been summarily taken from her and put up for adoption. Here she describes the aftermath of the birth: 'The three weeks, the six months after I had the child, all of it's just nightmarish, impossible. I didn't sleep, I didn't eat, I didn't do anything.... I just cried all the time.... I cried at an average of twelve, fourteen, sixteen times a day, until I didn't know you could cry like that. There wasn't anything left inside of me' (Hughes, 1961: 61). She identified with her infant daughter, who was 'drug-sick' at birth, and felt that although she was 'in no way prepared to be a mother, none whatsoever', that a strong and 'spontaneous love' had sprung up in her – for which there was simply no place in that historical moment. It is impossible to read Bishop's account without understanding the profound effect this reproductive loss had on her short life in mid-twentieth-century Chicago. Bishop was in an unusual position to relay her experiences prior to her untimely death just before publication of her book. We must assume that many other women met similar fates, given the prevalence of 'child removal' policies in the US, but had no channel through which to express their anguish.

Reproducing bodies and minds: Reducing demand and punishing patients

The relentless focus on women as reproducers, a focus derived directly from the public representation of drug-using women, has skewed policy in both the US and the UK towards criminalization. This section begins with a brief history of the federal response to the need for research and services centred on drug use by at-risk women of reproductive age, pregnant women, and women who are parenting. Recent efforts to change the policy climate in the US have been spearheaded not by the major feminist reproductive rights organizations, but by the National Advocates for Pregnant Women (NAPW), a tiny but tenacious organization that seeks to protect the human and reproductive rights of pregnant women, and which represents pregnant and parenting women from the most vulnerable communities, including drug-using pregnant women who have been criminally charged. The National Treatment

Agency in Britain has been the chief proponent of such rights within a nation in which healthcare is considered a universal social right.[10]

We must emphasize how unevenly drug-addicted pregnant women are treated in the US, where healthcare remains a non-universal privilege available to some and not others. While pregnant, drug-using women's lack of access to healthcare is compounded by intersections of difference into which race, ethnicity, social class, sexuality, and disability enter in varying admixtures, analyses of the prosecutions of pregnant, drug-using women consistently reveal that low income women and black women have been targeted (Flavin, 2009: 109).[11] Despite federal restraints, several states have attempted to pass laws charging pregnant women with various crimes on the grounds of "protecting the foetus" and some lawmakers have even tried to extend legal personhood to the foetus. Typically such attempts have failed once lawmakers understand that prosecution deters women from seeking healthcare and thus increases the health risks they face in bringing a pregnancy to term. However, the case for deterrent effects must be made again and again, and there seems to be little learning between incidents as the states have, in effect, their own political cultures and climates. We now turn to the federal effort to produce useable knowledge about the problems faced by drug-using pregnant women. Despite the lack of trickle-down, and a problematic structural division between research and treatment services, the US federal government has been one of the major underwriters of the knowledge about the problem that has been produced since the 1970s.

While we made the case earlier that gender defines the pregnant body,[12] what we would call 'gender' was rarely mentioned in the NIDA Research Issues series, which was published in 1974 prior to the commencement of the NIDA Research Monographs series. Two issues from that series, 'Drugs and Pregnancy' (Ferguson, Lennox, and Lettieri, 1974a) and 'Drugs and Sex' (Ferguson, Lennox, and Lettieri, 1974b) illustrate the shape that concerns about 'women' took at the outset of the Second Wave women's movement. In previous chapters we recounted how participants in the women's health movement took up their careers in alcohol and drug treatment. These women were of the same generation as the Student Association for the Study of Hallucinogens (STASH), a Madison, Wisconsin group that compiled several bibliographies for NIDA's National Clearinghouse for Drug Abuse Information, including one covering 'Women and Drugs' (1975). Judging from content covered in each of these booklets, which annotated or summarized extant articles in order to show in great detail what the state of knowledge looked like at the time, drug-using women were rarely mentioned *except* in the context of their social and sexual relationships with male addicts, or in their connection to 'neonates', babies or children.

Sexuality, sexual difference (the topic that came closest to gender), and sexual behaviour – both male and female homosexuality and heterosexuality – were covered in the bibliography. However, some entries were clearly about gender as a set of social and cultural norms shaping relationships. For instance, a study by June Clark et al. (1972) examined 40 black and 33 white wives of 73 heroin addicts in New Orleans, some of whom were also themselves addicted to heroin and maintained on methadone. The conclusion was reached that methadone maintenance offered 'immediate social rewards' resulting in 'increased stability' in family relations for 'the addict living with his family', a gain that 'may offset any failure to accomplish a complete 'cure' of the addiction' (Clark et al., 1972: 54). Many of the annotations centred male addict experiences, assuming women as ancillary victims to the 'relative 'loss' of sexuality' in their male partners, largely due to the pharmacological effects of the opiates (DeLeon and Wexler, 1973). However, some investigators (Irwin, 1973) found that the amount of sexual activity depended on the 'social context of addiction', including the availability of a sexual partner, and did not vary significantly from 'normal' non-addicts. The dominant cultural assumption, however, remained that the sexual lives of addicted individuals, male or female, were abnormal.

Among the most in-depth analyses of addict sexuality was Dan Waldorf's 1968 interview-based study of 226 male addicts from four New York State Narcotics Addiction Control Commission (NACC) facilities and 122 female addicts from the Manhattan Rehabilitation Center.[13] NACC was New York's civil commitment programme, which established 'rehabilitation centres' throughout the city.[14] Waldorf was one of the first to study these treatment facilities, which served men and women of all ethnicities (blacks outnumbered both whites and Puerto Ricans in NACC facilities). At first Waldorf found women more difficult to interview than men; he described interviews as pervaded by indifference and hostility (Waldorf, 1974: 70). However, this was overcome, interestingly, through the intertwined recognition of gender and sexuality as identity-based – men interviewed 'more feminine-appearing women' and women interviewed 'those appearing less feminine' (Waldorf, 1974, 70). 'Homosexual behavior at the Manhattan Rehabilitation Center was found to be more the norm than the exception. Liaisons were established by almost everyone whether she had been a lesbian on the outside or not. Much of this behavior seemed to be a way of overcoming the boredom and malaise that pervaded the center' (Waldorf, 1974: 70). The study was designed to get at 'specific differences between men and women addicts aside from obvious sex and role differences' (Waldorf, 1974: 69). Interesting from the perspective of later sociological work on gender was Waldorf's list of the principal differences between male and female addicts:

(1) More general disorganization of family life for females.
(2) Economic insecurity was greater for females while growing up.
(3) Females exhibited more sexual deviance.
(4) Women reported less criminality before heroin use.
(5) Women used treatment facilities less than men since it was easier for them to support themselves.

Waldorf offered prostitution as the reason offered for women's seemingly greater capacity to support their addiction; he noted that women 'seemed to suffer more guilt and remorse as a result of their addict life than men' and concluded that 'women suffer more from their addiction' because of how society defined women's roles. 'Society stigmatizes addicts, prostitutes and homosexuals, and often the female addict has at least two of these characteristics' (Waldorf, 1974: 71). Waldorf was clear that women's greater guilt and remorse grew from a gendered source but was historically contingent: while women had once outstripped men as the majority of addicts in the US, once the Harrison Act (1914) effectively criminalized addiction, women felt more constrained to abide by laws and social mores. Addict women were 'going against society's prescription for femininity as well as its laws and mores' (Waldorf, 1974: 74). While the summary of the relevant portion of Waldorf's book may have appeared in a publication titled 'Drugs and Sex,' it was clear that he differentiated analytically between 'sex' and gendered social roles, a distinction uncommon until much later among the women's and gender studies communities that began to form in order to carry the women's movement into academic institutions. Waldorf also commented on the relative neglect of female addicts and the sparse literature by comparison to the 'reams produced each year that deal with men' (Waldorf, 1974: 160).

Initially, interest in drugs and pregnancy in the US[15] was not propelled by an interest in women or gender, but because of rising concern over the possible teratogenic effects of drugs and speculation that genetic mutations might be due either to the effects of drugs of abuse or their metabolites (Falek and Einstein, 1973). Reports concerning chromosomal damage supposedly resulting from LSD circulated in the early 1970s; not only did efforts ensue to determine the extent of chromosomal damage, but there was a search for 'phenotypic abnormalities in new-born children of drug users' (Ferguson, Lennox, and Lettieri, 1974b).[16] This concern was not restricted to drug-using women but also centred on male drug addicts, as is evident in this summary: 'Since the risk of damage from the level of the gene to that of the clinically visible morphological defects is not only of significance as a population problem for future generations, but is of immediate concern to the individual and his offspring, the development and evaluation of methods for study of the genetic aspects of drug abuse is important' (Ferguson, Lennox, and Lettieri, 1974b: 6). Arthur Falek and Stanley Einstein (1973) argued that scientists should shoulder the responsibility of developing such methods, which where at least partly undertaken because of the possibility that newborn infants could provide incontrovertible evidence of genetic change in a single generation. Although this clarity did not arise, the discussion itself sheds insight into why concerns about drugs and pregnancy surfaced, and when and how they did.

In an anthology titled *Drugs and Youth*, edited by Ernest Harms, L. L. Neumann (1973) examined the effects of drug abuse during pregnancy on the foetus and newborn infants. Coming to terms with the historical evidence that many more women had once been addicted without obvious harms beyond a delimited narcotic withdrawal syndrome, she argued:

> The pregnant addict of 75 years ago was likely to be a middle-class housewife without major complicating social pathology ... Surviving infants were probably cared for by the mother in a reasonably normal home environment. In contrast, the pregnant addict today is more often living a life characterized by inadequate food and housing, neglected health, prostitution, frequent arrests, and an unstable or non-existent family life. The greatest risks faced by the infant of the present-day addict are not those of acute neonatal withdrawal, but those related to the adverse conditions which accompany the mother's drug habit.
>
> (Ferguson, Lennox, and Lettieri, 1974a: 18)

Some version of this sensible statement centring on the social conditions within which drug-using women lived their lives, along with insights from the relatively lengthy historical experience of female addicts in the US, was repeated throughout the summaries appearing in the 1974 publication. For instance, M. L. Stone et al. (1971) reported in the *American Journal of Obstetrics and Gynecology* that complications typically related to nutritional deficiencies, inadequate healthcare, and low socio-economic status, and advocated that pregnant addicts be met with special programmes for early case-finding and 'total socio-medical support' (Ferguson, Lennox, and Lettieri, 1974a: 68). This call for social as well as clinical support was echoed in many publications summarized in the annotated bibliography, almost all of which aimed to reduce mortality rates through early recognition and treatment of infants born to drug-addicted mothers. For instance, Carl Zelson et al. (1971) was an observational study of 384 infants born between 1960 and 1969 to heroin-addicted women at the Metropolitan Hospital Center at New York Medical College. The authors pointed out that congenital abnormalities did not occur any more frequently in this group than in the general population, but nevertheless concluded that 'maternal narcotic addiction seriously affects the fetus and has a damaging effect on the newborn infant' (Zelson et al., 1971). This sort of claim – in which lack of pathology was noted, but a conclusion of abnormality or damage was nevertheless drawn – was typical of the 1970s studies emerging from the increasing community of neonatologists, paediatricians, obstetricians, and gynaecologists who sought to document the effects not only of heroin and other addictions to illicit drugs, but also of methadone.

The 1970s was a period of great uncertainty in both the US and the UK regarding the effects of methadone on pregnant women and the foetuses they carried. Studies in the mainstream medical literature can be found ranging from little discernible effect (Wallach, Jerez, and Blinick, 1969) to methadone causing significantly *more* withdrawal signs than heroin (Zelson, Lee, and Casalino, 1973) to sudden infant deaths (Pierson, Howard, and Kleber, 1972). Carl Zelson et al. (1973) observed that the 'methadone babies had more withdrawal signs than the heroin babies', so the authors advised against using methadone 'indiscriminately during pregnancy' (Zelson, Lee, and Casalino, 1973: 125–6). Yet many more studies underlined the 'uniform return to a regular menstrual pattern' and a 'stabilization' of life that many women experienced once maintained on methadone (Wallach, Jerez, and Blinick, 1969). During the 1970s, the US experienced an expansion of methadone maintenance treatment for both male and female heroin addicts. However, methadone was far from the only treatment modality scaled up and tailored towards specific populations. As TCs reliant on confrontational techniques began to proliferate, the issue of pregnancy arose again.

In 1974 the NIDA Services Research Branch, then housed within the Division of Resource Development, launched The Women's Project, the national collaborative project addressed earlier in this book as a catalyst for the earliest women's treatment advocates. The project included five demonstration programmes and a central data collection and analysis system (National Clearinghouse, 1975: 5). Answers to some of the most basic questions about women's drug addiction and treatment were not yet known. The project was designed to study questions that had been raised early in the process, including the impact of societal attitudes on 'female self-concept'; legal problems, including child custody and alternatives to incarceration; educational and vocational training needs; 'breakdown in the family system'; 'the relationship between the female drug abuser in treatment and her children'; and the 'multi-generational transmission of drug problems' (National Clearinghouse, 1975: 6). The demonstration programmes served women and children, and were 'equipped to work with problems associated with pregnancy, parturition, and parenthood', making them quite different from treatment programmes serving male addicts. Recognizing at the outset that women had different problems and needs – and that negative societal attitudes towards women addicts and alcoholics hindered 'objective research' and 'proper medical treatment' (National Clearinghouse, 1975: 4) – the authors of the bibliography pitted their work against older arguments that 'women represent important social and moral symbols that are the bedrock of society. And when angels fall, they fall disturbingly far' (Hirsh, 1962; quoted in National Clearinghouse, 1975: 4). In understanding such 'governing mentalities' as impediments to their own more 'scientific', data-driven evaluation of women's treatment situation, these authors surely saw female addicts and alcoholics as caught within gendered social constraints.

The authors of the special bibliography on 'Women and Drugs' wrote that women's treatment 'has been somewhat less than ideal' due to staff holding societal attitudes viewing women as 'sicker' than men, as well as 'more emotional, limited by their biologic sex, and needing to please men' (National Clearinghouse, 1975: 5). Again, a nascent gender analysis in which hierarchical power dynamics between treatment providers and patients stood in the way of effective treatment for women pervaded this early call for 'attitudinal training of male staff members regarding the rights, roles, and special problems' that female addicts faced in treatment (National Clearinghouse, 1975: 5). The problems of women addicts were understood as closely related to the problems of women in general; the latter were attributed to societal attitudes.

Judianne Densen-Gerber, founder of Odyssey House, was a proponent of this view. In her book, *We Mainline Dreams: The Odyssey House Story* (1973), she described a 'women's marathon' encounter group session during which adolescents dealt with the concept of womanhood, a form of TC based on confronting feelings that women and girls have about being girls and women.

Well-known for her strong views on the subject of mandatory treatment for pregnant addicts as a form of 'protection of the unborn child', Densen-Gerber was one of the best-known feminist voices in the treatment arena. Trained as a lawyer and a physician, Densen-Gerber first encountered addicts at Metropolitan Hospital during her psychiatry residency when she herself was pregnant.[17] When she set up Odyssey House, she assumed custody of the children of addicts and argued – against other feminists such as Sheila Blume, whose views as New York State commissioner were addressed in Chapter 1 – that drug addiction should count as *prima facie* evidence of child abuse. Arguing that female addicts were not motivated to use birth control effectively, nor to abort resulting unplanned pregnancies, Densen-Gerber wrote that the addicted women she treated were driven by a 'fundamental desire to become pregnant, i.e., to become a normal woman with something to love and be loved by.... Because prevention and termination of pregnancy are not feasible to the addicts themselves, protection of the unborn child merits a mandatory treatment law for pregnant addicts' along with court-appointed guardians once children were born (Densen-Gerber, Wiener, and Hochstedler, 1972, quoted in National Clearinghouse, 1975: 26).

Despite being one of the most widely respected women in the treatment business, Densen-Gerber and her daughter, Tricia Baden, adopted the view that, 'Life is trust. Life is given to us to pass on, generation to generation. The taking of drugs can, we believe, cause the genetic material which passes human life from one person to another to be damaged, so that the baby is born retarded, or without arms and legs, or deformed, or in pain' (1972: 29). We see in Densen-Gerber's views a potent combination of support for women in treatment, including her belief that women-led groups were essential for effective women's treatment, along with social control-oriented attitudes about sexuality and unfounded beliefs about the effects of reproduction by female addicts. Despite understanding that women were socialized into 'dependent' social roles by virtue of gendered social expectations, Densen-Gerber and Charles C. Rohrs (1973) argued that 'Addiction must be designated as a prima facie criterion of unfitness as a parent. Only when this is done will children be protected by rights inherently theirs'.[18] At the same time that Densen-Gerber promulgated this position, with which many feminists involved in the field disagreed and saw as promoting conflicts of interest between women and their children, Odyssey House created in 1973 one of the first residential centres for pregnant addicts and children, which was called Mothers and Babies Off Narcotics (MABON). MABON was located on Ward's Island with another Odyssey House 'family centre' site in East Harlem. Today, Odyssey House bills itself as 'one of the largest treatment system[s] for drug-troubled families in the country', offering primary healthcare in addition to residential treatment through the TC model. Densen-Gerber herself was a controversial figure within the movement for women's drug treatment. When she delivered the memorable 1975 keynote speech at NIDA's first major national conference on women's drug treatment, held at the Fontainebleu Hotel in Miami Beach, Florida, many in the audience were appalled at the slides depicting dead, abused, and battered babies that she showed. Densen-Gerber's views on the topic were well-known; she believed that the 'majority of battered and brutalized babies who are identified as such – dead or alive – live in homes where the parents are using drugs'. As the wife of the Michael Baden, then New York City medical examiner, her words and the photos with which he supplied her carried some weight, and she had translated them into early actions by starting therapeutic communities for children ages 7–12, and for pregnant addicts. Densen-Gerber preferred to play a direct role in the supervision of Odyssey House, including in regional satellites such as the Odyssey House in Flint/Saginaw, Michigan.[19] According to the Michigan women, Densen-Gerber was reportedly threatened by NIDA's WDR Project, an effort to evaluate programme outcomes and collect data across sites in order to determine treatment effectiveness and directions to improve services for women. Yet her attitudes towards pregnant and addicted women were complicated by her understanding of their need to love and be loved, which was most apparent in Densen-Gerber's writings about her sense of futility regarding the provision of birth control and abortion services to addicted women (Densen-Gerber, Weiner, and Hochstedler, 1972). On the one hand, she advocated measures that most feminist treatment advocates came to see not only as excessively controlling, but as coercive state incursions not only into rights but also into the very bodily integrity of drug-using women. At the same time, Densen-Gerber created a network of therapeutic communities that recognized and cared for pregnant addicts and their babies and children; she was an eccentric and dramatic figure who inspired shrines, testimonials, and reportage in *New York* magazine.

By contrast physician Josette Mondanaro, founder of Wingspread Comprehensive Health Services for Women in Santa Cruz, California, contributed a perspective grounded in the notion that drug-using women deserved healthcare, including reproductive healthcare, that was cognizant of their specific and unique medical needs (1981: 281). What was striking about the two volumes NIDA published in 1981 was their avoidance of the lurid and hyperbolic constructions of drug-using women encountered elsewhere in the culture. These volumes were edited by Beth Glover Reed and Mondanaro, with backing from NIDA programme officer George Beschner, a long-time proponent of the view that *women* should be involved in NIDA's production and dissemination of knowledge about 'chemical dependency' in women. Although Mondanaro was diagnosed with a brain tumour during this time, and forced to scale back her activities at both the state and national levels, these volumes were important not only for the content and the measured tone with which they delivered practical knowledge, but because they helped secure space for women's treatment advocacy at the federal level even during the 1980s, a time of fiscal crisis that negatively affected the strategies by which drug-using women typically survived, coped with their responsibilities and sought to protect themselves from the hurtful effects of stigma (Murphy and Sales, 2001).

Despite attention to 'heroin mothers' in the 1970s, 'prenatal drug exposure' was constructed as a serious *new* problem in the 1980s. Sociologist of law Laura E. Gomez argues that this sense of novelty was produced by convergence between the 'War on Drugs' and the intensification of the abortion debate due to the religious right's championing of 'foetal rights' even *before* foetal viability (1997: 2). Indeed, pregnant addicts first came to strategic prominence during a domestic policy shift in the White House ONDCP, then headed by 'drug czar' William J. Bennett, to 'demand reduction'.[20] By the mid-1980s, as shown in previous chapters, woman-centred treatment programmes were experiencing fiscal pressure and retrenchment just as illegal drugs became 'America's number one domestic crisis' and federal policy was shifting from aiming to cut off supply to reducing consumer demand for illicit drugs. The federal policy shift to demand reduction relocated the War on Drugs from the 'cocaine jungles of South America where narco-terrorists prowl or on the inner-city street corners where the street gangs shoot it out' to the domestic or home front – the 'battlefield of values' within the family.[21]

Demand reduction policy conscripted women in the 'War on Drugs' differently depending on their social location. This policy shift towards changing hearts and minds coincided with the heightened public visibility of a population of poor, urban, primarily African-American women, both within the child welfare and drug treatment systems. Reproductive status was also differently implicated, as pregnant women are even more vulnerable to the mechanisms of discipline – formal and informal sanctions – than their counterparts who are not pregnant. 'Changing minds' – the stuff of demand reduction policies – involved coercive measures aimed at eliciting compliance by reminding individuals of their heightened vulnerability to state power. The wave of prosecutions in the late 1980s and early 1990s reminded all women of the precarious status of their legal rights of personhood, which are conditioned upon their discharge of the obligations of motherhood. As Drucilla Cornell argued in *The Imaginary Domain* (1995), unequal responsibility for men's sexuality, reproduction, (and, we add, for social reproduction) is imposed upon women, encoding an asymmetric power relation into the law that denies women equivalent respect, responsibility, sexual freedom, and imagination.

Public policies that 'normalize' the relationally gendered context of reproduction and privatize the costs of social reproduction also work to contain the feminist critique of this arrangement. At stake was women's responsibility for children and the fear, expressed in congressional hearings on maternal crack-cocaine use, that women were becoming unfit or unwilling to absorb the costs of social reproduction (Campbell, 2000). The assumption that individual, autonomous women control the circumstances under which they use drugs, become pregnant, decide to carry to term or not, or raise children is belied by the constraints that 'stratified reproduction' (Colen, 1995) makes on the agency and autonomy of all women. Social inequalities are made invisible in policy discourse by projecting social problems onto individuals who embody them – and pregnant, drug-using women were ripe to embody many social-structural problems. In addition 'foetal abuse' became used as political shorthand encoding a broader set of anxieties at work in the body politic concerning the reconfiguration of gender and race relations (Gomez, 1997: 3).

Like the story we told in previous chapters, California represented somewhat of a 'success story' for the feminist organizations and women's treatment advocates who countered the proposed punitive legislation at the time. Despite the climate of moral panic, the state of California and most other states – with the notable exception of South Carolina – were able to interrupt the cycle of 'blaming the victim' underway, despite the potency of the cultural figures deployed within the media and by the religious right. Feminist organizations and women's treatment advocates were able to argue successfully that the state should play a role that was more 'facilitative' than 'adversarial' in assuring the convergent interests of drug-using women and their babies (Johnsen, 1986). There is no doubt, reading the preambles to the 20-some bills before the California legislature by mid-1989, that the issue of 'prenatal drug exposure' was perceived to intersect with many other salient social problems and ancillary issues such as crime, welfare reform, HIV/AIDS, abortion, and reproductive autonomy. Many feminist activists, drug treatment providers, and pro-choice legislators interviewed by Gomez saw 'foetal abuse' as a construct advanced opportunistically by groups seeking to contain women's gains in the civil and reproductive rights arenas (1997: 38). For the individual women prosecuted, outcomes tended to be harsh and coupled with moral outrage on the part of prosecutor and public (Gomez, 1997: 101). It also appears in retrospect that addicted pregnant women were scapegoats for the downsizing of social services in the state of California (Murphy and Rosenbaum, 1999: 140).

While the wave of prosecutions about which Gomez was writing has subsided, many states continue to witness prosecution of pregnant, drug-using women well into the twenty-first century. According to the US Department of Health and Human Services, 12 states and the District of Columbia have laws that allow pregnant women who use illicit drugs to be charged with child abuse, and an additional 12 states have provisions allowing such charges when infants test positive for controlled substances at birth. Although some state high courts (Kentucky, 2010; Maryland, 2006; New Mexico, 2007; Texas, 2006) have struck down laws attempting to apply existing statutes on child abuse and neglect to drug use during pregnancy, lawmakers continue to propose 'mandating' the testing of pregnant women for illegal drug use as a route towards forcing them to 'seek' treatment. Often in these very same states there is documented public disinvestment in treatment or a distinct lack of treatment capacity for pregnant women.[22] Finally, states are able to depart from federal law by declaring 'drug emergencies' when problems with particular substances intensify regionally; at times these laws are targeted towards or have a 'disparate impact' upon women who are pregnant or parenting, as in Michigan's 2006 law defining any use or production of methamphetamine where children are present as *de facto* child abuse. Over 20 states have laws on the books defining some type of illegal drug use, distribution, or sale as child abuse and/or neglect. The state-level policy patchwork suggests a lack of social consensus and legal clarity that haunts this issue, making vigilant national surveillance of drug policy by treatment advocates as well as those who care about reproductive rights an ongoing necessity.

Women's drug and alcohol treatment advocates attempted to use the US Department of Health and Human Services, SAMHSA to provide some guidance, steering and stability at the federal level in the early 1990s. A consensus process leading to the 1993 publication of the first Federal TIP (TIP 2) focused on women, which was titled 'Pregnant, Substance-Abusing Women', suggests that at least on the federal level, pregnant, substance-using women were viewed as a 'special population' needing comprehensive services. How was it that both the federal effort to promote treatment for the most vulnerable pregnant women – 'often poor and suffering from multiple socioeconomic problems', according to the TIP 2 (1993: 1) – and the criminal prosecution of individual drug-using, pregnant women in nearly half of US states occurred at this moment? Part of the answer surely lies in regional variation – both Gomez (1997) and Lynn Paltrow (1992) point to significant geographic variation, with only two states (Florida and South Carolina) supplying most of the cases, and with zealous prosecutors being one of the critical factors for tipping the scales towards punitive responses. However, we suspect that the case made above concerning the symbolic salience of pregnant drug users and the peculiar forms of abjection and ambivalence to which they are subject was also operating. The flat, technocratic discourse of the TIP 2 guidelines could hardly be expected to combat the prosecutorial zeal to jail these women in attempts to gain control over their reproductive capacities. The consensus panel was at pains to remind readers that discrimination against pregnant women counted as gender or sex discrimination and even stated outright that 'the Panel does not support the criminal prosecution of pregnant, substance-using women. Furthermore, there is no evidence that punitive approaches work' (TIP 2, 1993: 2). Throughout the TIP 2, pregnant, substance-using women were depicted as neglected and tossed aside, meeting with closed doors despite their needs not being met.

> Some communities prosecute and jail women who abuse alcohol and other drugs while pregnant. These women may be legally separated from their children as well. More common, however, is the neglect they experience from health care and service delivery systems. The painful repercussions and neglect of pregnant, substance-using women and their children can be seen in shelters for battered women, among homeless populations, and in foster homes and child welfare institutions across the country.
>
> (TIP 2, 1993: 1)

Thus the TIP 2 recommended not only gender-specific but 'ethnically and culturally sensitive' service offered in a non-judgemental manner (1993: 7). Despite this, the panel recognized some women might have a 'basic distrust or dislike' of the healthcare system or physicians working within it, or be unused to seeking preventive care rather than 'emergency-necessitated' care. 'Her feelings of fear and guilt, and possible negative past experiences, may cause her to expect poor treatment. Sometimes she provokes a hostile interchange with health care professionals' (TIP 2, 1993: 8). Stressing that the very language used in healthcare settings may provoke further shame and guilt, the panel emphasized that 'every health care visit is an opportunity to provide positive reinforcement' to these reluctant patients, as well as support and even nurturance. Providers were also encouraged to assess the pregnant, substance-using woman's mental health, given the preponderance of dual diagnosis and women who had themselves been victims of domestic violence, abuse, victimization, and 'poor parenting' (TIP 2, 1993: 2, 26).

Involvement between pregnant substance users and Child Protective Services and other child welfare agencies was assumed to be ongoing and negative (TIP 2, 1993: 58). Child custody and placement issues of the very sort encountered at the US Narcotic Farm in the 1950s were understood to deter treatment programmes from accepting pregnant women in the 1990s. The TIP 2 mobilized a rhetoric of inclusion and anti-discrimination, emphasizing that 'criminal penalties should not be imposed on women based solely on their use of alcohol and other drugs during pregnancy' and arguing that pregnant women who had been incarcerated or detained for criminal offences should be granted access to treatment (1993: 54). CSAT/SAMHSA assumed itself to be setting the tone for state agencies, which were responsible for promulgating best practices and disbursing federal block grants throughout the treatment infrastructure. A top-down 'technology' or 'knowledge transfer' model was adopted and supported by innumerable trainings, continuing education credits within the licence and credentialing system, and publications. Yet all of this federal activity was ineffective when it came to forestalling the prosecutions, although women's treatment advocates were active in various local campaigns and state legislative hearings. Gulfs of understanding – indeed, 'epistemologies of ignorance' – widened between the 'mental health', 'drug and alcohol treatment', 'reproductive rights' and 'criminal justice' communities, and shared understandings continue to be rare in the US.

By contrast the issue in Britain has remained one of pushing not only to get gender on the agenda and gain access to treatment, but to emphasize the distinctiveness of women's bodies and the specific nature of their needs for treatment. As Hilary Klee wrote in concluding her reflections on the dilemmas posed by child welfare and drug dependence in the UK, some of the components of the US response would be appropriate in the UK, whereas 'others would be inappropriate in view of the UK orientation towards harm reduction, less punitive legislation and free access to treatment' (2002: 283). Reflecting on how attention to these issues has changed in the UK over the years, Susanne MacGregor sees progress in that

> [The notion of] women as reproductive organs . . . [is] coming through [the treatment field] and foetal alcohol syndrome is now getting more attention. So there is a ... concern with women's bodies. This is where it comes to neuropharmacology ... there has been more of a shift to the body – the distinctiveness of women's bodies.[23]

This distinctiveness is emphasized at many levels, but it is nowhere so emphatic as in the area of women's fitness as parents; questions about the capacity of male drug users to father have rarely been raised as a public matter. MacGregor recalls that concerns about the children of drug-using women being taken into care was initially raised by midwives in the UK:

> Are women fit mothers [who are] definitely heroin using? There's been attention to [the whole thing about babies born addicted and so on] ... It was recognised as a concern by midwives ... and quite a lot of children [were] taken into care because the mothers were seen.[24]

Indeed, interviews with midwives bear this out, but also show the ambivalent position in which many healthcare providers find themselves when dealing with women who are both pregnant and drug using. Consider Fay Macrory talking about her decade of experience in the drugs field:

> I was always a radical midwife ... fighting against the system ... it wasn't so much the doctors, it was my ... midwifery colleagues ... My previous role was drug liaison midwife, which we developed in the early 90's.... It wasn't long before I came back to St Mary's [that] I realised the attitude to women who were using drugs. [They] ... rarely turned up for antenatal care because that was [so] unacceptable. [In] 1992 I got together with some colleagues in the voluntary

> sector ... We used to sit in the Zion Art Centre ... and say, 'God, why do druggies and women get treated like sh*t?' ... I did a retrospective audit of fifty sets of notes of women who had been identified or had disclosed drug use ... We discovered all the babies would be admitted to special care and treated for withdrawal, usually, as we know now, unnecessarily.

Macrory noticed that her fellow healthcare workers had written 'pejorative, subjective remarks in their notes', as well as administered HIV tests and toxicology screens without even discussing it with their patients. This raises an issue that has been ongoing in both the US and the UK concerning the lack of trust and open communication between drug-using women and healthcare practitioners who care for them. Often this is expressed as a concern that there is something wrong with drug-using, pregnant women who avoid prenatal (US) or antenatal (UK) care prior to delivering babies. Macrory drew attention to the distinct lack of welcome such women receive when presenting for care:

> Why would they? When they'd come in the babies were taken to special care and because we had a resident social worker ... all babies were brought to their attention. So they were all admitted to special care and of course the chaos that came with that because what was happening ... was that they were having their antenatal assessment done postnatally. We knew nothing about them. Of course, the women didn't want to go there because they felt judged quite rightly... As one women said to me, 'I need to be off me face to get past that old bag in room two'... To me it was very clear. [The question] wasn't, Why didn't they attend for antenatal care? It was, Why on earth should they, when people treated them so badly?[25]

The phenomenon of drug-addicted women 'failing' to seek pre- or antenatal care, or leaving the hospital shortly after delivery 'against medical advice' has now been observed in the medical literature for over half a century.[26] This very issue led neonatologists in the US to create regimens responsive to this predicament in the late 1960s (Perlstein, 1947; Rosenthal, Patrick, and Krug, 1964; Stern, 1966) and to establish some of the earliest drug treatment programmes for pregnant and recently postpartum women (Finnegan, 1975; Finnegan et al., 1973, 1976). While it is clear that drug-using women avoid seeking healthcare for a variety of reasons, including shame, guilt, and fear of family breakup, it is also clear that their needs as patients have been fairly consistently unmet for decades. As Klee (2002) points out, it is essential for women to encounter a variety of 'family-based options' and to be supported in finding their way to a 'more rewarding lifestyle with their children that can ensure the safety of those children', but this 'Utopian state is a far cry from the experiences of drug-using mothers' (283). Until treatment is fully disentangled from punishment, stigmatization, and coercion, and becomes less bound up with the promulgation of gendered social norms, it is difficult to advocate its expansion.

Conclusion

When we consider exactly what aspects of gender and which gendered assumptions and knowledges operated to define drug treatment for pregnant women, it becomes apparent that women are assumed to be the linchpins of social order, family life, and biosocial (and cultural) reproduction. Women addicts were repeatedly exhorted to enter treatment in order to become stable enough to provide social stability for others – often for their male partners and children. Thus as a social problem, women's drug addiction has consistently fallen within the domain of social reproduction. What was women's treatment all about? Too often, it seems, women's treatment was not about women's health or even women's sense of themselves, but about what women need to do for others and what women need to do for society. This issue becomes all the more clear when it is set within the context of what Ruth Fletcher (2006) calls 'reproductive consumption'. While women are meant to consume reproduction as a site of politicisation and pleasure, their patterns of biological reproduction are most definitely affected by the acting out (or non-acting out in the case of pregnant drug users) cultural ideals about women, motherhood, parenting, and child rearing.

Yet it was also apparent to the women involved in creating, administering, and advocating for women-sensitive drug treatment programmes that children were particularly problematic, 'as children are important motivators for change in women and because responsibilities for children are such powerful disincentives to seeking treatment' (Reed, 1987: 163). On the one hand, inclusion of children could enrich their mothers' experiences in ways that benefit both parents and children. On the other hand, the presence of children forced programmes to broaden their scope and sometimes resulted in conflicts of interest and disruptions due to children's needs (Reed, 1987: 162). Children were sometimes viewed as addicts themselves, as in the 'junior junkies' scare that reportedly prompted Densen-Gerber to start up Odyssey

House branches for heroin addicts as young as nine years old in the early 1970s.[27] Far more often, however, children were seen as conduits to women – and as leverage by which to gain women's compliance with treatment programmes. In the UK context, recognizing children in the women and drug treatment mix generated not only discussions about 'hidden harms and vulnerabilities' but also opened up a powerful discourse on how 'qualitatively women's problems with drugs both direct and indirect can be more *complex* than men's (NTA, 2010). The perception that they are acting under threat of imminent 'reproductive loss' is implicated in all sorts of behaviours that women undertake to conceal their drug problems, from avoiding prenatal care and evading the scrutiny of the 'medical gaze' to giving birth to babies 'on the streets'. Rather than reading women's concealment as 'denial' or a symptom of the disease model of addiction, it should be viewed as a rational response to the extraordinarily persistent social stigma that pregnant drug-using women have historically faced, and the consequences that flow from that in terms of the erosion of women's human rights and their rights as 'reproductive citizens' (Flavin, 2009: 183).

Not only the basis of social citizenship, but the very personhood of pregnant women can be seen as under assault when pregnant or recently postpartum women are met with criminal charges brought on by those who claim to represent the rights of 'the unborn' or 'the foetus' against the rights of the pregnant woman or mother. Proponents of foetal rights have adopted a moral and religious agenda at odds with the women whose reproduction they wish to control. While litigation on behalf of the reproductive and human rights of pregnant women forms the core of its activities, NAPW operates basically as a think tank for the production of new feminist knowledges created to overcome the 'epistemologies of ignorance' that pervade the criminal justice system when it comes to all aspects of reproduction, including stillbirth, pregnancy, birth and delivery, and the immediate postpartum period.[28] When lack of knowledge about the activities and experiences of reproducing bodies and drug-using subjects is coupled with the pervasive stigmatization of drug use, this compounds the trouble faced by people whose very personhood has been reduced to their pregnancy or drug use status. Additionally, as NAPW points out, the women typically charged with criminal intent in cases of this kind often occupy the intersections of racial, ethnic, class, and other differences that combine to make them multiply vulnerable subjects before the forces of law and police.[29] Thus the organization has worked not only to litigate such cases and to oppose state legislation that would further criminalize pregnant women, but also to create a new body of knowledge and legal doctrine integrating all of the areas of knowledge upon which these cases touch under the rubric of 'reproductive justice' (Diaz-Tello, Paltrow and Moreno, 2010). Paltrow frames the problem as the dehumanization of pregnant women:

> We have learned that we cannot assure that pregnant women have full constitutional and human rights if we don't address race, class and drug issues, and if we don't recognize that the legal grounds for attacking abortion are really legal grounds for undermining the personhood of *all* pregnant women. We have come to realize that we cannot mobilize or act effectively if we do not acknowledge that 61 per cent of women who have abortions are already mothers and 84 per cent of women by 40 will become pregnant and give birth. While we don't want to be defined or limited by our capacity for motherhood, we can't ensure women's human rights if we don't deal with the fact the overwhelming majority of them are mothers.[30]

As we struggle with the dilemmas presented by mothers as persons,[31] we must recognize that not all women are or wish to become mothers; many women are mothers not by 'choice', but necessity; many women are forced to mother in ways that they themselves would not choose; still others cannot be the mothers they want to be for reasons far beyond 'choice' or control. An expansive notion of 'reproductive justice' will include all of these possible positions without qualification or condition. This chapter has shown how enduring the dehumanization and repetitive the struggles of drug-using women have been in the reproductive realm. While the toll of reproductive loss is high in this population, it has rarely been reckoned with *as* reproductive loss. Yet some of the most life-changing traumatic moments in the lives of individual drug-using women revolve around their losses in the reproductive realm. When we step back and realize how many women's lives have been affected over time, we are compelled to recognize the systemic nature of the institutional systems that intersect to produce such losses.

Conclusion: Making Gender Matter in an Age of Neurochemical Selves

We start with the question: *Does* gender still matter in an age of neurochemical thinking about self and other? We argue that gender does still matter because one of the most significant effects of understanding ourselves as 'neurochemical selves' has been a shift in the site of the deviance of 'others' from bodies to brains. The gendered body has long been the central site for the organization and performance of the social tasks of restraint, reproduction, regulation, and representation (Ettorre, 2007: 23 and 34; quoting Turner, 1996: 67). When the embodied routines through which these tasks are accomplished become disrupted or destabilized by social-structural shifts, institutional crisis, or changing social norms, the bodies who perform them are seen as maladapted and marked as 'deviant' (Ettorre, 2007: 33). Indeed the bodies of drug-using women have 'embodied deviance' for decades of public policy in both the US and the UK. However, a shift to understanding 'the brain' as the central site of 'embodied deviance' is now underway.

As a disembodied brain becomes increasingly understood as a core site of political struggles, deviance is now 'marked' in and on the brains and bodies of drug users. 'The brain' becomes the site of the production of this 'neurochemical deviance', a 'deranged' neurochemistry that causes social behaviour to 'go awry', in the words of Nora Volkow (2004), a top US neuroscientist who studies drug addiction and has used her long-running tenure as director of NIDA to advance neuroscientific approaches to the study of addictive behaviours, including problematic eating. In the course of framing the findings of neuroscientific work on the addictions for public consumption, Volkow uses a lexicon of 'derangement' and molecular 'disruption' occurring within 'the brain' and adopts the redefinition of addiction as a 'chronic, relapsing brain disease' or 'brain disorder'. We fear that this culturally loaded scientific lexicon skirts dangerously close to notions of 'brain damage' that invite the reinscription of social stigmas that the field has worked hard to dispel. In the midst of an intensified biomedicalization of culture through the figure of the 'addicted brain', we find ourselves awash in explanatory accounts and images claiming to provide neuroscientific 'evidence' for such claims. As long-time participant/observers in the fields of addiction research and treatment, we are concerned about the reinscription and reinforcement of notions of biological determinism and essentialism that once drew critical fire from anti-racist and anti-essentialist feminists. But this is not a bodily essentialism. For decades the field of addiction research has moved toward molecular and sub-cellular approaches. Researchers in these fields now claim to be studying 'gender' when they are studying neurotransmitter function and the molecular composition of women's bodies and brains, and leaving untouched the power differentials and the often hidden social, political, and economic relations within which people problematically use drugs or alcohol.

We advance a concept of gender to undo the essentialist/anti-essentialist dichotomy in favour of moving towards a more socially situated neuroscience. Our position is not 'anti-neuroscience' and cannot be dismissed as yet another critique of biological reductionism or determinism. By attuning ourselves to the conceptual approaches and tools offered by the new neurosciences – including accounts of neuroplasticity and neuroadaptation now central to neurochemistry and neurogenetics (Malabou, 2008) – we understand that neuroscientists are increasingly interested in 'social factors' occurring in the broader 'environment', but note their limited vocabulary for studying 'the social'. We must still be wary about the emergence of new brain-and-body-based neuro-determinisms that may obscure some of the older perceptions of difference that once undergirded the very inequities we are trying to address. As Evelyn Fox Keller writes in *The Mirage of a Space Between Nature and Nurture* (2010), questions of difference remain pressing because the 'major practical interest driving the search for the relative importance of different causal factors in producing a given phenomenon is to be found in the wish to effect *change* in that phenomenon' (83; emphasis ours).

As we have shown in the foregoing chapters, changing research and treatment cultures is an inescapably political process that depends on collective decisions about the allocation of resources – towards research and treatment and away from prosecution and criminalization, for instance. Policy designs and designations of 'target populations' assist in channelling resources in ways that advantage some 'contenders', and disadvantage others. As women's treatment advocates learnt, they were sometimes able to garner resources and put them to use in sustainable ways – but they often faced a frustrating process of 'reinventing the wheel' each time a new drug crisis produced a new 'target population' that would have to be 'legitimated' as a beneficiary of public services. What good are neuro-technologies for addressing the power differentials that we have demonstrated pervade the cyclic dismantling and reinvention of the sociocultural infrastructure of legitimation – and delegitimation – of gender-responsive and women-centred treatment? In order for these neuro-technologies to avoid becoming new 'epistemologies of ignorance', we suggest that a conscious and deliberate awareness of their potential to reinscribe deterministic thinking be held in tension with the practical and epistemological dilemmas faced by treatment providers and those whom they serve. Neuroscience can and will be put to political use – to set priorities, confirm or disconfirm knowledge claims emerging from other arenas, and, above all, to shed insight on which forms of intervention 'work' or 'don't work'. As notions of neuroadaptation and neuroplasticity are elaborated in today's neurosciences, they will be considered as a 'function of developmental age' (Keller, 2010: 75). That is, the relative fixity, malleability, permanence, and reversibility of particular traits (in our case, changes in the brain due to chronic drug exposure) varies over the life course; many aspects of drug addiction vary in complex interrelation with the social and cultural geography within which the person housing 'the addicted brain' lives out her life over time. Typically, both 'sex' and gender differences sculpt these terrains, and there is little or no space, to adopt Keller's lexicon, between those that can be attributed to 'nature' and those that can be attributed to 'nurture'. We must do a better job of talking about the both/and qualities of sex/gender differences, the intricate entanglements between persons, their brains, and the societies in which they live.

Epistemologies of ignorance

We argue that it is necessary to hold onto the notion that gender distinctions matter for how particular forms of healthcare and social provision are delivered in order to counter the epistemologies of ignorance encountered in the history recorded in these pages. We have argued throughout this book that distinct *social* consequences accrue to women addicts and alcoholics, particularly as regards their relationship to biosocial reproduction, that are not gender neutral. If gender is not specifically taken into account by those attempting to address the sources of those effects, the consequences will most likely be negative for women. We must ask what constitutes 'health' for such women in a neurochemical age when we all face increased mandates for self-regulation and pressures to take on board the 'recovery' of 'health' as an ongoing moral obligation, a project requiring 'constant self- and other public disciplining' (Clarke et al., 2010: 63). As the 'key site of responsibility' for health shifts from providers to individuals (variously cast as patients, 'users' or consumers), responsibility to 'recover' from addiction and alcoholism returns to the ground of moral obligation even in this most 'neurochemical' and 'molecular' age. The contradiction is clear: the governing mentalities that position addiction as a 'brain disease' also place responses to it within the purview of the moral obligations of citizenship, not unlike other such similar 'brain diseases' as obesity, alcoholism, and major and minor mental illnesses. Our societies may no longer view a 'disease of the will' or 'moral character flaws'[1] as predisposing individuals to alcoholism or addiction, but the compulsion to address alcoholism and addiction in ways that the dominant classes recognize as leading to 'recovery' is becoming the mandatory price of social inclusion.

Today there is unarguably an increasing moral compulsion for individuals to take personal responsibility for their health and health care. This moral responsibility takes on a punitive edge where resources for treatment are declining, or have never been available, and yet rights have become conditioned upon maintaining drug-free status. In the US, there have been myriad attempts to condition women's rights upon determinations of how well individual women discharge their personal, moral responsibility in regard to drug-use status. In the UK, the right to health has been translated into female individuals' right to produce healthy children within the heterosexual family matrix, as the needs of women have been obscured. The previous chapter showed how poorly women fared in US courts when brought up on drug charges associated with biological or social reproduction. Indeed Lynn M. Paltrow, the foremost litigator representing pregnant women who have been arrested and charged while trying to bring their pregnancies to term despite drug problems, provides numerous examples that such women are simply not treated like other defendants.[2] Such prosecutions are not gender neutral – such women are prosecuted *because* they are perceived to fall short on the gendered duties of citizenship.

While the 'degenerative' drug policies of the US appear more punitive, there appears to be paradoxically greater access to drug treatment structured specifically for women. Yet despite some exemplary women's treatment programmes flourishing in the US, most women in most states confront reduced access to treatment thanks to programmes forced to operate at reduced capacity relative to need due to periodic fiscal crises of the state and federal governments. This leaves drug-using women especially vulnerable to coercive actions by the state when pregnant and inhabiting a culture of fear that their children will be taken from them. Yet they are urged to actively seek healthcare and blamed when they do not do so – despite the potentially high costs triggered by their submission to scrutiny. The failure to see the toll that reproductive losses take in the lives of drug-using women both in the UK and US is part of an ongoing epistemology of ignorance with which they have been met.

Active embodiment of 'recovery' directed towards the reduction of drug-related harm is required both by dominant healthcare systems, and by advocates of practical alternatives such as harm reduction. What happens when we consider harm reduction drug policy from a feminist perspective? While there is relatively little talk about gender within the international harm reduction community, women's drug and alcohol use has long been viewed as more harmful than men's – more harmful to women themselves and their 'precious' wombs, more harmful to children and partners, more harmful to society and to the 'next generation'. Thus policy measures are more drastic when directed towards women, particularly when children, babies, or foetuses are involved. Women are both viewed as more at risk and as themselves 'riskier' and more potentially 'harmful' to others. Greater incursions into women's bodily integrity have been tolerated in the name of society's investment in 'families' and 'communities'. The notion 'hidden harms' itself masks the extent of these incursions. On the one hand, some think a 'harm maximization' regime has culminated in sterilizations, criminal prosecutions, child removal, and other draconian measures. On the other hand, others think of them as containment mechanisms, by which women's gains are contained and harnessed again towards making sure that women continue to play their 'traditional' role in social reproduction. Yet 'harms' and 'risks' are gendered, culturally produced and context-dependent, and the emphasis on 'personal responsibility' now dominant in the US and the UK typically requires that individuals take an active role in averting both.

As Chapter 5 demonstrated, embodiment is understood to be necessarily 'active' during pregnancy. Pregnant drug users are exhorted to become active in seeking prenatal care, addressing nutritional deficiencies, exercising, and engaging in other health-related practices that will support positive pregnancy 'outcome' – a 'healthy baby'. Yet the reduction of drug-related harm during pregnancy cyclically falls victim to an epistemology of ignorance, and there has been constant circulation of mythical claims concerning drug effects during pregnancy. Many people see enabling healthcare providers to advise drug-using women on how best to reduce drug-related harm while continuing to *use* rather than abstain from the use of illegal substances, tobacco, and alcohol as a moral contradiction. Yet that is exactly what needs to happen if the epistemologies of ignorance are to be overcome in this arena. If the political will to overcome objections to such moral contradictions is to be mustered, we argue that women's overwhelming responsibilities for social reproduction will have to be acknowledged in order for their recovery to be truly supported. The women's treatment advocates who grew up in the women's health movement were aware of this and remain engaged in producing new knowledges about the ways in which drug-using women experience social stratification, structural and personal violence, and trauma (Brown et al., 2000, 2002; Finkelstein, 2004; Finkelstein and Markoff, 2004).

Clashing views of 'medicalization' and 'feminism' as frames for drug treatment

Women's health movements – and the array of social movements configured around specific diseases or special patient populations following in their wake – take different stances towards medicalization. Many feminists who participated in the women's health movement viewed with scepticism the 'over-medicalization' of women's lives, in particular, the over-prescription of psychotropic medications to women as a symptom of the over-diagnosis of mental illness and mood disorders, as well as the medicalization of childbirth, which feminists considered an unwelcome imposition of patriarchal social norms aimed at controlling women. Feminist Phyllis Chesler's landmark book, *Women and Madness* (1972) joined the ongoing major critique of psychiatric approaches to treating mental illness initiated in the US by Thomas Szasz and in the UK by R. D. Laing under the rubric of antipsychiatry. One platform endorsed by antipsychiatry opposed congregate care, especially confinement to asylums or other 'total institutions' constructed for the sake of social control and discipline (Goffman, 1961). Enrolling not only patients but psychiatrists themselves, particularly graduates of 'community psychiatry' or 'community organizing' training programmes meant to staff the community mental health centres, the antipsychiatry movement was interested in reforming the whole society (Musto, 1975: 74–5). Similarly, feminists were intensely involved simultaneously in the critique of the gendered social order, the psychiatric profession, and in evolving a *feminist* or *gender-specific* or *woman-centred* therapeutic praxis.[3] When Susie Orbach and Luise Eichenbaum founded the Women's Therapy Centre in London in 1976 an important step was taken towards privileging feminist psychotherapy in the UK.

Heirs to the antipsychiatry movement, women's movement participants sharpened their own critique of hierarchical doctor-patient relationships and politicized the medicalization of a range of women's problems, from domestic drudgery to violence. Psychotropic drugs were not only seen as tools of patriarchy by feminists, but advertised as such within the medical press (Herzberg, 2009). Reviewing emergence of concerns over women's alcoholism in the 1970s in the UK, Betsy Thom (1997: 29) found a common thread running through responses to women's alcohol use which crosses cultural, temporal, and geographical barriers: the emphasis placed on women's gender-based roles, women's duties as mothers, wives, and caregivers. The same emphasis on women's normative roles in social reproduction can be glimpsed in responses to women's drug use. As providers of informal (and mainly unpaid) care work for purposes of biosocial reproduction, women in the UK have traditionally been placed in a particular relation to healthcare providers in the public sphere, with the medical profession exerting undue control over their lives (Oakley, 1980, 1981, 1984). This sort of social control has been reflected by authorities within the alcohol and drug treatment field, demonstrating that women's drug consumption and their related problems are bound up with their gendered positions in the structure of power relations in any given society (Sargent, 1992: 3). However, patient advocacy movements have shifted away from arguing against medicalization as a form of social discipline, and towards arguing for improved access to better-quality care as essential to their inclusion in the fruits and benefits of 'biomedicalizaton' (Clarke et al., 2010).

As healthcare came to be valued as a public good to which some had access in the US and as a public right in the UK, attitudes began to shift under conditions of neo-liberalism in ways that call medicalization into question as an adequate conceptual framework for making sense of the present. According to Nikolas Rose, the overarching term obscures the heterogeneity of biomedical knowledges, an important point for us because we view the women's health movement and women's treatment advocacy as articulating important alternatives to the epistemologies of ignorance that accompany medicine's ability to make us 'the kind of people we are' (Rose, 2009: 700). As Rose notes:

> The term medicalisation obscures the differences between placing something under the sign of public health ... placing something under the authority of doctors to prescribe ... and placing something within the field of molecular psychopharmacology. Nor does medicalisation help as critique, for why should it seem ethically or politically preferable to live one aspect or department of life under one description rather than another? The term medicalisation might be the starting point of an analysis, a sign of the need for an analysis, but it should not be the conclusion of an analysis.
>
> (Rose, 2009: 701–2)

Tracing what women's health movements have meant by 'medicalization' reveals that there have been changes in what Rose calls the 'political economy of subjectification'. Drug-using women may no longer be abjectly vilified in quite the same ways as they were in the 1950s, 1960s, and 1970s, but they are still denied the benefits of biomedicalization and unevenly subjected to criminal prosecutions and the more punitive and controlling forms of medicalization. Adele E. Clarke and Virginia Olesen (1999) argue that increased biomedicalization and an intensified role for technoscience in shaping the social worlds through which healthcare provision occurs have brought about new forms of suffering. They note cooptation of earlier feminist interventions, writing, 'Perhaps the major complication we confront as feminists concerned about women, health, and healing seeking to intervene around the legitimacy of difference is that this domain remains undertheorized and undercriticized while it becomes increasingly overbiomedicalized' (Clarke and Olesen, 1999: 4, 19).

The success of the women's health movement was complicated by a set of paradoxes, dilemmas, and contradictions that simultaneously produced a 'defeminized and dehumanized biomedicalization of women's health' (Clarke and Olesen, 1999: 5). These consequences are clearly set out in Steve Epstein's characterization of the rise to dominance of a group-based 'inclusion-and-difference paradigm' in the late twentieth century US. Epstein credits the feminist and women's health movement with leading a multifarious and disunified social movement composed of a 'heterogeneous and tacit coalition' of actors, including activists, patient advocates, and professional elites who pressured the federal biomedical research apparatus towards reforms of policy and practice that countered dominant tendencies towards standardization in biomedical research and enabled greater inclusion of those marked 'different' (Epstein, 2007: 53–4). Various constituencies representing women; sexual, ethnic, and racial minorities; children; the elderly; and sufferers of various diseases and conditions adopted similar cultural frames in ways that ultimately converged. Epstein credits the feminist movements of the 1970s and 1980s with reconfiguring the terrain of women's health, noting that political and ideological differences nonetheless converged in a 'deep scepticism towards the mainstream medical profession, a critique of many of its characteristic practices ... and a strong emphasis on women's personal autonomy and control over their bodies' (Epstein, 2007: 56).

Women's emphasis on gaining autonomy and control over 'our bodies' and 'ourselves' was in direct tension with assumptions made about women's alcoholism and drug abuse – for alcoholics and drug users were considered to lack restraint and regulation, moderation and self-control. For women this lack was compounded by the gender politics of autonomy and dependency.[4] The movement to politicize women's drug and alcohol treatment ran up against the major binary oppositions structuring gender politics, as well as western biomedical knowledge projects: active/passive; autonomy/dependency; and normal/pathological. Additionally, the field of drug policy is structured by a major opposition between 'criminalization' and 'medicalization', until the relatively recent emergence of 'harm reduction' as a pragmatic third-way position. Women's treatment advocates have typically argued for 'medical' or 'public health' approaches over and against 'criminalization'.

Drug and alcohol treatment advocates have thus had to occupy a position different from feminists on the question of medicalization, due to the stigma and marginalization with which they regularly contend. Some have been drawn to embrace disease models of alcoholism and addiction, arguing that medicalization could have the salutary effect of legitimating these disorders and undoing the far more negative effects of criminalization that have hounded and haunted women addicts and alcoholics. Medicalization was associated with modern scientific enlightenment, enabling them to attack the benighted but venerable notion of addiction as a flaw in moral character (disease concepts of alcoholism and drug addiction, of course, have long, intertwined histories beyond the scope of this book). If drug and alcohol problems achieved recognition as full-fledged and legitimate disease conditions, treatment would be better supported in the social as well as financial sense. For instance, Norma Finkelstein described weekly 'de-programming' sessions at her first job in the field that were designed to 'disabuse us of our past understanding of alcoholism as a symptom of a major mental illness and to learn about the disease of alcoholism'.[5]

The pervasive separation between the drug and alcohol worlds that women's treatment advocates experienced as they entered these worlds led them to see the necessity of bridging the gap and addressing the issues in an integrated fashion prior to many other entrants to the field. Proceeding unevenly in nations pursuing the merging of drug and alcohol treatment (see Bergmark in Klingemann and Hunt, 1998: 298–307), there are almost no data showing integration as highest in treatment systems most open to feminist perspectives. Yet we suspect that this is so, as the women's treatment advocates with whom we spoke often returned to the need for an integrated or 'holistic' approach, an approach which Susanne MacGregor and Elizabeth Ettorre (1987) proposed in the late 1980s. As Vivian Brown's concept of 'levels of burden' reminds us, when women in drug and alcohol treatment are asked to deal in a holistic fashion with complex histories of co-occurring mental health disorders and trauma – including revocation of parental rights and removal of their children – they are put into a treatment situation that disadvantages them relative to men who do not have to face up to so many difficulties at once. When women with relatively few resources are asked to carry the burden of integrating all of these forms of treatment, healthcare becomes burdensome. Feminist programmes that offer holistic approaches – parenting, education for children, and one-stop shopping for healthcare, including HIV tests – ask individual women to take on great burdens in addressing multiple, co-occurring issues. According to Nancy Paull, who directs treatment programmes in the states of Massachusetts and Rhode Island, primary care doctors often fail to enquire into substance abuse issues. As a result her treatment system has migrated towards providing primary healthcare and serving men, women, and children. While SSTAR no longer claims to be an overtly 'feminist' organization, Paull points to the incorporation of feminist principles into its very design. SSTAR, she notes, is structured along feminist lines, although those whom it serves may not know that.

This approach, known as 'gender mainstreaming' in other Anglophone countries, raises the question, 'At what point must a treatment program of "feminist design" declare as among its principles the empowerment of *women*?' Can treatment be a 'feminist technology' in the sense that Layne, Vostral, and Boyer (2010: 3) argue for – a set of technological 'tools' plus the 'knowledge that enhance[s] women's ability to develop, expand, and express their capacities'. It is clear that sometimes technologies that benefit women also benefit men; neither the gender of the designers nor the users is the definitive marker of a 'feminist technology' (Layne, Vostral, and Boyer, 2010: 23). But it may be more likely that women will design feminist technologies if the life experiences of other women inform their design. Another concern is the treatment workforce and whether or not those who work within it can be thought of as a 'feminist' force or as a force for the advocacy of drug-using women, given the constraints of federal and state funding. There it clearly depends on the history and principles of the treatment modality. The turn to trauma, then, is 'gendered' in problematic as well as promising ways, making women's problems seem much more complex, interconnected, and thus more intractable than men's. The recent 'medicalization' and even 'biomedicalization' of the concept of 'trauma' has added an additional layer to this complexity in the US.

Making feminist sense of the turn to trauma

While the relational model worked up by Finkelstein and others was clearly meaningful for making sense of connections between women's roles and responsibilities in biosocial reproduction and their drinking or drug use, one of its primary contributions was its ability to connect trauma, alcoholism, and addiction: 'Anyone who was doing women's treatment saw the connection. Sometimes women talked about violence and trauma more freely than they talked about being mother's in women's groups in the Seventies. I think it was something that women's programs who were really doing feminist work understood the connection. Women who were doing the work of listening to these women in groups were hearing this – it wasn't like women didn't talk about these issues. It became so central to work in addictions because there was a growing awareness. People began to write about it. There was a little research here and there. People began to develop treatment curricula – like Lisa Najavits who wrote "Seeking Safety", or Maxine Harris and TREM [Trauma Recovery and Empowerment Model]'.[6] Such curricula, or 'manualized protocols', had become central commodities within the response to women's drug and alcohol issues towards the end of the twentieth century.

We argue that the discourse of safety, trauma, and recovery has provided a 'respectable' way to talk about women's use of licit and illicit drugs. Speaking about these as *health issues* having *health consequences* opened up a way for feminist advocates to legitimate women's experiences of violence, as well as their turn to 'self-medication'. At the federal level, emphasis on trauma and violence emerged within the mental health field, and particularly at SAMHSA, during the 1990s, culminating in the Women, Co-occurring Disorders, and Violence Study (WCDVS), which was jointly funded in 1998 by the CSAT, CSAP, and CMHS. 'I think that was the fruition of many years of Susan Salasin's work at the Center for Mental Health Services', said Finkelstein, who chaired the WCDVS steering committee for the first two years. 'This national effort provided a whole other vehicle for those of us involved to spend another 5 or 6 years meeting four times a year. We formed a learning community and a consumer group. It was a very unique opportunity, very painful for a few years … because we were bringing together all kinds of people. This was a coalition from 14 different sites, as well as a coordinating centre and consultants and the funding agencies. Consumers were heavily involved. We called them CSRs – Consumer Survivor Recovering People – because everybody wanted the language from all three communities. It was really like the women's centre discussions of many years ago. It was people from the mental health community, people from the violence community, people from the substance use community'. The value of the effort, according to Finkelstein, was the redefinition of trauma as central to the formation of mental health and substance use disorders. This was contested ground for both the substance abuse and mental health communities. Finkelstein explained, 'There were still people from the substance abuse community who felt that if you said that trauma was central, it was as if addiction didn't matter …. There were a lot of fights, there were a lot of tears. I felt like I was back in the Sixties, or the Seventies'.

Although her sense was one of having come full circle in building a national attention to the core notion of trauma, Finkelstein could well have been in conversation with feminist sociologists Clarke and Olesen, who argue that 'ideas that were firmly held in the first moment of the women's health movement have given way to much more differentiated conceptualizations', as new and ever-partial knowledges displaced older frameworks (1999: 356). The challenge around which Clarke and Olesen's volume *Revisioning Women, Health, and Healing* (1999) was configured was one of tracing *where* 'knowledges about women, health, and healing are produced and utilized or not utilized' (356). Our purpose in re-tracing social movements involved in getting women's alcoholisms and addictions on the research and treatment agenda in the US and the UK has been to show how specific knowledges were produced in response to the 'epistemologies of ignorance', and how these moved from local to extra-local contexts and were reconfigured in the process as 'contending mentalities' in dynamic relation to the 'governing mentalities'. Adopting the concept of trauma as a way to talk about childhood sexual abuse, rape, domestic or family violence, and other forms of violence against women enabled feminists to define violence as a causal factor in women's drug and alcohol abuse. This in turn helped legitimate treatment by transforming the 'undeserving' into worthy subjects for public aid and state support.

The body politics of the health-oriented feminist social movement of the 1970s touched on myriad forms of feminized abjection, creating conditions of possibility for today's reconsideration of gender as 'trauma'. The creation of what would be in 2010 termed a 'trauma-informed treatment infrastructure' (Amaro et al., 2007) in the US was the culmination of efforts dating back to the 1970s to bring trauma, domestic violence or intimate partner violence, and battering not only to the attention of law enforcement authorities, but also make it a matter of women's health. The feminist effort ran parallel to other social movement efforts to get trauma on the agenda, namely those of Vietnam veterans and antiwar psychiatrists.[7] These efforts led to the first-time inclusion of PTSD in the *Diagnostic and Statistical Manual-III* (1980), which authoritatively defines diagnostic criteria for psychiatric disorders. The DSM-III is widely regarded to have revolutionized the mental health field, setting psychiatry on a scientific footing.[8]

Ironically, the feminist therapists with whom Jeanne Marecek and her students spoke adopted 'trauma talk' as a form of resistance to the diagnostic categories of conventional psychiatry, and to the so-called medical model (1999). While 'trauma talk' recapitulates the hegemonic register of psychopathology, an idiom that its adopters clearly meant to displace, 'trauma talk' enabled feminists to construct women patient/clients as *injured, not sick* and as *normal, not abnormal*. Thus the concept of trauma was used to oppose the very diagnostic system to which the trauma diagnosis (PTSD) was itself central. For some feminist therapists, trauma talk has subsumed all competing frameworks (Marecek, 1999: 170). What then is the cultural work accomplished by trauma talk, and why did feminist therapists find the trauma framework appealing? 'For many, trauma talk honors women's reality' (Marecek, 1999: 178). By attributing reality to traumatic events, the concept provided unity to a movement perceived to have lost the grounding once provided by the central concept of 'patriarchy'. While we see 'patriarchy' more as a disunifying concept than as a central narrative, we also see a remarkable uptake of 'trauma' in the US by a variety of enunciative communities for whom it provides both a causal narrative and a diagnostic effect (Fortun, 2001). Most of all, trauma does not fix blame but instead concentrates on the everyday experiences and the condition of the person suffering the effects of being traumatized. What to call this person has been contested, as 'victims', 'survivors', 'patients', 'clients', and 'consumers' each have differing connotations in the mental health arena.

In US popular culture, therapeutic enterprises, and in the emergence of the academic enterprise of 'trauma studies' or 'traumatology', the concept flourishes beyond the academic and scientific enterprises growing up around it.[9] Embedded in that concept are exceedingly nonspecific theories of causation (as no one has identified a mechanism through which trauma 'causes' drug and alcohol abuse). Yet 'trauma' is considered by many to be responsible for addiction. For instance, Susan Gordon Lydon's memoir of her heroin addiction, *Take the Long Way Home: Memoirs of a Survivor* (1993) 'demonstrates that Lydon's conceptualization of her addiction as a response to trauma reflects three key feminist contributions to trauma theory: the expansion of the conventional concept of trauma to include women's everyday and ongoing experiences; out of this expansion, the development of the concept of 'insidious trauma'; and the depathologization of adaptive, 'normal responses' to trauma' (Muzak, 2009). The cultural work performed by the concept of trauma is to transform conditions that seem 'pathological' into reasonable responses that fall within the range of normal adaptation. No longer are women who develop drug and alcohol problems 'victims of society' or subject to a gendered social order – they are experiencing trauma and translating their experiences into symptoms that can be treated through the modalities characterized earlier in this book.

'Where feminisms meet the world':[10] Treatment advocacy and feminist policy design

While it has seemed to us in writing this book that feminism is both more alive and more institutionalized in the US than it is in the UK, it was instructive to explore the nature of that aliveness. For feminism is alive in the US in different forms than were ever envisioned in the heady days of the 1970s when it seemed that the new knowledges being produced in the women's movement could and would transform social policy, clinical practice, and social relations. Yet women's drug and alcohol treatment did not become simply one among many 'defeminized and dehumanized biomedicalizations of women's health' (Clarke and Olesen, 1999: 5). The complicated successes of the women's health movement are beset by paradoxical cooptations, commodifications, and dilemmas borne of its precarious institutionalization in the US and the UK.

Writing ourselves – as feminist scholars who have long studied drug-using women and attempted to 'revision' women and drug use – into the study of health-oriented social movements, we have tried to indicate that the women's health movement grew from multiple roots while simultaneously conveying the generative dynamics of that movement (Morgen, 2002: 11). Today no one would quarrel with the idea that the women's health movements in the US or the UK attained the status of social movements, but may take issue with our claim that the attempt to gain gender-specific drug and alcohol treatment that actually recognizes women's real needs – based on their political and economic positions and social locations – can be seen as a social movement and not as an instance of the professionalization of social work or healthcare. It is simply that until now, this social movement has lacked its history, lacked the capacity to create and sustain narratives that fuse past, present, and future. For there to be a narrative, there must be a historical trajectory such as what we have presented in this book.

This conclusion places our foregoing chapters within the context of national social movements oriented towards health and wellness for a set of populations that have been considered socially problematic since the nineteenth century. As a history of the present, this book shows how the struggle for women's drug treatment was simultaneously the struggle of feminists trying to get women's needs taken seriously, making good cases that women needed 'special' or 'differential' treatment due to their socially-designated responsibilities for biosocial reproduction and their 'complex' social needs, and turning to regional, state, and national governments for the necessary resources. They argued that treatment for women had to take women's specific and differential needs into account, rather than arguing on the universalistic grounds of fairness or women's equality with men, in ways that would have recapitulated the 'male standard' of which they were so critical. They had to blaze what David J. Hess (2007) has called 'alternative pathways' in order to offer treatment as a technological product and to modify dominant treatment modalities such as the so-called therapeutic community. Yet, at the same time as they engaged in a process of creative reconstruction of dominant treatment modalities, particularly those in the US had to make their efforts sustainable within the structures of health and human services of the state and federal governments or, they learnt from bitter experiences such as those of the Women's Action Alliance in New York State, their efforts would wither on the vine if they could not create a new status quo (Meyerson and Scully, 1995).

Since the 1990s in the US, criticisms around the cooptation of the women's health movement have lessened in the face of the overwhelming commodification of healthcare, which rests upon a potent combination of privatization within the healthcare and insurance industries, as well as widespread access to pharmaceuticals. There is less concern with 'radical feminism' or separatism than there once was; gender awareness is still expanding and even becoming respectable in the US federal research apparatus; yet in the 1980s and 1990s a shift towards 'the family' in both the US and UK meant the inclusion of men and children in women's treatment, an acknowledgement of the existence of non-normative or 'multicultural' family models, and the need for treatment practices that are cognizant of cultural differences between groups. While this emphasis on 'the family' often obscures or dilutes the visibility of women's needs, and may hamper women's claims upon the state, it also became clear to us that the 'tempered radicals' (Meyerson and Scully, 1995) about whom we write used 'the family' to increase women's access to care, including healthcare, and as a way to expand what counts as treatment. There has also been statutory pressure to include men, as the need to prove that care is not ideologically 'feminist' can make funding situations unstable because it marks programmes as needing to prove that they are inclusive. An irony of inclusivity is that programmes sometimes pay a toll in terms of gender specificity in terms of their capacity to address women's needs and in terms of their explicit commitment to feminist discourse on equality. By widening what is meant by 'gender,' and making of 'gender' a mainstream term inclusive of masculinity as well as femininity, it seems that 'gender' has become a 'respectable' way to talk about women. As Angela McRobbie argued in her critique of the 'gender mainstreaming' position espoused by Sylvia Walby and others, 'gender' has become a way of claiming a position of respectability and academic legitimacy. Has the 'tempering' gone too far?

We argue that how drug-using women are treated very much depends on the macro-structural drug policy environment. Within the 'degenerative' policy-making context of drug policy, women are not only not seen as important, rights-bearing policy 'target populations', but are dehumanized when represented as 'abusing themselves' or 'poisoning' others through their use of alcohol and drugs. As 'embodied deviants', any problems they have are seen as self-inflicted, leading to an unstable institutionalization of programmatic remedies that are always in danger of being taken away. This has led to an unsustainable treatment policy in both nations – with relatively few exceptions, the mix of voluntary organizations such as DAWN in the UK, or state or federally-funded organizations in the US cannot sustain themselves beyond initial funding periods. Thus enormous resources are put into 'reinventing the wheel' through grant writing, fundraising, and short-term crisis management – rather than into creating sustainable programmes that can weather the next fiscal crisis of the state or the reduced public and political interest that follows declining media visibility until the next 'drug panic'. Yet at the same time, as long as women are taken to be 'good enough' mothers and grandmothers who play their assigned roles in social reproduction, their needs are 'depoliticized' and considered unimportant in terms of social support. Those seen as 'addicted' or 'abusing' or sometimes even just 'using' alcohol and or drugs are deemed unworthy of public support and thus begrudged access even to short-term and typically under-funded programmes.

Caught between the horns of this dilemma, we consider, again with McRobbie, how feminists have worked to have their ideas taken into account to the point where the practices they advocate are institutionalized – the point at which 'contending mentalities' become 'governing mentalities'. Over time different ideas about gender and women's needs have been incorporated in different ways in the political cultures of the US and the UK. 'Gender aware' and 'gender sensitive' forms of governmentality have evolved in both countries. Under the names of gender-specific, gender-responsive, or gender-informed treatment, this incorporation sometimes works through the displacement of gender, as it has in the US, where trauma can be seen as having displaced gender just as gender is sometimes mistakenly viewed as displacing women. 'Harm' may possibly be an even weaker way to name 'gender' than 'trauma'. As movement actors in the US and the UK moved directly into government positions, they gained professional credentials as policy makers, mental health workers, and social workers who helped turn the ship of state towards women's issues. While they have achieved some success, some see it as having come at a price. And in the UK, the introduction of the coalition's 'Big Society' will surely signal more reliance on women to do 'the government's work' without any support or funding to build cultural capacity or to continue supporting gender equality.

The substitution of 'trauma' for gender – such that women's treatment advocates now speak of a 'trauma informed treatment infrastructure' in the United States – presents both problems and opportunities. As 'talking about oppression' became 'talking about trauma', and 'trauma' was understood as a core issue for drug and alcohol-using women, trauma was also in the process of being medicalized in the psychiatric arena. While women's treatment advocates are quite clear that in using the term 'trauma', they are speaking to broader issues than the narrow issue of the psychiatric diagnosis of PTSD, the slippage is easily made. Advocates gesture towards matters of structural violence, as well as intimate partner violence, childhood sexual abuse, and other forms of psychological and sexual trauma. However, there is a great gap between 'best practices' supposed to enable programmes to address such broader issues, and the situation that most women face as they navigate social service agencies towards finding effective and accessible drug and alcohol treatment. This is, we argue, more than the usual gap between ideal-typical and actually existing treatment due to a unique confluence of social differences – including race, ethnicity, class, sexuality, ability/disability, and gender – that structure drug policy and have implications for how treatment is accessed.

Feminist treatment advocacy and feminist policy design are both useful for thinking not only about past drug policies and the vicissitudes of state support for a variety of treatment modalities, but also for the future. We argue that there simply has to be longer-term thinking about how best to support women in drug and alcohol treatment, and how to deliver this form of healthcare so that is both more effective and more efficient in reaching those who need it. The cyclic, drug crisis-driven reinventions of the wheel are rarely if ever sustainable, especially where a sociocultural infrastructure lacks social acceptance, legitimacy, or credibility – and therefore sustainability. We end with a contradiction that has haunted us throughout the research and writing of this book. In arguing for a 'gendered' treatment infrastructure, we run the risk that such a system will again be stigmatized and marginalized as it has been wherever women's drug and alcohol treatment programmes have been started up in the past. In insisting that gender-specific treatment be made available as part of the healthcare options open to all women, regardless of social status and cultural difference, we run the risk of falling into the trap of the 'special population'. How gender-specific do treatment programmes need to be in order to appeal to women? Does gender specificity translate into more accessible treatment? More attractive options for women? More effective outcomes? More sustainable programmes? We argue that if drug use is gendered in its biosocial effects and consequences, it must be gendered in its treatment. We argue that even in this most 'neurochemical' era, the sense of self is gendered and so, too, are the social rights and responsibilities perceived to be part and parcel of personhood. The 'rights of personhood', in other words, are gendered and gender defines the rights of pregnant persons as well. Denying this makes little sense; instead, we insist upon gender as an epistemology from which to build new knowledges and forms of political recognition.

What does the feminist mantra 'Our bodies, ourselves' now look like under the combined weight of advanced or 'neo' liberalism, which insists on personal responsibility for *your* body and *your* brain, the supplantation of addiction as a 'social problem' by the technoscientific account of it as a 'brain disorder', and new cultural constructs of 'neurochemical selves'? It is important to understand the non-essentialist and non-deterministic characteristics of new constructs of 'the brain' as an epistemic actor. We argue that the old feminist critique of biogenetic determinism does not quite fit these emerging accounts of the ever-changing brain, accounts which assume the plasticity of the brain and its ongoing adaptations not only to neurochemistry but to social and cultural – even political and economic – circumstances. In a phrase we owe to conversation with Deborah Steinberg, the claim here is that 'you make your essence over' constantly, in and through social and symbolic interactions. This brain is a different brain from the brain that was once the subject of phrenology, and it is a mistake to read current neuro-imaging practices as simply reiterating that history. Yet at the same time, history sticks to the 'embodied deviants' who are female addicts and alcoholics, long represented as threats to civilization itself, and the cultural narratives and social histories within which they are embedded are unlikely to evaporate without a trace in the face of neuro-imagery.

Finally, we need to think in terms of an 'embodied' rather than a 'disembodied' brain. While we are the midst of an epistemic shift towards an abstraction or abjection of brain from body, assisted mightily by neuro-imaging technologies, it is also the case that the brain leads back to the body. For the brain is housed in a body – there are so far no bodiless brains, and body and brain are isomorphically attached to the person as a social and political category. The argument put forth by Rose is that 'we are becoming neurochemical selves' responded primarily to licit pharmaceutical drugs prescribed and used for the purposes of self-modification. Considering Rose's argument in light of illicit drugs requires some inflection. We believe that it has become important to understand the move from the body as the site of deviance to the brain as the site of deviance, and to begin to connect claims made about the neurochemistry of the brain to our argument about biosocial reproduction.

We have used the literature on 'reproductive loss' and addicts as the 'embodiment of risk' to understand what the new reformulations of alcoholism and addiction as 'brain diseases' betoken for women, and particularly for pregnant women. In a culture in which, in the hierarchy of organs, our brains now take precedence over our hearts and our wombs, the implications must be considered. The legitimation of addiction as a 'brain disease' has been held out by neuroscientists who study addiction as a way to de-stigmatize addiction. There has long been an uneasy relationship between addiction, alcoholism, and mental disorders more typically thought of as 'brain disorders.' In the early twentieth century, as documented by historians of science, addiction was a problem 'owned' by psychoanalysis; there was much consideration of the 'psychopathologies', 'personality configurations' or 'character' flaws that supposedly 'predisposed' some individuals to addictive states. 'Psychopathological' explanations persisted in addiction psychiatry, which still 'owns' a significant share of the addiction problem in the US, but remains particularly prominent in the UK. Psychiatric explanations continue to enjoy a significant share of the 'sociocultural infrastructure of legitimation' (Clarke et al., 2010) through which addictive disorders are understood and treated in both countries. In recent years this explanatory infrastructure has been extended to a variety of disorders, including obesity and other 'appetitive' disorders. For instance, while 'trauma' is understood as an event that occurs in the context of the social world, PTSD is understood as a diagnosis that implies a response to trauma so problematic that it becomes a 'brain disease'. As women are increasingly understood to be multiply problematic psychiatric subjects – female substance abusers are typically diagnosed with 'co-occurring' disorders or 'co-morbidities' at rates exceeding 70 per cent – it will become important to see how feminist treatment advocates respond to the construct of addiction and alcoholism as 'brain disorders'.

We suspect, given the history of social challenges faced by addicted and alcoholic women and their advocates, that 'new brain disorders' exhibited by newly problematic 'neurochemical selves' may well meet new forms of stigma and deviance related to women's failure to discharge their 'personal responsibilities' as moral persons inhabiting a neurochemical age. We remind our readers that history is a sticky business, for today's new sciences transmute into tomorrow's 'epistemologies of ignorance'. However, our analysis opens up alternative pathways. Feminist treatment advocates created new forms of practical knowledge and expertise based on insights generated from listening closely to the populations they sought to serve. The new neurosciences are essentially being asked to 'translate' their findings into clinical applications. Taking a page from the colonial history of Western scholarship and science, feminist philosopher Sandra Harding (2008: 153) argues that research disciplines have long 'serviced the dominant groups through providing the conceptual categories and preferred causal relations between them through which public policy has functioned. They have provided the "conceptual practices of power"' (citing Smith, 1990). However, Harding then goes on to argue that 'if that service to power is to cease', such sciences will have to recognize their complicity with the political projects of 'over-advantaged' groups to the exclusion of marginalized groups. The politics of neuroscience and the biomedicalization of women's health are entangled with the politics that keep some women poor and enmeshed in circumstances where they and their children have little choice but to participate in the drug economies that overwhelm their cultural geographies. Where is the neuroscience of poverty? Of the alterations of brain structure and function and the behavioural changes attributable to chronic exposure to boredom, misery, and violence? Of the 'brain diseases' caused by the innumerable day-to-day insults of institutional racism, homophobia and sexism? Why do we not study the brains of those who seek to dominate others, who further blame those who have borne the brunt of social exclusion for so long, who have a proclivity to translate difference into inequality, or chronic tendencies to punish, oppress, or prosecute? Let us hope the answers to these questions will be informed by a deep awareness of gender as a valued epistemology from which new knowledges and expressions of political praxis are shaped and made possible.

Notes

Introduction: Making Gender Matter: Drug-Using Women, Embodiment, and the Epistemologies of Ignorance

1. N. Tuana (2006) in 'The Speculum of Ignorance: The Women's Health Movement and Epistemologies of Ignorance' argues that social movements have often resisted 'epistemologies of ignorance' and that this tactic was a 'key strategic technology of the women's health movement'. Tuana urges scholars studying knowledge production practices, as we are in this book, to 'account for *not* knowing, that is, for our *lack* of knowledge about a phenomena [*sic*] or, in some cases, an account of the practices that resulted in a group *unlearning* what was once a realm of knowledge'.
2. This term first appeared in the editorial introduction to *Deviant Bodies*, edited by Jacqueline Urla and Jennifer Terry (1995), and was defined as 'the historically and culturally specific belief that deviant social behaviour (however that is defined) manifests itself in the materiality of the body, as a cause or an effect, or perhaps as merely a suggestive trace' (2).
3. D. Weinberg (2002), 'On the Embodiment of Addiction', *Body and Society*, 8, 4: 1–19.
4. Throughout we use 'postclassical paradigm' and 'epistemological paradigm' or 'mode of knowledge' interchangeably to emphasize the *epistemology of embodiment* on which knowledges of the gendered body are based.
5. Riska (2010) lays these out in 'Gender and Medicalisation Theories', in A. E. Clarke, L. Mamo, J. R. Fosket, J. R. Fishman, and J. K. Shim (eds), *Biomedicalization: Technoscience, Health, and Illness in the U.S.* Durham, NC: Duke University Press.
6. The emphasis on drug addiction changing brain structure and function in permanent and irreversible ways (Leshner, 1997) has been superseded by dominant notions of neuroplasticity and adaptation (Malabou, 2008). What effect these will have on the drug field remains to be seen, as we are aware of few scholars who take these ideas up outside the neurosciences.
7. For an example of the divergence between two movements that share mutual interests, see L. M. Paltrow (2001), 'The War on Drugs and the War on Abortion: Some Initial Thoughts on Their Connections, Intersections, and the Effects', *Southern University Law Review*, 28, 201.
8. See http://www.avaproject.org.uk/our-projects/stella-project.aspx (accessed 7 October 2010) (emphasis ours).
9. See 'Report of National Advocates for Pregnant Women, Submission to the United Nations Universal Periodic Review, Ninth Session of the Working Group, Human Rights Council', April 2010 at http://advocatesforpregnantwomen.org/NAPW_UPRSubmissionUSA.pdf (accessed 1 August 2010). The NAPW report documents human rights abuses to pregnant women in the US, stating that 'pregnancy can make women the target of criminal investigation, incarceration, counterproductive civil child welfare interventions, and forced

medical procedures in the United States. At the same time, access to services that ensure dignity and informed medical decision-making are being limited arbitrarily' (1).

10. For instance, see ACMD (2007b) *Drug Facilitated Sexual Assault.*
11. The conceptual underpinnings of epigenetics concern gene-environment interactions. Today the field often conflates epidemiology and genetics – and has been offered as a potential harbinger of a new era of attention to 'social' or environmental factors in genetic research.
12. See also for example, Jellinek (1960); Vaillant (1973); Edwards et al. (1976); and Plant (1981).
13. Interview conducted by E. Ettorre with C. Fazey, 15 November 2009.
14. In the US, medical care for pregnant women is referred to as 'prenatal care', whereas in Britain it is called 'antenatal care'.
15. Interview conducted by N. Campbell with B. G. Reed, 16 January 2008.
16. Interview conducted by N. Campbell with B. G. Reed, 16 January 2008.
17. Although the terms 'expressive' and 'instrumental' are often attributed to Talcott Parson, they are from the work of Morris Zelditch (1955) that appeared in a co-edited book of which Talcott Parsons was an editor. For Parsons' own work on the family, see T. Parsons (1942), 'Age and Sex in the Social Structure of the United States', *American Sociological Review*, 7, 5: 604–16; T. Parsons (1959), 'The Social Structure of the Family', in R. Ashen (ed.), *The Family: Its Functions and Destiny*, New York: Harper and Row.
18. Interview conducted by Elizabeth Ettorre with Betsy Thom, 13 November 2009.
19. TRANX was the National Tranquilliser Advisory Council, which was funded for two years by the Department of Health in December 1983. It was founded by the co-ordinator, Joan Jerome, who had been a benzodiazepine user for 17 years (see Ettorre 1986e).
20. Concerns about suicidality and increased 'suicidal ideation' of both adults and children on antidepressants have mitigated the triumphalism in both the US and the UK.
21. See Spivak's 1993 interview with Sara Danius and Stefan Jonsson in *Boundary* 2, 20.2, 24–50.
22. In the UK, the national agencies are the Department of Health, the Department for Work and Pensions, and the Department of Communities and Local Government. The NTA is a special health authority within the National Health Service, established by the British Government in 2001 to improve availability, capacity and effectiveness of treatment for drug misuse in England. As part of the NTA, the National Drug Treatment Monitoring System (NDTMS) collects, collates, and analyses information from and for those involved in the drug treatment sector. The NDTMS is a development of the Regional Drug Misuse Databases, which have been in place since the late 1980s (see: http://www.nta.nhs.uk/ndtms.aspx (accessed 7 October 2010). In the US, the federal Department of Health and Human Services houses SAMHSA, which contains the Center for Substance Abuse Prevention and the Center for Substance Abuse Treatment. Research is located in the National Institute on Drug Abuse, an institute within the National Institutes of Health, which also contains the National Institute on Alcohol Abuse and Alcoholism. State agencies, which combine drug and alcohol

prevention and treatment services, have oversight of treatment provision and service delivery, which is administered at the local county level in the US as well as through private healthcare providers. Treatment services vary state to state, so women's access to treatment depends largely upon in which state they reside.

23. However, SAMHSA and some of the state agencies, such as California and Massachusetts, have been friendly to women's movement actors and thus women's treatment guidelines in the US have adopted an approach consonant with the 'relational' aspects of the postclassical epistemology (see Treatment Improvement Protocol 51, which we analyse later).

1 Getting Gender on the Agenda: A History of Pioneers in Drug Treatment for Women in the United States and the United Kingdom

1. The New York City Welfare Council indicated a 700 per cent increase in 1950 over 1946, although the total number of teenagers involved remained unknown. No one knew how many addicts there were. The figures came from the Research Center for Human Relations, New York University, then conducting the classic study published as *The Road to H* (New York: Basic Books, 1964).
2. L. Bender (1961). 'State Care of Emotionally and Socially Disturbed Adolescents', in E. M. Thornton (ed.). *Planning and Action for Mental Health*. London: World Federation for Mental Health. 200–15; and 'Drug Addiction in Adolescence', *Comprehensive Psychiatry*, 4, 3 (1963): 181–94. The first peak arose in the wake of the Harrison Act from 1918–19.
3. The institution at Bedford Hills was named the Westfield State Farm from 1932 to 1970, when it was changed to the Bedford Hills Correctional Facility. It is now a maximum security facility for approximately 800 women over age 16. The original New York state reformatory for women was legislated in 1892, and operated by the State Board of Charities once it opened in 1901. One year after the name was changed to Westfield, a separate prison section was opened – thus there was both a prison and a reformatory operating on the site. The facility was also referred to as 'Hudson'.
4. Segregation of specific populations was not a new idea at the Westfield State Farm, which had operated a Division for Mentally Defective Delinquent Women on the site of the former Rockefeller Laboratory of Social Hygiene after news of ungovernable inmates became a public scandal between 1915 and 1919. From 1920 to 1932 women found to be of 'low intelligence' were transferred to the DMDDW. After 1932 the name of the institution was changed to the Bedford Hills Correctional Facility. See http://www.archives.nysed.gov/a/research/res_topics_legal_corrections_inst_bedford.shtml (accessed 10 April 2011).
5. Correspondence from J. Lowry to J. V. Bennett, 27 January 1955.
6. Memo to US Marshals from J. V. Bennett, 9 April 1957; cf. 26 June 1956. All correspondence quoted in this section from the National Archives and Records Administration in College Park, Maryland, RG 129, Box 25, 'Lewisburg to Lexington, Bureau of Prisons'.

7. Connecticut had one of the earliest state-funded public inebriate hospitals in the country, founded on the notion that inebriety was a disease appropriately treated through medical means (see S. W. Tracy (2005). *Alcoholism in America: From Reconstruction to Prohibition*. Baltimore, MD, Johns Hopkins University Press. 123–9).
8. Mann was one of the most powerful women within Alcoholics Anonymous, working to found NIAAA in 1970. Her book was an important touchstone for those seeking to treat alcoholics.
9. On Blume's role in the fight for labels warning consumers of alcoholic beverages of their dangers during pregnancy, see J. Golden (2005). *Message in a Bottle: The Making of Fetal Alcohol Syndrome*. Cambridge, MA: Harvard University Press, 88–9.
10. The 1957 article was based on study of 46 alcoholic women and 55 alcoholic men in Connecticut outpatient clinics and an additional 37 alcoholic women committed to State Farm. Lisansky's second article (1958) on the topic was 'The Woman Alcoholic', *Annals of the American Academy of Political and Social Science*, 315: 73–81.
11. Correspondence from Gomberg to Waxman, 27 April 1981b. All quotations in this paragraph are from this letter, which can be found in the Edith Gomberg Papers, Bentley Library, University of Michigan, Box 3, Presentations, US House of Representatives.
12. Testimony, 11 March 1981: 3. All quotations in this paragraph are from Gomberg's testimony before this subcommittee, a copy of which can be found in the Edith Gomberg Papers, Bentley Library, University of Michigan, Box 3, Presentations, US House of Representatives.
13. Testimony, 27 July 1981: 2. Edith Gomberg Papers, Bentley Library, University of Michigan, Box 3, Presentations, US Senate.
14. Testimony, 27 July 1981: 3. Edith Gomberg Papers, Bentley Library, University of Michigan, Box 3, Presentations, US Senate.
15. Testimony, 27 July 1981: 5. Edith Gomberg Papers, Bentley Library, University of Michigan, Box 3, Presentations, US Senate.
16. Edith Gomberg Papers, Bentley Library, University of Michigan, Box 4, Folder 3, Presentations, Women and Alcoholism, Outlines and Notes.
17. According to the 2002 General Household Survey, women had an average of six General Practitioner (GP) consultations per year whereas men had four. Also, over the years since 1971, there is consistently a higher percentages of females than males consulting an NHS GP in the 14 days prior to interview for the survey. See http://www.statistics.gov.uk/cci/nugget.asp?id=827(accessed 17 October 2010).
18. See http://www.nta.nhs.uk/about/default.aspx. (accessed 17 October 2010).
19. *Spare Rib* was a collective magazine of the Second Wave women's movement in the UK. The first issue was published in June 1972.
20. Interview by E. Ettorre with D. Black on 2 November 2009.
21. Interview by E. Ettorre with D. Black on 2 November 2009.
22. Interview by E. Ettorre with D. Black on 2 November 2009.
23. Interview by E. Ettorre with D. Black on 2 November 2009.
24. Hazelden's women's programmes were updated in the 1970s and 1980s with inclusion of services for mental health disorders, trauma, and eating

disorders, as well as the opening of the Women and Children Recovery Community in New Brighton, Minnesota in 1997 and the 2006 opening of a Women's Recovery Center on the main Hazelden campus, which consists of two 22-bed primary treatment units.

2 Raising Consciousness or Controlling Women? Women's Drug and Alcohol Treatment Re-emerges

1. In the UK, the ideology of the post World War II patriarchal family emphasized women's central role in the socialisation of 'normal' children. John Bowlby's influential theories stressed the importance of the mother/child dyad and the significance of a woman's place in the home/domestic sphere (Bowlby, 1951; Smart, 1981). Early in the twentieth century, experts in the Society for the Study of Inebriety were talking about 'ante-natal pathology' (Shaw, 1903).
2. Interview conducted by N. Campbell and J. Spillane with L. P. Finnegan on 19 June 2005.
3. Interview conducted by N. Campbell and J. Spillane with L. P. Finnegan on 19 June 2005.
4. Interview conducted by N. Campbell and J. Spillane with L. P. Finnegan on 19 June 2005.
5. Interview conducted by E. Ettorre with A. Dixon on 22 October 2009.
6. Compare the differences between this emphasis on life skills, and the relational emphasis of later programmes encapsulated in the Nurturing Program, a curriculum designed to teach women in recovery to nurture themselves and others (see Chapter 4).
7. Interview by N. Campbell with B. G. Reed on 16 January 2008.
8. From the WDR Newsletter, No. 6, May 1979, p. 2.
9. According to Alice Echols, proponents of consciousness-raising (CR) distinguished it from psychotherapy, arguing the goal of CR was to 'analyze male oppression in order to dismantle it, while the purpose of therapy was to carve out personal solutions to women's oppression' (1989: 87).
10. In 1988 WHIC and WRRIC merged to form the Women's Health and Reproductive Rights Information Centre. In 1992 the name was shortened to Women's Health. See http://www.netdoctor.co.uk/pregnancyandfamily/support_groups/006274.htm accessed 8 October 2010.
11. See J. Herman, 'History of the Somerville Women's Health Project', Gene Bishop Papers, Schlesinger Collection, Radcliffe Institute, Harvard University, 90-M52, Folder 1.
12. Vaillant had been on staff at the US Public Health Service Narcotic Farm in Lexington, Kentucky, which had an active women's detox and treatment unit from 1941 to 1974. See Vaillant (1995). *The Natural History of Alcoholism Revisited*, arguing that alcoholism is both a social and medical condition.
13. Interview conducted by N. Campbell with N. Finkelstein on 16 September 2009.
14. Interview conducted by N. Campbell with N. Finkelstein on 16 September 2009.
15. Interview conducted by N. Campbell with N. Finkelstein on 16 September 2009.

16. Within British radical feminism, separatism in the early days (i.e. the first National Women's Liberation Conference in 1972) was envisaged as a strategic necessity rather than a political goal. It was not anti-man but pro-woman. Later expressions of radical feminism were more separatist than the earlier days of the movement. A group of British radical feminists spearheaded separatism when in 1977 Sheila Jeffreys translated the political theory of radical feminism into a revolutionary feminist strategy. Women must 'not collaborate at all with the enemy' (i.e. men) and identify as revolutionary feminists. (See Coote and Campbell, 1982: 21–2).
17. The Greater London Council was the top-tier local government administrative body for Greater London from 1965 to 1986. It replaced the earlier London County Council, which had covered a much smaller area. It had a number of sub-committees. The Women's Committee was set up in 1982 under Ken Livingston's administration.
18. Elizabeth Ettorre was on the DAWN Management Committee and was elected Chair very early on.
19. Interview conducted by E. Ettorre with D. Black on 2 November 2009.
20. See also Mold and Berridge (2010: 83–100) for a recent historical interpretation of the CFI. Their approach is based on the idea that 'modernist' rehabilitation is a practice of moulding subjects to conform with dominant social norms.
21. Interview conducted by E. Ettorre with D. Black on 2 November 2009.
22. Interview conducted by E. Ettorre with D. Black on 2 November 2009.
23. Interview conducted by E. Ettorre with D. Black on 2 November 2009.

3 Undue Burdens: The Emergence of Feminist Treatment Advocacy in a Masculinist System

1. NARA was a liberalization of drug laws that began with the Kennedy administration's Commission on Narcotic and Drug Abuse, which in 1963 recommended a federal civil commitment programme akin to those of California and New York. Initially this was to fund supervised aftercare for those discharged from federal hospitals, and to enable the establishment of state residential treatment systems. The Kennedy administration was also responsible for a similar shift towards a decentralized mental health care system with the landmark Community Mental Health Centers Act or CMHCA (1965). Musto (1975) points to similar implementation challenges of the CMHCA due to heightened expectations and a dearth of professionals trained in 'community psychiatry' to work outside the state hospital system. Uneven implementation was the result of NARA, which allowed three different types of civil commitment. Some jurisdictions simply found NARA too complex to implement, while others relied heavily on it starting in 1967. For the five years before NARA fell into disuse in the face of scaled-up state and local treatment, the programme admitted more than 10,000 patients. Administration was the responsibility of the NIMH, under the direction of psychiatrist Stanly F. Yolles, who heralded NARA with these words, 'Now for the first time, the emphasis is placed on treating addicts in their home communities'. The administrator responsible for field offices in Chicago,

New York, Los Angeles, and later Philadelphia and Atlanta, Sherman N. Kieffer noted, 'The number of patients receiving treatment under the Act during the first year demonstrates the gap which existed in referral and commitment procedures before the Act passed. Many of the addicts now receiving treatment under the legislation would have been sent to jail with little hope of receiving rehabilitative services under the old system' ('New Program for Drug Addicts', *American Journal of Public Health*, 58, 12, December 1968: 2353).

2. Interview by N. Campbell with B. G. Reed on 16 January 2008.
3. Interview by N. Campbell with B. G. Reed on 16 January 2008.
4. For an account of the periodic threats to federal funding for women's treatment in the US, see V. R. Brown (1995). 'Interview with Maggie Wilmore, Chief of Women and Children's Brach, Center for Substance Abuse Treatment', *Journal of Psychoactive Drugs*, 27.4 (Oct.–Dec.): 321–3.
5. ADAMHA was 'restructured' out of existence in the early 1990s, with responsibility for direct services taken on by the newly formed Substance Abuse and Mental Health Services Administration and divided from responsibility for research. NIDA, NIAAA, and NIMH became part of NIH, the federal basic science research apparatus.
6. This comes from the third page of an exhibit submitted by the Eagleville Hospital and Rehabilitation Center in Eagleville, Pennsylvania, which appeared on page 420 of the exhibits for the 1976 hearing, in reference to alcoholic women who return home after brief stays 'because my children need me'.
7. Noted in 'The Alcoholism Report', 5, 13 (22 April 1977): 8.
8. Interview conducted by N. Campbell with N. Finkelstein on 16 September 2009.
9. See the Urban Institute's report authored by K. Finegold, L. Wherry, and S. Schardin (2004). 'Block Grants: Historical Overview and Lessons Learned' (No. A-63 in 'New Federalism: Issues and Options for States', 21 April).
10. Perhaps the most well-known women's treatment facility in the US is The Betty Ford Center, which opened in 1982 with one of four residence halls designed specifically for women. According to Iliff et al. (2007), 'The question of whether to treat all clients in gender-specific units was frequently debated by Mrs. Ford and the Board of Directors. In 1988, the question of whether to offer gender specific treatment was posed to the staff of 14 counselors. The outcome was seven in favor of separate sex treatment and seven in favor of co-ed treatment. Mrs. Ford cast the deciding vote: the Center would work toward providing separate treatment units for men and women. Fully implementing this decision took considerable time'. Approximately 40 per cent of patients treated at 'The Betty' have been women.
11. Two 500-page volumes were published under the title *Treatment Services for Drug Dependent Women*, G. M. Beschner, B. G. Reed, and J. Mondanaro (eds). Rockville, MD: National Institute on Drug Abuse, 1981. Contributions to these edited volumes were practical in nature, summarizing the state-of-the-art techniques known at the time, on topics ranging from assertiveness training to health promotion to 'sexuality and fears of intimacy as barriers to recovery'. Chapters considered populations including drug-dependent lesbians, 'mothers and children together', and men working with drug-dependent women in

therapeutic communities or other treatment settings. What is clear from an analysis of these volumes is that concerns about pregnancy or any particular group of drug-dependent women did not dominate in the mid-1980s, and indeed the implications of 'chemical dependency' were situated within the broader context of women's lives. As the editors make clear, 'many problems and issues that treatment of drug dependent women must address are related more to their being women than to their chemical dependency' (1981: 7).

12. Interview by N. Campbell with B. G. Reed on 16 January 2008.
13. For further recent history of policies enabling expansion of women's treatment, see C. E. Grella (2008). 'From Generic to Gender-Responsive Treatment: Changes in Social Policies, Treatment Services, and Outcomes of Women in Substance Abuse Treatment', *Journal of Psychoactive Drugs*, SARC Supplement 5 November: 327–43.
14. Interview conducted by N. Campbell with B. Primm on 18 June 2006.
15. Historical Note, Women's Action Alliance Records, Sophia Smith Collection, Smith College, Northampton, Mass.
16. See http://asteria.fivecolleges.edu/findaids/sophiasmith/mnsss76_bioghist.html (accessed 15 July 2010).
17. Interview conducted by N. Campbell with B. Primm on 18 June 2006.
18. We address the content of CSAT's TIP 2, 'Pregnant, Substance-Using Women' (1993), which was the outcome of a consensus panel chaired by Janet Mitchell, in Chapter 5. The TIPs reflect a 'technology transfer' model that provides best-practice guidelines created by the federal agency that steer states receiving federal block grants towards state-of-the-art treatment protocols. Our thanks to Cindy Fazey for providing us with the TIP 2, which is no longer available online, having been 'replaced' by the TIP 51, which we also analyse. Part of the reason that women's treatment advocates are forced continually to reinvent their knowledge practices is due to lack of continuity exacerbated by the periodic federal reorganizations to which the US government is prone. We should also point out that material listed on CSAT's current website no longer includes the word 'women', but instead categorizes women and gender-related topics under the topic heading 'Children and Family'.
19. California was one such place. David Smith, M.D. recalled working with Josette Mondanaro, M.D. when they were both running free clinics in the Haight-Asbury in San Francisco during the 1970s. Mondanaro became deputy director of the state Drug Abuse Treatment Department, a position from which she started two regional coalitions, the Northern and Southern California Alliances of Women's Treatment Programs, which spawned hundreds of programmes. Mondanaro was also active at the federal level. See Eden E. Mondanaro (2004). 'A Pioneer of Chemical Dependency Treatment: Dr Mondanaro Takes No Prisoners', *Am J. Public Health*, August; 94, 8: 1300–2.
20. Interview by N. Campbell with B. G. Reed on 16 January 2008.
21. The NIMH Epidemiological Catchment Area (ECA) study was a multi-sited, collaborative attempt to map regional variation and national prevalence of various psychiatric disorders during the 1980s. Although the cartographic impulse was credited to Carter's 1978 Presidential Commission on Mental Health, the project capitalized on the field's decades-long shift towards

'objective diagnostic methods' and standardized operational criteria, both of which the ECA helped to consolidate and stabilize. The study began in the 1980s and its final report, *Psychiatric Disorders in America* (1991) was authored by Lee N. Robins and Darryl Regier. Their last chapter considered the implications of 'co-occurrence of disorders', the 'other disorders [that] may defeat the therapeutic efforts or increase risks of relapse of the treated disorder' (Robins and Regier, 1991: 356). Epidemiological investigation revealed that certain disorders occurred together at rates well above chance – the question then became whether these disorders had common aetiology or whether one functioned as a risk factor for another.

22. Interview conducted by N. Campbell with V. Brown on 20 January 2010.
23. Interview conducted by N. Campbell with V. Brown on 20 January 2010.
24. Interview conducted by N. Campbell with V. Brown on 20 January 2010.
25. Interview conducted by N. Campbell with V. Brown on 20 January 2010.
26. Interview conducted by N. Campbell with V. Brown on 20 January 2010.
27. Interview conducted by N. Campbell with V. Brown on 20 January 2010.
28. Interview conducted by N. Campbell with V. Brown on 20 January 2010.
29. Bavolek encouraged adaptation of his curriculum to specific groups, and citations may refer to one or many among these different adaptations. The Nurturing Program for Families in Substance Abuse Treatment and Recovery curriculum was developed by the Coalition on Addiction, Pregnancy and Parenting (now the Institute for Health and Recovery), and tested with the following Massachusetts women's treatment programmes: New Day, Somerville; Women, Inc., Dorchester; Edwina Martin House, Brockton; F.I.R.S.T., Springfield; and Steppingstone, Inc., Fall River. The project was funded by CSAP through a grant administered by the Health Research Institute, as well as the Commonwealth of Massachusetts Department of Public Health and Bureau of Substance Abuse Services. Originally published in 1995, the first curriculum is listed under Moore et al. (1995) in the references. The second edition was developed by The Institute for Health and Recovery and is listed under Bogage et al. (2006). The two editions differed in format, but few differences in content were noted.
30. For a full account of interconnections between Gilligan, Miller, and other feminist theorists in this circle, see Christina Robb (2006). *This Changes Everything: The Relational Revolution in Psychology*. New York, Farrar, Straus and Giroux.
31. Quote from newsletter 'Innovations from the Sites', April 2002, 1.
32. Interview conducted by N. Campbell with V. Brown on 20 January 2010.
33. In 1992 NIDA moved to NIH, which required an emphasis on the 'basic research' orientation. Remaining in the US Department of Health and Human Services, SAMHSA took responsibility for 'behavioral health' and was relegated to investing in programme evaluations that had become so complex that they bordered on research in the 1990s. As the disaggregation of research and service delivery proceeded, NIDA got out of the treatment business, and the division of labor within the Office of Treatment Improvement (OTI)/ADAMHA, which ultimately became CSAT/SAMHSA, affected the directions in which the new division could move.
34. Interview conducted by N. Campbell with V. Brown on 20 January 2010.
35. Interview conducted by N. Campbell with V. Brown on 20 January 2010.

36. 'Motivational interviewing' is considered an Evidence-Based Practice in the US (Miller, 2002). On 'motivational interviewing', see Carr (2010) and Carr, E. S. (n.d.). 'From Denial to Ambivalence: The Shifting Semiotics of American Addiction Counseling', in E. Raikhel and W. Garriott (eds). *Addiction Trajectories*. Under review.
37. H. H. S. Publication No. (SMA) 09-4426. Rockville, MD: Substance Abuse and Mental Health Services Administration, 2009). Published TIPs are available at http://www.kap.samhsa.gov (accessed on 11 April 2011).
38. Interview conducted by N. Campbell with V. Brown on 20 January 2010.
39. This 'self-in-relation' concept – as opposed to the concept of an 'autonomous' self formed through individuation – pervades the writings of all of the theorists of women's psychological development associated with Gilligan, Miller, and the Stone Center.
40. Personal communication with N. Finkelstein, 3 November 2010.
41. For information on this innovative organization, see Mosely, 1996 and http://www.prototypes.org/ (accessed on 11 April 2011).
42. Interview conducted by N. Campbell with V. Brown on 20 January 2010.
43. Interview conducted by N. Campbell with V. Brown on 20 January 2010.
44. Interview conducted by N. Campbell with V. Brown on 20 January 2010.
45. Interview conducted by N. Campbell with N. Paull on 4 January 2010.
46. Interview conducted by N. Campbell with N. Paull on 4 January 2010.
47. Interview conducted by N. Campbell with N. Paull on 4 January 2010.
48. Interview conducted by N. Campbell with N. Paull on 4 January 2010.
49. Interview conducted by N. Campbell with N. Paull on 4 January 2010.
50. Interview conducted by N. Campbell with N. Paull on 4 January 2010.
51. Interview conducted by N. Campbell with N. Paull on 4 January 2010.
52. Interview conducted by N. Campbell with N. Paull on 4 January 2010.
53. Interview conducted by N. Campbell with N. Paull on 4 January 2010.
54. Interview conducted by N. Campbell with N. Paull on 4 January 2010.
55. I. Vogt (1998). 'Gender and Drug Treatment Systems', in H. Klingemann and G. Hunt (eds), *Drug Treatment Systems in an International Perspective: Drugs, Demons, and Delinquents*. London: SAGE Publications, 291.

4 'Unearthing Women' in Drug Policy: Where Do Women Fit – Or Do They?

1. The Society changed its name to the Society for the Study and Cure of Inebriety in 1884, and again in 1887 to the Society for the Study of Inebriety (SSI).
2. This is the precursor of the contemporary journal, *Addiction*.
3. Today this phenomena is referred to as Sudden Infant Death Syndrome (SIDS).
4. Inebriates were men or women 'charged with drunkenness four times in one year'. *The 1902 Licensing Act* placed habitual inebriates on a 'Black List' so their photographs and descriptions would be circulated to the police and licensed publicans who would be fined if they knowingly served the 'Listed' (Holmes, 1903).
5. Bramwell Booth was the oldest son of William Booth, the British Methodist minister who founded the Salvation Army in 1865.

6. The Normyl cure was a medicinal mixture containing strychnine and brucine, which were then purported to cure alcohol and drug addiction. The former is a very toxic alkaloid while the latter is a bitter alkaloid less poisonous than the former. See Anonymous (1912 a and b).
7. In 1902 at Finnigan's Dance Studio in Manchester, a group of 21 dance masters formed the United Kingdom Alliance of Professional Teachers of Dancing and Kindred Arts (UKA). In those early days it covered Dance, Opera and Sword Fencing and everyone paid an entry fee of half a guinea (52½p). See http://www.ukadance.co.uk/about.htm (accessed 14 November 2010).
8. It reported that addicts were not numerous, mainly therapeutic addicts, middle aged and middle class. Additionally, numbers had diminished (Stimson, 1973: 24–5). Spear (1967: 248) contended that a proportion of addicts were members of the medical profession and he termed them 'professional addicts'.
9. *1920 Dangerous Drugs Act.*
10. During World War I, civilians could buy morphine and cocaine kits for soldiers, which were labelled 'A useful present for friends at the front' and sold complete with syringe and spare needles, in Harrods (Barton, 2003: 16).
11. The Committee defined an addict as 'a person who as a result of repeated administration has become dependent upon a controlled drug under the Dangerous Drugs Act and has an overpowering desire for its continuance, but who does not require it for the relief of organic disease'. (Section 17)
12. In 1965 there was no 'relevant research institute in the UK' in the field of addiction because 'there had been no problem of a magnitude to justify investment' (Edwards, 2010: 984). It was not until 1967 that the Ministry of Health decided to fund a research centre, the Addiction Research Unit at the Institute of Psychiatry, and Griffith Edwards was made Director designate for the soon-to-be-established research centre (Edwards, 2010: 985).
13. Stimson noted that he was only able to study 13 of the 15 London DDUs (51).
14. The author notes that they take those from Holloway Prison 'who come to us on a year's Condition of Residence on a Probation Order, having been before the Court charged with offences usually committed while they have been under the influence of drink or drugs' (80).
15. This Act legislated stricter controls on General Practitioners (GPs) prescribing and required the Home Office to be notified of new addicts
16. This established the ACMD. It made a distinction between supply and possession offences as well as soft and hard drugs. Substances were divided into classes A, B, and C.
17. This required doctors treating addicts to notify the Chief Medical Officer if they suspected a patient to be an addict and again GPs were restricted in terms of prescribing.
18. Predecessor of the current Department of Health.
19. Interview conducted by E. Ettorre with S. MacGregor on 3 December 2009.
20. Interview conducted by E. Ettorre with A. Dixon on 22 October 2009.
21. Interview conducted by E. Ettorre with A. Dixon on 22 October 2009.
22. Strang's (1991) article had a picture of a woman injecting heroin with the caption, 'We must put aside morality and focus on harm caused by injecting drugs'.

23. *The Drug Trafficking Offenses Act 1986* evidenced a shift to a more punitive response.
24. Interview conducted by E. Ettorre interview with B. Thom on 13 November 2009.
25. Interview conducted by E. Ettorre interview with B. Thom on 13 November 2009.
26. Margaret Thatcher was elected British Prime Minister on 4 May 1979.
27. Interview conducted by E. Ettorre with F. Measham on 26 November 2010.
28. Mention was made of how 'the number and location of prisons for women create particular problems where the response to drug misuse is concerned' (6). This report acknowledged that 'the drug's strategy of a women's prison and the profile of activity which illustrates it would need to be different from that of a male prison' (6).
29. Other reports that were published by ACMD during this phase were: ACMD (1995) *Volatile Substance Abuse*; ACMD (1993) *Drug Education in Schools: The Need for New Impetus*; ACMD (1992) *The Care and Treatment of Drug Misusers: A Guidance Note* and ACMD (1990) *Problem Drug Use, a Review of Training*.
30. Interview conducted by E. Ettorre with S. MacGregor on 3 December 2009.
31. Interview conducted by E. Ettorre with S. MacGregor on 3 December 2009.
32. Interview conducted by E. Ettorre with S. MacGregor on 3 December 2009.
33. Interview conducted by E. Ettorre with S. MacGregor on 3 December 2009.
34. Interview conducted by E. Ettorre with F. Measham on 26 November 2010.
35. Interview conducted by E. Ettorre with F. Measham on 26 November 2010.
36. See Ettorre (1992), 145–9.
37. Interview conducted by E. Ettorre with F. Measham on 26 November 2010.
38. Interview conducted by E. Ettorre with A. Delargy, Team Leader, Embrace – Families and Domestic Violence Project, Alcohol Concern on 25 May 2010.
39. This policy emphasis eventually led to an awareness of the 'hidden harms' of drug use and an awareness of the policy need to hear the 'voices' of the children of problem drug users. See ACMD (2003: 11) and ACMD (2007a).
40. There were 174 documents listed including nine posters which were eliminated from this exercise. See http://www.nta.nhs.uk for publication list (accessed 14 November 2010).
41. Interview conducted by E. Ettorre with S. MacGregor on 3 December 2009.
42. Adfam is a non-statutory agency 'committed to representing the needs of families on a national policy level, as well as helping local service delivery for the families of drug and alcohol users. Adfam helps to ensure that the needs of families are accounted for on various forums, steering groups and advisory bodies, including the Department of Health, Department for Children, Schools and Families (DCSF – now the Department for Education), the National Institute for Clinical Excellence (NICE), the National Treatment Agency (NTA), and various forums alongside other drug and alcohol charities'. See: http://www.adfam.org.uk/about_us/about_us/policy (accessed 14 November 2010).
43. Interview conducted by E. Ettorre with V. Evans 9 February 2010.
44. Interview conducted by E. Ettorre with V. Evans 9 February 2010.
45. See http://www.nta.nhs.uk/nta-join-phs-jul10.aspx (accessed 14 November 2010).

46. It should be pointed out that from 1948 until the formation of SAMHSA in 1990, the NIMH was a unique exception in providing centralized professional supervision over *both* research and psychiatric services, as Robert H. Felix, founding director of the NIMH, had prevailed in keeping mental health a unique exception to the federal division between service and research (Musto, 1975: 63).
47. That the alcohol and drug abuse treatment workforce defines itself as on the 'frontlines' of a 'war on drugs' (of which many are deeply critical) is illustrated by the title of NIAAA's newsletter for the profession, *Frontlines* (McCarty, 2002: 1–2).
48. The US treatment workforce consists of nearly 70,000 practitioners. In the late 1970s, fewer than one in four counsellors had graduate degrees. Today more than half do, with most coming out of community colleges. Annual turnover is high (close to 18 per cent). Typical clinicians are white, middle-aged women – almost 70 per cent of the workforce is comprised of individuals with this profile. Few have doctoral degrees but over half have master's degrees (Harwood, 2002: 3).
49. The impact of these initiatives is measured as a function of the number of educational contacts (such quantitative measures were mandated by the Government Performance Results Act of 1993).

5 Reproducing Bodies and Governing Motherhood: Drug-Using Women and Reproductive Loss

1. Z. Eisenstein (1998). *The Female Body and the Law*, Berkeley, CA: University of California Press, argues that 'gender plays an active role in defining the pregnant body' (79). While her argument rests on a conflation between the female body, the 'mother's body' and the pregnant body, her understanding is that all of these are *women's* bodies constructed as different.
2. See Layne, 2003 for a discussion of this concept.
3. Surveying American and British publics to probe how exactly stigma, embedded in cultural contexts, works towards the mentally ill, Martin, Lang and Olafsdottir (2008) found that national contexts – including macro-structural policies – shape social norms governing responses to people who live with stigmatized conditions. Specifically, social stigma shapes access to social power and resources, the social acceptability of 'othering' the mentally ill, and, ultimately, their chances for recovery. Scholars 'rethinking stigma' have also examined attitudes towards drug addicts generally. Martin, Pescosolido, and Tuch (2000) found Americans least willing to interact with drug and alcohol dependent people (71.8% and 55.7% unwilling, respectively), as compared to their unwillingness to interact with schizophrenics (48.4% unwilling) or depressives (37.4% unwilling). Room (2005) found that a 'generalized and ubiquitous stigma of alcoholism and addiction' after surveying 14 countries for the World Health Organization. See also Link et al. (1999).
4. On this point, see Ettorre (2007: 55) in conversation with the work of Rosi Braidotti (1994; 2002).
5. In the US, one of the most controversial debates has been over 'Project Prevention', also known as Children Require A Caring Kommunity (CRACK).

The National Advocates for Pregnant Women (NAPW) has argued that this programme, initiated by Barbara Harris, an adoptive mother of several 'crack babies' who incentivizes contraception and sterilization for drug-addicted women, is based on control, not empowerment. Several articles on CRACK appear on the NAPW website http://www.advocatesforpregnantwomen.org/ (accessed 1 April 2011).

6. This statement (quoted in Painter, Riley-Buckley, and Whittington 2000: 18) was written by the British midwife Cath Siney from Liverpool who was influential in raising awareness of pregnant users for midwives in the UK. She helped to expose the need for proper treatment of women substance users and carried out a national survey of maternity services in England and Wales (Morrison and Siney, 1995). The survey found that 11 per cent of notified female drug users had given birth in the study year (N = 568). But, only 52 per cent had antenatal discussions and less than one third had links with drug agencies (see also Crome et al., 2005: 432).
7. Research carried out by the Oasis Project, a drug service in Brighton, England revealed that 18 per cent of student midwives and 29 per cent of qualified midwives in the local area described their personal attitude as 'biased against substance misusers', while at the same time being aware it was their role to provide help to these women (Painter, Riley-Buckley, and Whittington, 2000: 18)
8. In the Oasis study mentioned above, pregnant substance users reported that the main reasons for not disclosing their substance use were fear of both negative staff attitudes and social service intervention (Painter, Riley-Buckley, and Whittington, 2000: 18).
9. This text, which was dictated to sociologist Howard S. Becker by Marilyn Bishop, whose pseudonym was Janet Clark, was transcribed from audiotape and edited by Helen MacGill Hughes. The study was conducted under the auspices of the Institute for Juvenile Research and the Chicago Area Project with financial assistance from the National Institute of Mental Health. See Nancy D. Campbell's 2005 interview with Becker at http://sitemaker.umich.edu/substance.abuse.history/oral_history_interviews&mode=single&recordID=00000000000000000000000000000000000000002287158&nextMode=list (accessed 14 April 2011) and Bennett (1988).
10. However, this is a right which is increasingly being eroded through the implementation of stringent health and social policies introduced by successive governments including both Conservative and Labour governments as well as the current Coalition Government.
11. This is also becoming apparent in the UK where research revealed that black women fared the worst in Drugs Testing and Treatment Orders (DTTOs) representing only three per cent of those placed on orders. In other words, black defendants are more likely to be given a custodial sentence than their white counterparts. (See Heneghan, 2000.)
12. Race also defines the pregnant body, but discussion of race and ethnicity is strikingly absent from the material on gender, drugs, and pregnancy produced in the 1970s. Race is sometimes included as a demographic variable in the studies we quote, but it was rarely if ever an explicit topic until much later in the development of the field.
13. His work was ultimately published in book form as *Careers in Dope* (Englewood Cliffs, NJ: Prentice-Hall, 1973).

14. In the UK at the time, the ACMD (1968) published a report *The Rehabilitation of Addicts* which consistently referred to 'heroin addicts' as 'he' or 'him', although in Appendix B: 'Hospital return of heroin addicts undergoing treatment' comparisons were made between male and female outpatients. While the total number of male patients was 883, the number for female patients was 213'.
15. In the UK, an interest in obstetrics, pregnancy, and opiate use began to become visible in the late 1960s when pregnant drug users were being identified in treatment. The main concern at that time was 'tolerance and therefore failure to provide adequate analgesia and exacerbation of dependence on drugs' (95) (see Crawley and Pawson, 1969). The biochemistry of addiction became a concern in the 1970s (see, for example, Sassoon, 1978). Very often concerns in the UK for the effects of alcohol on pregnancy overshadowed concern for pregnant addicts (Pratt, 1981).
16. It is important to note that in the 1950s, 1960s, and even into the 1970s, LSD was used as an adjunct to sex therapy and couples counselling. See R. Alpert (1969). 'Drugs and Sexual Behavior', *Journal of Sex Research*, 5, 1: 50–6.
17. According to Ronald Brown, quoted in a 2003 obituary by Janice Hopkins Tanne published in the *British Medical Journal*.
18. This article responded to a 1972 report titled 'The Children of Addicts: Unrecognized and Unprotected' by the New York State Assembly Select Committee on Child Abuse. Densen-Gerber and Rohrs argued that social responsibilities to the 'unwilling victims of drug abuse' were not being due to previous underestimates of the scope and extent of the problems represented by 'drug addicted parents'.
19. Interview conducted by N. Campbell with B. G. Reed on 16 January 2008 and interview conducted by N. Campbell and E. Ettorre with B. G. Reed and C. Boyd on 11 March 2010.
20. US Senate (1990). *Drug Treatment and Prevention, Hearings before the Senate Committee on Labor and Human Resources*, 101st Cong., 2nd sess., 24 April at 9.
21. US Department of Justice (1989). Office of the Attorney General of the United States, *Drug trafficking: A report to the President of the United States*, 2.
22. On this point, see NAPW Analysis of Tennessee Bills SB1065 and HB0890 (2009) at http://www.advocatesforpregnantwomen.org/issues/civil_child_welfare_cases_and_issues/ (accessed 1 August 2010).
23. Interview conducted by E. Ettorre with S. MacGregor on 3 December 2009.
24. Interview conducted by E. Ettorre with S. MacGregor on 3 December 2009.
25. Interview conducted by E. Ettorre with F. Macrory on 2 October 2009.
26. Becker and Duffy (2002) demonstrate how in the UK this phenomenon is being challenged gradually. In their survey which identified services targeting women problem drug users in England and Scotland, they found that of the 18 organizations surveyed, two were identified as targeting 'pregnant women and women with children' and a further six 'pregnant women' specifically. They argue for 'women-friendly service provision', echoing DAWN's demands of almost 20 years earlier.
27. *Time Magazine* (1970). 'Behavior: The Junior Junkie', *Time* 16 February. At http://www.time.com/time/magazine/article/0,9171,904165-2,00.html (accessed 14 December 2010).

28. In the UK, the Together Women Project, dotted around England, and the Stella Project in London have expanded the production of feminist knowledges on substance use in the criminal justice field.
29. For an excellent account of the wide variety of women whose reproductive capacities are policed through the 'patriarchal regulation of motherhood' in the US, see NAPW Board President Jeanne Flavin's book, *Our Bodies, Our Crimes: The Policing of Women's Reproduction in America*, New York University Press, 2009.
30. Personal communication with Lynn Paltrow, 16 December 2010.
31. See S. Bordo (1995). 'Are Mothers Persons? Reproductive Rights and the Politics of Subjectivity', in *Unbearable Weight: Feminism, Western Culture and the Body*, Berkeley, CA, University of California Press.

Conclusion: Making Gender Matter in an Age of Neurochemical Selves

1. The literature on social stigma indicates that substantial portions of populations surveyed continue not only to think that drug users bear personal responsibility for negative health outcomes, but also that there is an intimate connection between the stigmatization and moralization of substance abuse and intoxication (Room, 2005, 149).
2. See L. M. Paltrow and K. Jack (2010). 'Pregnant Women, Junk Science, and Zealous Defense', *The Champion Magazine*, National Association of Criminal Defense Lawyers, May at http://advocatesforpregnantwomen.org/main/publications/articles_and_reports/pregnant_women_junk_science_and_zealous_defense.php (accessed December 2010).
3. On the lack of thoroughgoing feminist critiques of psychiatry and psychiatric institutions, see Burstow (1992). However, feminists such as Kate Millet in *The Loony-bin Trip* and Shulamith Firestone produced writing critical of the treatment of mentally ill women.
4. Historical shifts in the meanings of 'dependency' and its relationship to subordination are pointed to in N. Fraser and L. Gordon (1994). 'A Genealogy of "Dependency": Tracing a Keyword of the US Welfare State', *Signs: Journal of Women in Culture and Society*, 19.2: 309–36.
5. Interview by N. Campbell with N. Finkelstein, 16 September 2009.
6. Interview by N. Campbell with N. Finkelstein, 16 September 2009.
7. See D. Fassin and R. Rechtman (2007). *The Empire of Trauma*, especially 78–84.
8. Both the DSM-III itself and the diagnostic category PTSD were the objects and outcomes of an ongoing contestation; see Kirk and Kutchins (1992); Young (1997).
9. See the work of the National Trauma Consortium, particularly, Finkelstein (2004). 'Enhancing Substance Abuse Recovery Through Integrated Trauma Treatment' and other publications accessed at http://www.nationaltraumaconsortium.org/.
10. Clarke and Olesen, 1999: 5.

References

Addiction Technology Transfer Center. (2000). *The Change Book: A Blueprint for Technology Transfer.* Kansas City, MO: Addiction Technology Transfer Center.
Advisory Council on the Misuse of Drugs (ACMD) (2007a). *Hidden Harm: Three Years On: Realities, Challenges and Opportunities.* London: HMSO.
ACMD (2007b). *Drug-Facilitated Sexual Assault.* London: HMSO.
ACMD (2005). *Methylamphetamine Review.* London, HMSO.
ACMD (2003). *Hidden Harm: Responding to the Needs of Children of Problem Drug Users.* London: HMSO.
ACMD (2000). *Reducing Drug-Related Deaths.* London: HMSO.
ACMD (1998). *Drug Misuse and the Environment.* London: HMSO.
ACMD (1996). *Drug Misusers and the Criminal Justice System Part III: Drug Misusers and the Prison System: An Integrated Approach.* London: HMSO.
ACMD (1995). *Volatile Substance Abuse.* London: HMSO.
ACMD (1994). *Drug Misusers and the Criminal Justice System Part II: Police, Drug Misusers and the Community.* London: HMSO.
ACMD (1993). *Drug Education in Schools: The Need for New Impetus.* London: HMSO.
ACMD (1992). *The Care and Treatment of Drug Misusers: A Guidance Note.* London: HMSO.
ACMD (1991). *Drug Misusers and the Criminal Justice System Part I: Community Resources and the Probation Services.* London: HMSO.
ACMD (1990). *Problem Drug Use, a Review of Training.* London: HMSO.
ACMD (1989). *AIDS and Drug Misuse, Part 2.* London: HMSO.
ACMD (1988). *AIDS and Drug Misuse, Part 1.* London: HMSO.
ACMD (1984). *Prevention.* London: HMSO.
ACMD (1982). *Treatment and Rehabilitation.* London: HMSO.
ACMD (1968). *The Rehabilitation of Addicts.* London: Her Majesty's Publication Office (HMSO).
Ahmed, S. and Stacey, J. (2001). 'Testimonial Cultures: An Introduction', *Cultural Values*, 5, 1: 1–6.
Alpert, R. (1969). 'Drugs and Sexual Behavior', *Journal of Sex Research*, 5, 1: 50–6.
Amaro, H. (1999). 'An Expensive Policy: The Impact of Inadequate Funding for Substance Abuse Treatment', *American Journal of Public Health*, 89, 5: 657–9.
Amaro, H., Chernoff, M., Brown, V., Arevalo, S., and Gatz, M. (2007). 'Does Integrated Trauma-Informed Substance Abuse Treatment Increase Treatment Retention?' *Journal of Community Psychology*, 35, 7: 845–62.
American Bar Association (ABA) (1957). *Joint Legislative Committee on Narcotics Study*, November 25 (transcript of the meeting held on 25 November).
Andersen, M. D. (1979). 'Health Needs of Drug Dependent Clients', *WDR Newsletter*, 13. School of Social Work, Ann Arbor, MI: University of Michigan.
Anderson, T. (2008). *Neither Villain nor Victim: Empowerment and Agency among Women Substance Abusers.* New Brunswick, NJ: Rutgers University Press.

Anderson, T. (2005). 'Dimensions of Women's Power in the Illicit Drug Economy', *Theoretical Criminology*, 9, 4: 371–400.

Anderson, T. (1998). 'A Cultural Identity Theory of Drug Abuse', *Sociology of Crime, Law and Deviance*, 1: 233–62.

Anderson, T. (1995). 'Toward a Preliminary Macro Theory of Drug Addiction', *Deviant Behavior: An Interdisciplinary Journal*, 16: 353–72.

Annandale, E. (1998). *The Sociology of Health and Medicine: A Critical Introduction.* Cambridge: Polity Press.

Anonymous (1912a). 'The "Normly" Cure for Alcohol and Drug Addictions', *British Medical Journal*, 27 April: 959–60.

Anonymous (1912b). 'The "Normly" Cure for Alcohol and Drug Addictions, Second Report', *British Medical Journal*, 12 October: 981.

Apple, R. D. (2006). *Perfect Motherhood: Science and Childrearing in America.* Piscataway, NJ: Rutgers University Press.

Armstrong, D. (1979). 'The Emancipation of Biographical Medicine', *Social Science and Medicine*, 13A: 1–8.

Backer, T. E. (1991). *Drug Abuse Technology Transfer.* Rockville, MD: National Institute on Drug Abuse.

Barton, A. (2003). *Illicit Drugs: Use and Control.* London: Routledge.

Bean, P. (2004). 'Linking Treatment Services to the Criminal Justice System', in P. Bean and T. Nemitz (eds). *Drug Treatment: What Works?* London: Routledge, pp. 219–35.

Bean, P. (1974). *The Social Control of Drugs.* London: Martin Robertson.

Becker, H. S. (2005). Interview conducted by N. D. Campbell. *History of a Public Science: History of Substance Abuse Research.* Ann Arbor, MI: University of Michigan Substance Abuse Research Center at http://sitemaker.umich.edu/substance.abuse.history/home.

Becker, J. and Duffy, C. (2002). *Women Drug Users and Drugs Service Provision: Service Level Responses to Engagement and Retention.* London: Home Office.

Bender, L. (1963). 'Drug Addiction in Adolescence', *Comprehensive Psychiatry*, 4, 3: 181–94.

Bender, L. (1961). 'State Care of Emotionally and Socially Disturbed Adolescents', in E. M. Thornton (ed.). *Planning and Action for Mental Health.* London: World Federation for Mental Health.

Ben-Yehuda, N. (1994). 'The Sociology of Moral Panics: Toward a New Synthesis', in R. Coomber (ed.). *Drugs and Drug Use in Society: A Critical Reader.* London: Greenwich University Press, pp. 201–20.

Bennett, J. (1988). *Oral History and Delinquency: The Rhetoric of Criminology.* Chicago: University of Chicago Press.

Best, S. and Kellner, D. (1991). *Postmodern Theory: Critical Interrogations*, New York: The Guilford Press.

Bergmark, A. (1998). 'Expansion and Implosion: The Story of Drug Treatment in Sweden', in H. Klingemann and G. Hunt (eds). *Drug Treatment Systems in an International Perspective: Drugs, Demons and Delinquents.* London: Sage Publications.

Berridge, V. (1999). *Opium and the People: Opiate Use and Drug Control Policy in Nineteenth and Early Twentieth Century England.* London: Free Association.

Berridge, V. (1984). 'Drugs and Social Policy: The Establishment of Drug Control in Britain 1900–1930', *British Journal of Addiction*, 79, 17–29.

Berridge, V. (1979). 'Morality and Medical Science: Concepts of Narcotic Addiction in Britain, 1820–1926', *Annals of Science*, 36, 67–85.

Berridge, V. and Edwards, G. (1981). *Opium and the People: Opiate Use in 19th Century England.* London: Allen Lane.

Beschner, G., Reed, B. G., and Mondanaro, J. (eds) (1981). *Treatment Services for Drug Dependent Women.* Rockville, MD: National Institute on Drug Abuse.

Best, D. and Abdulrahim, D. (2005). *Women in Drug Treatment Services* (Research Briefing: 6). London: National Treatment Agency.

Blumberg, H. (1981). 'Characteristics of People Coming to Treatment', in I. G. Edward and C. Busch (eds). *Drug Problems in Britain: A Review of Ten Years.* London: Academic Press, pp. 77–115.

Blume, S. B. (2006). 'Conversation with Sheila Blume', *Addiction*, 101, 1: 31–9.

Blume, S. B. (1985a). 'Conversation with Mark Keller', *British Journal of Addiction*, 80, 5–9.

Blume, S. B. (1985b). 'Women and Alcohol: A Review', *JAMA*, 256: 1467–70.

Blume, S. B. (1981). 'Drinking and Pregnancy: Preventing Fetal Alcohol Syndrome', *New York State Journal of Medicine*, 81: 95–8.

Bogage, T., Marron, B., Donald, T., Finkelstein, N., and Abrams, B. (2006). *The Nurturing Program for Families in Substance Abuse Treatment and Recovery.* Park City, UT and Asheville, NC: Family Development Resources.

Booth, Mrs. B. (1911). 'The Management of the Inebriate Woman', *The British Journal of Inebriety*, 9, 2: 53–108.

Bordo, S. (1995). 'Are Mothers Persons? Reproductive Rights and the Politics of Subjectivity', in *Unbearable Weight: Feminism, Western Culture and the Body.* Berkeley, CA: University of California Press.

Boston Women's Health Book Collective (1971). *Our Bodies, Ourselves: A Course by and for Women.* Boston: New England Free Press.

Boston Women's Health Book Collective (1970). *Women and Their Bodies: A Course.* Boston: Boston Women's Health Book Collective.

Bowlby, J. (1951). *Maternal Care and Mental Health.* Geneva: World Health Organisation.

Boyd, S. C. (1999). *Mothers and Illicit Drugs.* Toronto: University of Toronto Press.

Braidotti, R. (2002). *Metamorphoses: Towards a Materialist Theory of Becoming*, Cambridge: Polity Press.

Braidotti, R. (1994). *Nomadic Subjects: Embodiment and Sexual Difference in Contemporary Feminist Theory.* New York: Columbia University Press

Brown, V. B. (1995). 'Interview with Maggie Wilmore, Chief of Women and Children's Branch, Center for Substance Abuse Treatment', *Journal of Psychoactive Drugs*, 7, 4: 323–4.

Brown, V. B., Huba, G. J., and Melchior, L. A. (1995). 'Level of Burden: Women with More Than One Co-Occurring Disorder', *Journal of Psychoactive Drugs*, 27, 4: 339–46.

Brown, V. B., Melchior, L. A., Panter, A. T., Slaughter, R., and Huba, G. J. (2000). 'Women's Steps of Change and Entry into Treatment: A Multidimensional Stages of Change Model', *Journal of Substance Abuse Treatment*, 18, 231–40.

Brown, V. B., Melchior, L. A., Waite-O'Brien, N., and Huba, G. J. (2002). 'Effects of Women-Sensitive, Long-Term Residential Treatment on Psychological Functioning of Diverse Populations of Women', *Journal of Substance Abuse Treatment*, 23, 133–44.

Brown, V. B., Najavits, L. M., Cadiz, S., Finkelstein, N., Heckman, J. P., and Rechberger, E. (2007). 'Implementing an Evidence-Based Practice: Seeking Safety Group', *Journal of Psychoactive Drugs*, 39, 3: 231–40.

Brown, V. B., S. Sanchez, J. E. Zweben, and Aly, T. (1996). 'Challenges in Moving from a Traditional Therapeutic Community to a Women and Children's TC model', *Journal of Psychoactive Drugs*, 28, 1: 39–46.

Brummit, H. (1963). 'Observations on Drug Addicts in a House of Detention for Women', *Corrective Psychiatry and Journal of Social Therapy*, 9, 2: 62–70.

Burstow, B. (1992). *Radical Feminist Therapy: Working in the Context of Violence*. London: Sage Publications.

Camberwell Council on Alcoholism (CCA) (1980). *Women and Alcohol*. London: Tavistock Publications.

Campbell, N. D. (2010). 'Situated Pharmaco-Logics: How Addiction Became Lodged in the Brain'. Unpublished paper given at the conference on 'Addiction(s): Social or Cerebral?' Sponsored by the European Neuroscience and Society Network, European Science Foundation and the Academy of Finland. Majvik, Finland. September 9.

Campbell, N. D. (2007). *Discovering Addiction: The Politics of Substance Abuse Research*. Ann Arbor, MI: University of Michigan Press.

Campbell, N. D. (2000). *Using Women: Gender, Drug Policy, and Social Justice*. New York: Routledge.

Campbell, N. (1999). 'Regulating "Maternal Instinct": Governing Mentalities of Late Twentieth-Century US Illicit Drug Policy', *SIGNS: Journal of Women in Culture and Society*, 24, 4: 895–923.

Campbell, N., Olsen, J. P., and Walden, L. (2008). *The Narcotic Farm: The Rise and Fall of America's First Prison for Drug Addicts*. New York: Abrams.

Carr, E. S. (n.d.). 'From Denial to Ambivalence: The Shifting Semiotics of American Addiction Counseling', in E. Raikhel and W. Garriott (eds). *Addiction Trajectories*. Under review.

Carr, E. S. (2011). *Scripting Addiction: The Politics of Therapeutic Talk and American Sobriety*. Princeton, NJ: Princeton University Press.

Center on Addiction and Substance Abuse (CASA) (1996). *Substance Abuse and the American Woman*. New York: National Center on Addiction and Substance Abuse at Columbia University.

CSAT (2009). *Substance Abuse Treatment: Addressing the Specific Needs of Women*. Treatment Improvement Protocol (TIP) Series 51. HHS Publication No. (SMA) 09-4426. Rockville, MD: Substance Abuse and Mental Health Services Administration.

CSAT (1994). *Comprehensive Treatment Model for Alcohol and Other Drug-Abusing Women and Their Children*. Rockville, MD: Substance Abuse and Mental Health Services Administration.

CSAT (1993). *Pregnant, Substance-Using Women*. Treatment Improvement Protocol (TIP) Series 2. HHS Publication No. (SMA) 93-1998. Rockville, MD: Substance Abuse and Mental Health Services Administration.

Cetina, K. K. (2007). 'Sociality with Objects: Social Relations in Postsocial Knowledge Societies', *Theory, Culture and Society*, 14.4: 1–30.

Chavkin, W., Breitbart, V., Elman, D., and Wise, P. H. (1998). 'National Survey of the States: Policies and Practices Regarding Drug-Using Women', *American Journal of Public Health*, 88, 1: 117–19.

Chein, I., Gerard, D. L., Lee, R. S., and Rosenfeld, E. (1964). *The Road to H: Narcotics, Delinquency, and Social Policy*. New York, Basic Books.

Chesler, P. (1972). *Women and Madness*. New York: Doubleday and Co.

Clark, J. S., Capel, W. C., Goldsmith, B. M., and Stewart, G. T. (1972). 'Marriage and Methadone: Spouse Behavior Patterns in Heroin Addicts Maintained on Methadone', *Journal of Marriage and Family Issues*, 34, 3: 496–502.

Clarke, A. E., Mamo, L., Fosket, J. R., Fishman, J. R., and Shim, J. K. (2010). *Biomedicalization: Technoscience, Health and Illness in the U.S.* Durham, NC: Duke University Press.

Clarke, A. E. and Olesen, V. L. (1999). 'Revising, Diffracting, Acting', in A. E. Clarke and V. L. Olesen (eds). *Revisioning Women, Health and Healing: Feminist, Cultural and Technoscience Perspectives*. New York: Routledge, pp. 3–48.

Clarke, K. and J. Formby (2000). 'Feeling Good, Doing Fine'. *DrugLink*, 15, 5: 10–13.

Clement, S. (1989). 'The Community Drug Team: Lessons from Alcohol and Handicap Service', in D. Bennent (ed.). *Treating Drug Abusers*. London: Routledge, pp. 171–89.

Coalition on Addiction, Pregnancy and Parenting (1997). *Gender Specific Substance Abuse Treatment*. Alexandria, VA: National Women's Resource Center for the Prevention and Treatment of Alcohol, Tobacco and Other Drug Abuse and Mental Illness.

Colen, S. (1995). '"Like a Mother to Them": Stratified Reproduction and West Indian Childcare Workers and Employers in New York', in F. D. Ginsburg and R. Rapp (eds). *Conceiving the New World Order: The Global Politics of Reproduction*. Berkeley, CA: University of California Press, pp. 78–102.

Cohen, S. (1972). *Folk Devils and Moral Panics*. London: MacGibbon and Kee.

Collins, R. (2004). *Interaction Ritual Chains*. Princeton, NJ: Princeton University Press.

Coomber, R. and South, N. (2004). 'Drugs, Cultures and Controls in Comparative Perspective', in R. Coomber and N. South (eds). *Drug Use and Cultural Contexts 'Beyond the West': Tradition, Change and Post-Colonialism*. London: Free Association Books, pp. 13–26.

Cooperstock, R. (1978a). 'Sex Differences in Psychotropic Drug Use', *Social Science and Medicine*, 12B: 179–86.

Cooperstock, R. (1978b). 'The Epidemiology of Psychotropic Drug Use in Canada', *Canadian Family Physician*, 24: 889–92.

Cooperstock, R. and H. L. Lennard (1979). 'Some Social Meanings of Tranquillizer Use', *Sociology of Health and Illness*, 1, 331–47.

Cooperstock, R. and M. Sims (1971). 'Mood-Modifying Drugs Prescribed in a Canadian City: Hidden Problems', *American Journal of Public Health*, 61: 1007–16.

Cooperstock, R. and P. Parnell (1982). 'Research on Psychotropic Drug Use: A Review of Findings and Methods', *Social Science and Medicine*, 16, 12: 1179–96.

Coote, A. and Campbell, B. (1982). *Sweet Freedom, the Struggle for Women's Liberation*. Oxford: Basil Blackwell.

Coppolillo, H. P. (1975). 'Drug Impediments to Mothering Behavior', *Addictive Diseases*, 2, 1: 201–8.

Cornell, D. (1995). *The Imaginary Domain: Abortion, Pornography and Sexual Harassment*. New York: Routledge.

Covington, S. S. (2002). 'Helping Women Recover: Creating Gender-Responsive Treatment', in S. L. A. Straussner and S. Brown (eds). *The Handbook of Addiction Treatment for Women: Theory and Practice*. Hoboken, NJ: Jossey-Bass.

Covington, S. S. and Surrey, J. (1997). 'The Relational Model of Women's Psychological Development: Implications for Substance Abuse', in S. Wilsnack and R. Wilsnack (eds). *Gender and Alcohol: Individual and Social Perspectives*. New Brunswick, NJ: Rutgers University Press, pp. 335–51.

Cramer, M. A. (2002). 'Under the Influence of Unconscious Process: Countertransference in the Treatment of PTSD and Substance Abuse in Women', *American Journal of Psychotherapy*, 56, 2: 194–210.

Crawley, B. E. and Pawson, M. (1969). 'Analgesia in Narcotic Addiction', *British Journal of Addiction*, 64: 95–7.

Crome, I., Khaled, M. K., Ghetau, E., McAuley, R., Bhloor, R., Jones, P., and O'Brien, P. M. S. (2005). 'Opiate Misuse in Pregnancy: Findings of a Retrospective Study', *Drugs: Education, Prevention and Policy*, 12, 6: 431–6.

Cuskey, W. R., Premkumar, T., and Sigel, L. (1972). 'Survey of Opiate Addiction among Females in the United States between 1850 and 1970', *Public Health Reviews*, 1: 7–39.

Dally, A. (1990). *A Doctor's Story*, Basingstoke: Macmillan.

Davis, K. (2007). *The Making of Our Bodies, Ourselves: How Feminism Travels across Borders*. Durham, NC: Duke University Press.

Drugs, Alcohol, and Women Nationally (DAWN) (1986). *Women and Stimulants*. London: DAWN.

DAWN (1985a). *Women and Alcohol*. London: DAWN.

DAWN (1985b). *Women and Tranquillisers*. London: DAWN.

DAWN (1985c). *DAWN's Evidence Presented to the House of Common's Social Services Committee*, January.

DAWN (1984a). *Women and Heroin*. London: DAWN.

DAWN (1984b). *Survey of Facilities for Women Using Drugs Including Alcohol in London*. London: DAWN. Compiled by DAWN workers with assistance from Dr. E. M. Ettorre, Institute of Psychiatry, London.

DAWN (1980). *Report from the First Symposium*. 28 November 1980, London, DAWN.

deBelleroche, J. (2002). 'Molecular Basis of Addiction', in W. Caan and J. deBelleroche (eds). *Drink, Drugs and Dependence: From Science to Clinical Practice*. London: Routledge, pp. 123–33.

Daniels, C. (1996). *At Women's Expense: State and the Politics of Fetal Rights*. Cambridge, MA: Harvard University Press.

Deedes, W. (1970). *The Drug Epidemic*. London: Tom Stacey.

Deitch, D. A. and Zweben, J. E. (1981). 'Synanon: A Pioneering Response in Drug Abuse Treatment and a Signal for Caution', in J. Lowinson and P. Ruiz (eds). *Substance Abuse: Clinical Problems and Perspectives*. Baltimore, MD: Williams and Wilkins, pp. 289–302.

DeLeon, G. and Wexler, H. K. (1973). 'Heroin Addiction: Its Relation to Sexual Behavior and Sexual Experience, *Journal of Abnormal Psychology*, 81, 1: 36–8.

Densen-Gerber, J. (1973). *We Mainline Dreams: The Odyssey House Story*. Baltimore, MD: Penguin Books.

Densen-Gerber, J. and Rohrs, C. C. (1973). 'Drug Addicted Parents and Child Abuse', *Contemporary Drug Problems*, 2, 683–96.

Densen-Gerber, J. and Baden, T. A. (1972). *Drugs, Sex, Parents, and You.* Philadelphia and New York: J. B. Lippincott Co.

Densen-Gerber, J., Wiener, M., and Hochstedler, R. (1972). 'Sexual Behavior, Abortion, and Birth Control in Heroin Addicts: Legal and Psychiatric Considerations', *Contemporary Drug Problems*, 1, 4: 72.

Denton, B. and O'Malley, P. (1999). 'Gender, Trust and Business: Women Drug Dealers in the Illicit Economy', *British Journal of Criminology*, 39, 4: 513–30.

Diaz-Tello, F., Paltrow, L., and Moreno, A. (2010). NAPW Working Paper: Birth Justice as Reproductive Justice. Accessed on 20 December 2010 at http://advocatesforpregnantwomen.org/main/publications/articles_and_reports/napw_working_paper_birth_justice_as_reproductive_justice.php.

d'Orban, P. (1970). 'Heroin Dependence and Delinquency in Women – A Study of Heroin Addicts in Holloway Prison', *British Journal of Addiction*, 65: 67–78.

Douglas, M. (1987). 'A Distinctive Anthropological Perspective', in M. Douglas (ed.). *Constructive Drinking: Perspectives on Drink from Anthropology*. Cambridge: Cambridge University Press, pp. 3–15.

Douglas, M. (1966). *Purity and Danger: An Analysis of the Concepts of Pollution and Taboo.* London: Routledge and Kegan Paul.

Doyal, L. (1995). *What Makes Women Sick: Gender and the Political Economy of Health.* Basingstoke: Macmillan Press Ltd.

Doyal, L. (1983). 'Women, Health and the Sexual Division of Labour: A Case Study of the Women's Health Movement in Britain', *Critical Social Policy*, 3: 21–32.

Doyal, L. (with I. Pennell) (1979). *The Political Economy of Health.* London; Pluto Press.

DrugScope (2010). *DrugScope Responds to Government's Decision to Abolish the National Treatment Agency: NTA's Functions to be Transferred to the New Public Health Service.* London: DrugScope (Press Release 26 July 2010).

Duke, K. (2010). 'Clashes in Culture: The Professionalization and Criminalization of the Drugs Workforce', *British Journal of Community Justice*, Special Edition, 8, 2: 31–43.

Duke, K. (2009). 'The Focus on Crime and Coercion in UK Drugs Policy', in S. MacGregor (ed.). *Responding to Drug Misuse: Research and Policy Priorities in Health and Social Care*. London: Routledge.

Eccles, W. (1942). 'The Society for the Study of Inebriety its Past and Present: What of its Future', *British Journal of Inebriety*, 40: 1–10.

Echols, A. (1989). *Daring To Be Bad: Radical Feminism in America, 1967–1975* Minneapolis, MN: University of Minnesota Press.

Edwards, G. (2010). 'Seeing America: Diary of a Drug-Focused Study Tour Made in 1967', *Addiction*, 105: 984–90.

Edwards, G. (2004). *Matters of Substance: Drugs: Is Legalisation the Right Answer or the Wrong Question?* London: Allen Lane.

Edwards, G. (1981). 'The Background', in G. Edwards and C. Busch (eds). *Drug Problems in Britain: A Review of Ten Years*. London: Academic Press, pp. 5–23.

Edwards, G. (1978). 'Drug and the Questions that Can be Asked of Epidemiology', in J. Fishman (ed.). *The Bases of Addiction*. Berlin: Dahlem Konferenzen.

Edwards, G., Russell, M. A. H., Hawks, D., and MacCafferty, M. (eds) (1976). *Drugs and Drug Dependence*. Farnborough, Hants: Saxon House, D.C. Heath.

Eisenstein, Z. (1998). *The Female Body and the Law.* Berkeley, CA: University of California Press.

Epstein, S. (2007). *Inclusion: The Politics of Difference in Medical Research*. Chicago, IL: University of Chicago Press.

Erickson P.G., Butters J., McGillicuddy P., and Hallgren A. (2000). 'Crack and Prostitution: Gender, Myths, and Experiences', *Journal of Drug Issues*, 30, 4: 767–88.

Ernst, S. and Goodison, L. (1997). *In Our Own Hands: A Book of Self-Help Therapy*. London: The Women's Press Ltd.

Ettorre, E. M. (2010). 'Bodies, Drugs and Reproductive Regimes', in E. Ettorre (ed.). *Culture, Bodies and Sociology of Health*. Surrey, UK: Ashgate, pp. 155–72.

Ettorre, E. M. (2007). *Revisioning Women and Drug use: Gender, Power and the Body*. Basingstoke: Palgrave Macmillan.

Ettorre, E. M. (2004). 'Revisioning Women and Drug Use: Gender Sensitivity, Gendered Bodies and Reducing Harm', *International Journal of Drugs Policy*, 15, 5–6: 327–35.

Ettorre, E. M. (1997). *'Women and Alcohol Women and Alcohol: From a Private Pleasure to a Public Problem?* London: Women's Press.

Ettorre, E. M. (1992). *Women and Substance Use*. Houndmills: Macmillan.

Ettorre, E. M. (1989). 'Women and Substance Use/Abuse: Towards a Feminist Perspective or How to Make Dust Fly', *Women's Studies International Forum*, 12, 6: 593–602.

Ettorre, E. M. (1988). 'A Follow-Up Study of Alcoholism Treatment Units', *British Journal of Addiction*, 83: 57–65.

Ettorre, E. M. (1987). 'Drug Problems and the Voluntary Sector of Care', *British Journal of Addiction*, 82: 469–76.

Ettorre, E. M. (1986a). 'Women and Drunken Sociology: Developing a Feminist Analysis', *Women's Studies International Forum*, 9, 5: 515–20.

Ettorre, E. M. (1986b). 'Women, Substance Abuse and Self-Help', in S. MacGregor (ed.). *Drugs and British Society: Responses to a Social Problem in the 1980s*. London: Routledge, pp. 101–15.

Ettorre, E. M. (1986c). 'Self-Help Groups as an Alternative to Benzodiazepine Use', in J. Gabe and P. Williams (eds). *Tranquillisers: Social, Psychological and Clinical Perspectives*. London and New York: Tavistock Publications, pp. 180–93.

Ettorre, E. M. (1985a). 'A Study of Alcoholism Treatment Units: Links with the Community', *British Journal of Addiction*, 79,181–9.

Ettorre, E. M. (1985b). 'A Study of Alcoholism Treatment Units: Some Findings on Patients', *Alcohol and Alcoholism*, 20, 361–9.

Ettorre, E. M. (1985c). 'A Study of Alcoholism Treatment Units: Some Findings on Unit and Staff', *Alcohol and Alcoholism*, 20, 371–8.

Ettorre, E. M. (1984). 'A Study of Alcohol Treatment Units: Treatment Activities and the Institutional Response', *Alcohol and Alcoholism*, 19, 243–55.

Ettorre, B., Griffiths, R., Kent, R. and Waterson, J. (eds) (1987). *Proceedings of a Conference on Women's Problems with Alcohol and Other Drugs: Improving Our Response*. Canterbury: University of Kent.

Ettorre, E. M. and Miles, S. (2001). 'Young People, Drug Use and the Consumption of Health', in S. Henderson and A. Petersen (eds). *Consuming Health: The Commodification of Health Care*. London: Routledge.

Ettorre, E. M. and Riska, E. (2001). 'Long-Term Users of Psychotropic Drugs: Embodying Masculinized Stress and Feminized Nerves', *Substance Use and Misuse*, 36, 9 and10: 1187–211.

Ettorre, E. M. and Riska, E. (1995). *Gendered Moods*. London: Routledge.

European Monitoring Centre for Drugs and Drug Addiction (EMCDDA) (1999). *Annual Report of the drugs problem in the European Union*, Luxembourg, Office for Official Publications of the European Communities.

Evans, R. D., Forsyth, C. J., and Gauthier, D. K. (2002). 'Gendered Pathways into and Experiences within Crack Cultures Outside of the Inner City', *Deviant Behavior: An Interdisciplinary Journal*, 23, 6, 483–510.

Falek, A. and Einstein, S. (1973). 'Genetics and Drug Abuse: A Primer for Workers in the Field'. *Drug Forum*, 2, 4: 377–94.

Fassin, D. and Rechtman, R. (2007). *The Empire of Trauma: An Inquiry into the Condition of Victimhood*. Princeton, NJ: Princeton University Press.

Faulder, C., Jackson, C., and Lewis, M. (1976). *The Women's Directory*. London: Virago.

Fazey, C. (1977). *The Aetiology of Psychoactive Substance Use*. Paris: UNESCO Press.

Ferguson, P., Lennox, T., and Lettieri, D. (1974a). *Drugs and Pregnancy: The Effects of Nonmedical Use of Drugs on Pregnancy, Childbirth, and Neonates*. (ADM, 75–187). Research issues 5. Rockville, MD: National Institute on Drug Abuse (NIDA).

Ferguson, P., Lennox, T., and Lettieri, D. (1974b). *Drugs and Sex: The Nonmedical Use of Drugs and Sexual Behavior*. (ADM, 76–184). Research issues 2. Rockville, MD: National Institute on Drug Abuse (NIDA).

Ferrell, J. and Sanders, C. R. (1995). 'Culture, Crime and Criminology', in J. Ferrell and C. R. Sanders (eds). *Cultural Criminology*. Boston: Northeastern University Press, pp. 3–21.

Figueroa, R. and Harding, S. (eds) (2003). *Science and Other Cultures: Issues in Philosophy of Science and Technology*. New York, Routledge.

Finegold, K., Wherry, L., and Schardin, S. (2004). 'Block Grants: Historical Overview and Lessons Learned', Urban Institute Report No. A-63, in 'New Federalism: Issues and Options for States', April 21.

Finkelstein, N. (2004). *Enhancing Substance Abuse Recovery through Integrated Trauma Treatment*. Sarasota, FL: National Trauma Consortium.

Finkelstein, N. and Markoff, L. S. (2004). 'The Women Embracing Life and Living (WELL) Project: Using the Relational Model to Develop Integrated Systems of Care for Women with Alcohol/Drug Use and Mental Health Disorders with Histories of Violence', *Alcoholism Treatment Quarterly*, 22, 3 and 4: 63–80.

Finkelstein, N., VanDeMark, N., Fallot, R., Brown, V. B., Cadiz, S., and Heckman, J. (1996). 'Using the Relational Model as a Context for Treating Pregnant and Parenting Chemically Dependent Women', *Journal of Chemical Dependency Treatment* (The Haworth Press), 6, 1 and 2: 23–44.

Finkelstein, N. and Piedade, E. M. (1993). 'The Relational Model and the Treatment of Addicted Women', *The Counselor*, May/June, pp. 8–10.

Finnegan, L. P. (1975). 'Narcotic Dependence in Pregnancy', *Journal of Psychedelic Drugs*, 7: 299.

Finnegan, L. P., Emich, J. P., Connaughton, J. F., and Wieland, W. (1973). 'Comprehensive Care of the Pregnant Addict and its Effect on Maternal and Infant Outcome', *Contemporary Drug Problems*, 1: 795–809.

Finnegan, L. P., Bookhart, P. R., Moten, L., Cohen, C., Goodman, N. (1976). 'Comprehensive Services to Drug Dependent Women and their Children', in

A. Schecter, H. Alksne, and E. Kaufman (eds). *Critical Concerns in the Field of Drug Abuse*. New York, NY: Marcel Dekker, Inc., pp. 745–49.

Flavin. J. (2009). *Our Bodies, Our Crimes: The Policing of Women's Reproduction in America*. New York: New York University Press.

Flemen, K. (2004). 'Gimme Shelter: WinterComfort Five Years On', *Druglink*, 19, 5: 12–13.

Fletcher, R. (2006). 'Reproductive Consumption', *Feminist Theory*, 7, 1: 27–47.

Fortun, K. (2001). *Advocacy after Bhopal: Environmentalism, Disaster, New Global Orders*. Chicago, IL: University of Chicago Press.

Fraser, N. and Gordon, L. (1994). 'A Genealogy of "Dependency": Tracing a Keyword of the U.S. Welfare State', *SIGNS: A Journal of Women in Culture and Society* 19, 2: 309–36.

Friedman, J. and Alicea, M. (2001). *Surviving Heroin: Interviews with Women in Methadone Clinics*. Gainesville, FL: University Press of Florida.

Frye, M. (1983). *The Politics of Reality: Essays in Feminist Theory*. Trumansburg, NY: Crossing Press.

Ghodse, A. H. (1977). 'Drug-Dependent Individuals Dealt With by London Casualty Departments', *British Journal of Psychiatry*, 131: 273–80.

Gilligan, C. (1982). *In a Different Voice: Psychological Theory and Women's Development*. Cambridge, MA: Harvard University Press.

Gilman, M. R. (1991). 'Beyond Opiates ... and into the '90s', *Druglink*, November/December: 16–18.

Gil-Rivas, V., Fiorentine, R., and Anglin, M. D. (1996). 'Sexual Abuse, Physical Abuse, and Posttraumatic Stress Disorder among Women Participating in Outpatient Drug Abuse Treatment', *Journal of Psychoactive Drugs*, 28, 1: 95–102.

Glatt, M. M. (1972). *The Alcoholic – and the Help He Needs*. London: Priory Press.

Glynn, T. J., Pearson, H. W., and Sayers, M. (1983). *Women and Drugs*. NIDA Research Monograph: Rockville, MD, DHHS Pub. No. (ADM), 83–1268.

Goffman, E. (1961). *Total Institutions: Essays on the Social Situation of Mental Patients and Other Inmates*. New York: Anchor Books.

Golden, J. (2005). *Message in a Bottle: The Making of Fetal Alcohol Syndrome*. Cambridge, MA: Harvard University Press.

Gomberg, E. S. L. (1986). The Edith S. Gomberg Papers, the Bentley Historical Library, University of Michigan, Ann Arbor, Michigan.

Gomberg, E. S. L. (1984). 'Femininity and Women's Alcohol Abuse', presented at the 92nd Annual Meeting of the American Psychological Association, Toronto, Canada.

Gomberg, E. S. L. (1982). 'Historical and Political Overview: Women and Drug Use', *Journal of Social Issues*, 38, 2: 9–23.

Gomberg, E. S. L. (1980). 'Women, Alcohol, and Drugs: The Life Cycle', Paper presented at the Institute of Pennsylvania Hospital, February 15, Symposium titled 'The Woman Next Door', sponsored by the Coordinating Office for the Drug and Alcohol Abuse Programs, Department of Public Health, City of Philadelphia.

Gomberg, E. S. L. (1979). *Gender and Disordered Behavior: Sex Differences in Psychopathology*. New York: Brunner/Mazel.

Gomberg, E. S. L. (1975). 'Alcoholism and Women: The State of Knowledge Today'. Paper presented at the National Alcoholism Forum, April 29, Milwaukee, Wisconsin.

Gomez, L. E. (1997). *Misconceiving Mothers: Legislators, Prosecutors, and the Politics of Prenatal Drug Exposure*. Philadelphia, PA: Temple University Press.

Green, A., Day, S., and Ward, H. (2000). 'Crack Cocaine and Prostitution in London in the 1990s', *Sociology of Health and Illness*, 22, 1: 27–39.

Grella, C. E. (2008). 'From Generic to Gender-Responsive Treatment: Changes in Social Policies, Treatment Services, and Outcomes of Women in Substance Abuse Treatment', *Journal of Psychoactive Drugs*, SARC Supplement 5, pp. 327–43.

Griffin, C. (1997). 'Troubled Teens: Managing Disorders of Transition and Consumption', *Feminist Review*, 55: 4–21.

Hammersley, M. (2001). 'Which Side was Becker on? Questioning Political and Epistemological Radicalism', *Qualitative Research*, 1, 1: 91–110.

Hammersley, R. and Reid, M. (2002). 'Why the Pervasive Addiction Myth is Still Believed', *Addiction Research and Theory*, 10, 1: 7–30.

Haraway, D. J. (1988). 'Situated Knowledges: The Science Question in Feminism as a Site of Discourse on the Privilege of Partial Perspective', *Feminist Studies*, 14, 3: 575–600.

Harding, S. (2008). *Sciences from Below: Feminisms, Postcolonialities, and Modernities*. Durham, NC: Duke University Press.

Harding, S. (2006). *Science and Social Inequality: Feminist and Postcolonial Issues*, Urbana and Chicago, IL: University of Illinois Press.

Harding, S. (1998). *Is Science Multicultural? Post-Colonialisms, Feminisms, and Epistemologies*. Bloomington, IN: Indiana University Press.

Harding, S. (1991). *Whose Science? Whose Knowledge? Thinking from Women's Lives*. Ithaca, NY: Cornell University Press.

Harding, S. (1987). 'Conclusions: Epistemological Questions', in S. Harding (ed.). *Feminism and Methodology*. Bloomington, IN: Indiana University Press and Milton Keynes, Open University Press, pp. 181–90.

Harding, S. (1986). *The Science Question in Feminism*. Ithaca, NY: Cornell University Press.

Hartsock, N. C. M. (1985). *Money, Sex and Power: Toward a Feminist Historical Materialism*. Boston: Northeastern University Press.

Harwood, H. J. (2002). 'Survey on Behavioral Health Workplace', *Frontlines*, November.

Henderson, S. (1999). 'Drugs and Culture: The Question of Gender', in N. South (ed.). *Drugs: Cultures, Controls and Everyday Life*. London: Sage Publications, pp. 36–48.

Henderson, S. (1996). 'E Types and Dance Divas: Gender Research and Community Prevention', in T. Rhodes and R. Hartnoll (eds). *AIDS, Drugs and Prevention: Perspectives on Individual and Community Action*. London: Routledge.

Henderson, S. (1993). 'Fun, Frisson and Fashion', *International Journal of Drug Policy*, 4, 3: 122–9.

Heneghan, M. (2000). 'Race, Women and Treatment: Alternatives to Custody', *Druglink*, 15, 5: 21–3.

Her Majesty's Government (HMG) (2010). *The Cross Government Research Strategy*, (February). London: Home Office.

HMG (2008). *Drugs: Protecting Families and Communities*. London: Home Office.

Herman, J. L. (1992). *Trauma and Recovery: The Aftermath of Violence – from Domestic Abuse to Political Terror.* New York: Basic Books.

Herzberg. D. (2009). *Happy Pills in America: From Miltown to Prozac*. Baltimore, MD: The Johns Hopkins University Press.

Hess, D. J. (2007). *Alternative Pathways in Science and Industry: Activism, Innovation and the Environment in an Era of Globalization*. Cambridge, MA: The MIT Press.

Hill, S. Y. (2000). 'Alcohol and Drug Abuse in Women', in M. Streiner, K. Yonkers and E. Eriksson (eds). *Mood Disorders in Women*. London: Martin Dunitz, pp. 449–68.

Hirsh, J. (1962). 'Women and Alcoholism', in W. C. Bier (ed.). *Alcoholism and Narcotics*. New York: Fordham University Press, pp. 108–15.

Home Office (1986). *Tackling Drugs Misuse: A Summary of the Government's Strategy*. London: HMSO.

Holmes, T. (1903). 'The Criminal Inebriate Female', *The British Journal of Inebriety*, 1, 2: 69–72.

Hughes, H. M. (1961). *The Fantastic Lodge: The Autobiography of a Girl Drug Addict*. Boston and Cambridge, MA: Houghton Mifflin Co. and The Riverside Press.

Humm, M. (ed.) (1992). *Feminism: A Reader*. New York: Harvester Wheatsheaf.

Hunt, G., Joe-Laidler, K., and Evans, K. (2002). 'The Meaning and Gendered Culture of Getting High: Gang Girls and Drug Use Issues', *Contemporary Drug Problems*, 29, 2: 375–411.

Iliff, B., Siatkowski, C., Waite-O'Brien, N., and White, W. (2007). 'The Treatment of Addicted Women: Modern Perspectives from the Betty Ford Center, Caron Treatment Centers and Hazelden', *Counselor*, 8, 3: 42–8.

Irwin, J. K. (1973). 'The "Normal" Life of the Addict and the Consequences of Addiction'. NIDA Grant RO-1-DA-00280: 77–90.

Irwin, K. (1995). 'Ideology, Pregnancy and Drugs: Differences between Crack-Cocaine, Heroin and Methamphetamine Users', *Contemporary Drug Problems*, 22: 613–37.

Jamieson, A., Glanz, A., and MacGregor, S. (1984). *Dealing with Drug Misuse: Crisis Intervention in the City*. London: Tavistock Publications.

Jellinek, E. M. (1960). *The Disease Concept of Alcoholism*. New Haven: Hill House Press.

Jerome, J. with L. Bilgorri (1991). *The Lost Years: Tranquillisers and After*. London: Virgin Publishing.

Johnsen, D. (1986). 'The Creation of Fetal Rights: Conflicts with Women's Constitutional Rights to Liberty, Privacy, and Equal Protection', *Yale Law Journal*, 95: 599–625.

Johnson, B. and A. Manwar (1991). 'Towards a Paradigm of Drug Eras: Previous Drug Eras Help to Model the Crack Epidemic in New York City During the 1990s'. Paper presented at American Society of Criminology, San Francisco, November.

Kalant, O. J. (1980). 'Introduction', in O. J. Kalant (ed.), *Alcohol and Drug Problems in Women*. New York: Plenum Press. (Volume 5 *Research Advances in Alcohol and Drug Problems*).

Kandall, S. (1996). *Substance and Shadow: Women and Addiction in the United States*. Cambridge, MA: Harvard University Press.

Keane, H. (2002). *What's Wrong with Addiction?* New York: New York University Press.

Keller, E. F. (2010). *The Mirage of a Space between Nature and Nurture*. Durham, NC: Duke University Press.

Kessel, N. and Walton, H. (1965). *Alcoholism*. Harmondsworth: Penguin Books.

Kieffer, S. N. (1968). 'New Program for Drug Addicts', *American Journal of Public Health*, 58, 12: 2353.
Kirk, S. A. and Kutchins, H. (1992). *The Selling of DSM: The Rhetoric of Science in Psychiatry.* New York: Aldine de Gruyter.
Klassen, P. (2001). 'Sacred Maternities and Postbiomedical Bodies: Religion and Nature in Contemporary Home Birth', *SIGNS: Journal of Women in Culture and Society*, 26, 3: 775–810.
Klawiter, M. (2008). *The Biopolitics of Breast Cancer: Changing Cultures of Disease and Activism.* Minneapolis: MN University of Minneapolis Press.
Klee, H. (2002). 'Drugs and Parenting', in H. Klee, M. Jackson, and S. Lewis (eds). *Drug Misuse and Motherhood.* London: Routledge, pp. 145–64.
Klee, H., Jackson, M., and Lewis, S. (eds) (2002). *Drug Misuse and Motherhood.* London: Routledge.
Klingemann, H. and Hunt, G. (eds) (1998). *Drug Treatment Systems in an International Perspective: Drugs, Demons and Delinquents.* London: Sage Publications.
Koedt, A. (1973). 'The Myth of the Vaginal Orgasm', in. A. Koedt, E. Levin, and A. Rapone (eds). *Radical Feminism.* New York: Quadrangle Books, 198–207.
Lacey, R. and Woodward, S. (1984). *That's Life! Survey on Tranquillisers.* London: British Broadcasting Corporation in association with MIND.
Ladd-Taylor, M. and Umanksy, L. (eds) (1998). *'Bad' Mothers: The Politics of Blame in Twentieth-Century America.* New York: New York University Press.
Langman, L. (2003). 'Culture, Identity, and Hegemony: The Body in the Global Age', *Current Sociology*, 52, 3/4: 223–47.
Larner, J. and R. Tefferteller (1966). *The Addict in the Street.* Harmondsworth: Penguin Books.
Laurie, P. (1967). *Drugs.* Harmondsworth: Penguin Books.
Layne, L. L. (2002). *Motherhood Lost: A Feminist Account of Pregnancy Loss in America.* New York: Routledge.
Layne, L. L., Vostral, S. L., and Boyer, K. (2010). *Feminist Technology.* Chicago, IL: University of Illinois Press.
Leshner, A. I. (1997). 'Addiction is a Brain Disease, and It Matters', *Science*, 278, 5335: 45–7.
Li, L., Ford, J. A. and Moore, D. (2000). 'An Exploratory Study of Violence, Substance Abuse Disability, and Gender', *Social Behavior and Personality*, 28, 1: 61–71.
Link, B. G., Phelan, J. C., Bresnahan, M., Stueve, A., and Pescosolido, B. A. (1999). 'Public Conceptions of Mental Illness: Labels, Causes, Dangerousness and Social Distance', *American Journal of Public Health*, 89, 9: 1328–33.
Lisansky, E. S. (1958). 'The Woman Alcoholic', *Annals of the American Academy of Political and Social Science*, 315: 73–81.
Lisansky, E. S. (1957). 'Alcoholism in Women: Social and Psychological Concomitants', *Quarterly Journal of Studies on Alcohol*, 18: 588–623.
Lisansky, E. S. (1954). 'The Clinical Psychologist in a Clinic for Alcoholics', In *Survey of Clinical Practice in Psychology.* New York: International Universities Press, pp. 209–17. (Box 6, Folder 'Publications, 1950s').
Litman, G. (1986). 'Women and Alcohol Problems: Finding the Next Questions', *British Journal of Addiction*, 81: 601–3.

Litman, G. (1978). 'Clinical Aspects of Sex Role Stereotyping', in J. Chetwynd and C. Hartnett (eds). *The Sex Role System*. London: Routledge and Kegan Paul, pp. 109–26.

Litman, G. (1975). 'Women and Alcohol: Facts and Myths', *New Behaviour*, 24, 126–9.

Litman, G. and Wilson, C. (1978). *A Review of Services for Women Alcoholics in the UK*. Paper presented at the 24th International Institute on the Prevention and Treatment of Alcoholism, Zurich, Switzerland.

Littlewood, R. (2002). *Pathologies of the West*. London: Continuum.

Lydon, S. G. (1993). *Take the Long Way Home: Memoirs of a Survivor*. San Francisco, CA: Harper.

McClelland, E. C., Davis, W. N., Kalin, R., and Warner, E. (1972). *The Drinking Man*. London: Collier Macmillan.

MacDonald, R., Shildrick, T., and Simpson, M. (2007). 'Drugs in Britain: Discussion and Conclusions', in R. MacDonald, T. Shildrick, and M. Simpson (eds). *Drugs in Britain: Supply, Consumption and Control*. Basingstoke, Palgrave Macmillan.

MacGregor, S. (2010). 'Policy Responses to the Drugs Problem', in S. MacGregor (ed.). *Responding to Drug Misuse: Research and Policy Priorities in Health and Social Care*. London: Routledge, pp. 1–13.

MacGregor, S. (1995). *Drugs, Policy, Community and the City, Occasional Paper from Series of the School of Sociology and Social Policy*. London: University of Middlesex, 23.

MacGregor, S. (1989). 'The Public Debate in the 1980s', in S. MacGregor (ed.). *Drugs and British Society: Responses to a Social Problem in the 1980s*. London: Routledge, pp. 1–19.

MacGregor, S. and Ettorre, E. M. (1987). 'From Treatment to Rehabilitation: British Policy on the Treatment and Care of Drug Takers', in N. Dorn and N. South (eds). *A Land Fit for Heroin: Drug Policies, Prevention and Practice*. Basingstoke: Macmillan Press, Ltd., pp. 125–45.

MacGregor, S., Ettorre, B., Coomber, R., Crosier, A., and Lodge, H. (1991). *Drug Services in England and the Impact of the Central Funding Initiative*. London: Institute for the Study of Drug Dependence.

MacGregor, S. and Smith, L. (1998). 'The English Drug Treatment System: Experimentation or Pragmatism', in H. Klingemann and G. Hunt (eds). *Drug Treatment Systems in an International Perspective*. London: Sage Publications, pp. 69–80.

McCarty, D. (2002). 'The Alcohol and Drug Abuse Treatment Workforce', *Frontlines,* November.

McRobbie, A. and Thorton, S. L. (1995). 'Rethinking "Moral Panic" for Multi-Mediated Social Worlds', *British Journal of Sociology*, 46, 4: 559–74.

Mahan, S. (1996). *Crack, Cocaine, Crime, and Women: Legal, Social, and Treatment Issues*. Thousand Oaks, CA: Sage Publications.

Maher, L. (1992). 'Punishment and Welfare: Crack Cocaine and the Regulation of Mothering'. *Women and Criminal Justice*, 3, 2: 35–70.

Malabou, C. (2008). *What Should We Do With Our Brain?* New York: Fordham University Press.

Mann, M. (1968). *The New Primer on Alcoholism*. New York, Holt, Rinehart and Winston.

Marecek, J. (1999). 'Trauma Talk in Feminist Clinical Practice', in S. Lamb (ed.), *New Versions of Victims: Feminists Struggle with the Concept*. New York, New York University Press, pp. 158–70.
Martin, J. K., Lang, A., and Olafsdottir, S. (2008). 'Rethinking Theoretical Approaches to Stigma', *Social Science and Medicine*, 67, 3: 431–40.
Martin J. K., Pescosolido, B. A., and Tuch, S. A. (2000). 'Of Fear and Loathing: The Role of Disturbing Behavior, Labels and Causal Attributions in Shaping Public Attitudes Toward Persons with Mental Illness'. *Journal of Health and Social Behavior*, 41, 2: 208–33.
Mayes, L. C., Granger, R. H., Bornstein, M. H., and Zuckerman, B. (1992). 'The Problem of Prenatal Cocaine Exposure: A Rush to Judgment'. *Journal of the American Medical Association*, 267, 3: 406–8.
Maynard, M. (1994). 'Method, Practice and Epistemology: The Debate about Feminism and Research', in M. Maynard and J. Purvis (eds). *Researching Women's Lives from a Feminist Perspective*. London: Taylor and Francis.
Measham, F. (2002). '"Doing Gender" – "Doing Drugs". Conceptualizing the Gendering of Drug Cultures', *Contemporary Drug Problems*, 29, 2, 335–73.
Measham, F., Aldridge, J., and Parker, H. (2001). *Dancing on Drugs: Risk, Health and Hedonism in the British Club Scene*. London: Free Association Books.
Melville, J. (1984). *The Tranquilliser Trap and How to Get Out of it*. London: Fontana Paperbacks.
Member of the Community of St. Mary (1944). 'The Moral Mental and Physical Background of Female Inebriates', *British Journal of Inebriety*, 42, 1: 3–20.
Mertens, J. R. and Weisner, C. M. (2001). 'Predictors of Substance Abuse Treatment Retention among Women and Men in an HMO', *Alcoholism: Clinical and Experimental Research*, 24, 10: 1525–33.
Meyerson, D. E. and Scully, M. A. (1995). 'Tempered Radicalism and the Politics of Ambivalence and Change', *Organization Science*, 6, 5: 585–600.
Miller, J. B. (1986). *Toward a New Psychology of Women*. Second Edition. Boston: Beacon Press.
Miller, J. B. (1976). *Toward a New Psychology of Women*. Boston: Beacon Press.
Mills, C. W. (1997). *The Racial Contract*. Ithaca, NY: Cornell University Press.
Miller, W. R. (2002). *Motivational Interviewing: Preparing People for Change*. New York: The Guilford Press.
Ministry of Health (1965). *Drug Addiction: The Second Report of the Interdepartmental Committee*. London: HMSO.
Ministry of Health (1961). *Drug Addiction: Report of the Interdepartmental Committee*. London: HMSO.
Ministry of Health (1926). *Report of Departmental Committee on Morphine and Heroin Addiction. Rolleston Report*. London: HMSO.
Mitchell, J. (1974). *Psychoanalysis and Feminism*. New York: Pantheon Books.
Mold, A. (2008). *Heroin: The Treatment of Addiction in Twentieth Century Britain*. DeKalb, IL: Northern Illinois University Press.
Mold, A. and Berridge, V. (2010). *Voluntary Action and Illegal Drugs: Health and Society in Britain since the 1960s*. Basingstoke: Palgrave Macmillan.
Monaghan, L. (2001). *Body Building, Drugs and Risk*. London: Routledge.
Mondanaro, E. E. (2004). 'A Pioneer of Chemical Dependency Treatment: Dr Mondanaro Takes No Prisoners', *American Journal of Public Health*, August, 94, 8: 1300–2.

Mondanaro, J. E. (1981). 'Reproductive Health Concerns for the Treatment of Drug Dependent Women', in *Treatment Services for Drug Dependent Women* I, Rockville, MD: National Institute on Drug Abuse, DHHS Publication No. (ADM) 81–1177: 258–81.

Moore, J., Buchan, B., Finkelstein, N., and Thomas, K. E. (1995). *Nurturing Program for Families in Substance Abuse Treatment and Recovery.* Park City, UT: Family Development Resources, Inc.

Morgen, S. (2002). *Into Our Own Hands: The Women's Health Movement in the United States, 1969–1990.* New Brunswick, NJ: Rutgers University Press.

Morrison, C. and Siney, C. (1995). 'Maternity Services for Drug Misusers in England and Wales: A National Survey', *Health Trends*, 27: 15–17.

Mosely, T. M. (1996). 'PROTOTYPES: An Urban Model Program of Treatment and Recovery Services for Dually Diagnosed Perinatal Program Participants', *Journal of Psychoactive Drugs*, 28, 4: 381–8.

Murphy, S. and Rosenbaum, M. (1999). *Pregnant Women on Drugs: Combating Stereotypes and Stigma.* New Brunswick, NJ: Rutgers University Press.

Murphy, S. and Rosenbaum, M. (eds) (1995). 'The Rhetoric of Reproduction: Pregnancy and Drug Use', *Contemporary Drug Problems*, 22, 4.

Murphy, S. and Sales, P. (2001). 'Pregnant Drug Users: Scapegoats of the Reagan/Bush and Clinton Era Economics', *Social Justice*, 78, 4: 72–95.

Musto, D. F. (1999). *The American Disease: Origins of Narcotics Control.* Oxford University Press. (Third Edition).

Musto, D. F. (1975). 'Whatever Happened to Community Mental Health?' *The Public Interest*, 39: 53–79.

Muzak, J. (2009). 'Trauma, Feminism, and Addiction: Cultural and Clinical Lessons from Susan Gordon Lydon's *Take the Long Way Home: Memoirs of a Survivor*', *Traumatology*, 15, 4: 24–34.

Najavits, L. M. (2007). 'Seeking Safety: An Evidence-Based Model for Substance Abuse and Trauma/PTSD', in K. A. Witkiewitz and G. A. Marlatt (eds). *Therapists' Guide to Evidence-Based Relapse Prevention: Practical Resources for the Mental Health Professional.* San Diego, CA: Elsevier Press, pp. 141–67.

Najavits, L. M. (2002). 'Seeking Safety: A New Psychotherapy for Posttraumatic Stress Disorder and Substance Use Disorder', in P. Oiumiette and P. Brown (eds). *Trauma and Substance Abuse: Causes, Consequences, and Treatment of Comorbid Disorders.* Washington, DC: American Psychological Press, pp. 147–70.

Najavits, L. M. (2001). *Seeking Safety: A Treatment Manual for PTSD and Substance Abuse.* New York: Guilford Press.

National Clearinghouse for Drug Abuse Information (1975). *Women and Drugs: An Annotated Bibliography* (ADM, 76–289). National Institute on Drug Abuse (NIDA).

National Treatment Agency for Substance Misuse (NTA) (2010). *Women in Drug Treatment: What the Latest Figures Reveal.* London: NTA. Accessed at www.nta.nhs.uk 14 November 2010.

NTA (2009a). *Diversity: Learning From Good Practice in The Field.* London: NTA. Accessed at www.nta.nhs.uk.

NTA (2009b). *The Story of Drug Treatment.* London: Home Office.

Neill, A. and Hymers, J. (1972). *Alcoholism, the Ignored Illness.* Edinburgh: Alna Press.

Nellis, M. (1980). *The Female Fix.* New York: Houghton Mifflin.

Neumann, L. L. (1973). 'Drug Abuse in Pregnancy: Its Effects on the Fetus and Newborn Infant', in E. Harms (ed.). *Drugs and Youth: The Challenge of Today.* New York: Pergamon Press, 1–32.

New York Academy of Medicine (1951). *Drug Addiction among Adolescents.* New York Academy of Medicine with Josiah Macy, Jr. Foundation, 30 November 1951 and 13–14 March 1952.

New York State Narcotics Investigation (1951–2). *Report.* (Housed in the New York State Archives.)

Noether, C. D., Finkelstein, N., VanDeMark, N. R., Savage, A., Reed, B. G., and Moses, D. J. (2005). 'Design Strengths and Issues of SAMHSA's Women, Co-occurring Disorders and Violence Study', *Psychiatric Services*, 66, 10: 1233–6.

Nolan, G. and Day, C. (1988). *Alcohol and the Black Community: Providing an Anti-Racist Service.* London: DAWN.

Oakley, A. (1984). *The Captured Womb: A History of the Medical Care of Pregnant Women.* Oxford: Basil Blackwell.

Oakley, A. (1981). *Subject Women.* Oxford: Martin Robertson.

Oakley, A. (1980). *Women Confined: Towards a Sociology of Childbirth.* Oxford: Martin Robertson.

Oakley, A. (1979). *From Here to Maternity.* Harmondsworth: Penguin Books.

Olson, N. (2003). *With a Lot of Help from Our Friends: The Politics of Alcoholism.* Lincoln NE: Writer's Club Press.

O'Malley, P. and Valverde, M. (2004). 'Pleasure, Freedom and Drugs: The Uses of "Pleasure" in Liberal Governance of Drug and Alcohol Consumption', *Sociology*, 38, 1, 25–42.

O'Sullivan, S. (1987). 'Addicting Forces', in S. O'Sullivan (ed.). *Women's Health: A Spare Rib Reader.* London: Pandora, p. 318.

Page, A. (1980). 'Counselling', in Camberwell Council on Alcoholism, *Women and Alcohol.* London: Tavistock Publications, pp. 159–75.

Painter, J., Riley-Buckley, D., and Whittington, D. (2000). 'Practical Considerations: Making Women's Services Available', *Druglink*, 15, 5: 18–20.

Paltrow, L. M. (2001). 'The War on Drugs and the War on Abortion: Some Initial Thoughts on the Connections, Intersections and the Effects', *Southern University Law Review*, 28, 201.

Paltrow, L. M. (1992). *Criminal Prosecutions of Pregnant Women: National Update and Overview*, New York: Reproductive Freedom Project, American Civil Liberties Union Foundation.

Parker, H., Aldridge, J., and Measham, F. (1998). *Illegal Leisure: The Normalization of Adolescent Drug Use.* London: Routledge.

Parker, H. and Measham, F. (1994). 'Pick "n" Mix: Changing Patterns of Illicit Drug Use among 1990s Adolescents', *Drugs: Education, Prevention and Policy*, 1, 1: 5–13.

Parker, H., Measham, F., and Aldridge, J. (1995). *Drug Futures: Changing Patterns of Drug Use amongst English Youth.* London: Institute for the Study of Drug Dependence.

Parker, H., Williams, L., and Aldridge, J. (2002). 'The Normalisation of "Sensible" Recreational Drug Use: Further Evidence from the Northwest England Longitudinal Study', *Sociology*, 36, 4: 941–64.

Parra, G. (2002). 'Welfare Reform and Substance Abuse Treatment: Innovative State Strategies', National Health Policy Forum. No. 771.

Parsons, T. (1959). 'The Social Structure of the Family', in R. Ashen (ed.), *The Family: Its Functions and Destiny*, New York: Harper and Row.
Parsons, T. (1942). 'Age and Sex in the Social Structure of the United States', *American Sociological Review*, 7, 5: 604–16.
Pearson, G. (1999). 'Drug Policy Dilemmas: Partnership, Social Exclusion and Targeting Resources', in A. Marlow and G. Pearson (eds). *Young People, Drugs and Community Safety*. Lyme Regis: Russell House Publishing.
Perlstein, M. A. (1947). 'Congenital Morphinism: Rare Cause of Convulsions in Newborn', *JAMA*, 135: 633.
Perry, L. (1979). *Women and Drug Use: An Unfeminine Dependency*. London: Institute for the Study of Drug Dependence.
Pescor, M. J. (1944). 'A Comparative Study of Male and Female Drug Addicts', *American Journal of Psychiatry*, 100: 771–4.
Peters, T. and Preedy, V. (2002). 'Alcohol and Genetic Predisposition', in W. Caan and J. De Belleroche (eds). *Drink, Drugs and Dependence: From Science to Clinical Practice*. London: Routledge, pp. 27–37.
Phillips, A. and Rakusen, J. (1978). *Our Bodies, Ourselves: A Health Book by and for Women*. London: Penguin Books, Ltd.
Pierson, P. S., Howard, P. and Kleber, H. D. (1972). 'Sudden Deaths in Infants Born to Methadone-Maintained Addicts', *Journal of the American Medical Association*, 220, 13: 1733–44.
Plant, M. (1981). 'What Aetiologies?', in G. Edwards and C. Busch (eds). *Drug Problems in Britain: A Review of Ten Years*. London: Academic Press.
Plant, M. (1975). *Drugtakers in an English Town*. London: Tavistock Publications.
Pratt, O. (1981). 'Alcohol and the Woman of Childbearing Age – A Public Health Problem', *British Journal of Addiction*, 76: 383–90.
Raine, P. (2001). *Women's Perspectives on Drugs and Alcohol: The Vicious Circle*. Aldershot: Ashgate.
Reed, B. G. (1987). 'Developing Women-Sensitive Drug Dependence Treatment Services: Why So Difficult?' *Journal of Psychoactive Drugs*, 19, 2: 151–64.
Reid, J. (1929). 'The Treatment of Female Inebriates and Drug Addicts', *The British Journal of Inebriety*, 24, 2: 58–62.
Reid, M. and Hammersley, M. (2000). 'Sociopsychological Issues in Understanding Gender Relations and Gender Differences', *Psychology, Evolution and Gender*, 2, 2: 167–73.
Reinarman, C. (2005). 'Addiction as Accomplishment: The Discursive Construction of Disease', *Addiction Research and Theory*, 13, 4: 307–20.
Reinarman, C. (1994). 'The Social Construction of Drug Scares', in P. and P. Adler (eds). *Constructions of Deviance: Social Power, Content, and Interaction*. Wadsworth Publishing, pp. 92–103.
Rich, A. (1980). 'Toward a Woman-Centered University (1973–74)', in A. Rich, *On Lies, Secrets and Silence: Selected Prose 1966–78*. London: Virago, pp. 125–55.
Rich, A. (1976). *Of Woman Born: Motherhood as Experience and Institution*. New York: W. W. Norton.
Riska, E. (2010). 'Gender and Medicalization and Biomedicalization Theories', in A. E. Clarke, J. R. Fosket, J. R. Fishman, and J. K. Shim (eds). *Biomedicalization: Technoscience, Health, and Illness in the U.S.* Durham, NC: Duke University Press.
Riska, E. (2001). *Medical Careers and Feminist Agendas: American, Scandinavian and Russian Women Physicians*. New York: Aldine Gruyter.

Riska, E. and Ettorre, E. (1999). 'Mental Distress – Gender Aspects of Symptoms and Coping', *Acta Oncologica*, 38, 6: 757–61.

Robb, C. (2006). *This Changes Everything: The Relational Revolution in Psychology*. New York: Farrar, Straus and Giroux.

Roberts, A. Jackson, M., and Carlton-Laney, I. (2000). 'Revisiting the Need for Feminism and Afrocentric Theory when Treating African-American Female Substance Abusers', *Journal of Drug Issues*, 30, 4: 901–18.

Robins, L. N. and D. Regier (eds) (1991). *Psychiatric Disorders in America: The Epidemiologic Catchment Area Study*. New York: The Free Press.

Room, R. (2005). 'Stigma, Social Inequality and Alcohol and Drug Use', *Drug and Alcohol Review*, 24, March: 143–55.

Room, R. (2004). 'Alcohol and Harm Reduction, Then and Now', *Critical Public Health*, 14: 329–44.

Rose, N. (2007). 'Beyond Medicalisation', *The Lancet*, 369, 9562: 700–2.

Rose, N. (2006). *The Politics of Life Itself: Biomedicine, Power, and Subjectivity in the Twenty-First Century*. Princeton, NJ: Princeton University Press.

Rose, N. (2003). 'Becoming Neurochemical Selves', in N. Stehr (ed.). *Biotechnology between Commerce and Civil Society*. New Brunswick, NJ: Transaction Publishers.

Rosenbaum, M. (1981). *Women on Heroin*. New Brunswick, NJ: Rutgers University Press.

Rosenthal, T., Patrick, S. W., and Krug, D. C. (1964). 'Congenital Neonatal Narcotics Addiction: A Natural History', *American Journal of Public Health*, 54, 8: 1252–62.

Roth, P. (1991a). *Alcohol and Drugs Are Women's Issues: A Review of the Issues*. Vol. I. Women's Action Alliance Series. Metuchen, NJ: Scarecrow Press.

Roth, P. (1991b). *Alcohol and Drugs Are Women's Issues: A Model Program Guide*. Vol. II. Women's Action Alliance Series. Metuchen, NJ: Scarecrow Press.

Rowbotham, S. (1973). *Women's Consciousness, Man's World*. Harmondsworth: Penguin Books.

Ruggerio, V. (1999). 'Drugs as a Password and the Law as a Drug: Discussing the Legalisation of Illicit Substances', In N. South (ed.). *Drugs: Cultures, Controls and Everyday Life*. London: Sage Publications, pp. 123–37.

Sargent, M. (1992) *Women, Drugs and Policy in Sydney, London and Amsterdam*. Aldershot: Avebury.

Sassoon, H. F. (1978). 'Addictions: Some Reasons for Investigating Their Hematology', *British Journal of Addiction*, 73: 61–7.

Scharlieb, M. (1907). 'Alcohol and the Children of the Nation', *The British Journal of Inebriety*, 5, 2: 59–71.

Schneider, A. L. and Ingram, H. (1997). *Policy Design for Democracy*. Lawrence, KS: University Press of Kansas.

Schneider, A. L. and Ingram, H. (1993). 'The Social Construction of Target Populations', *American Political Science Review*, 87, 2: 334–46.

Schneider, A. L. and Sidney, M. (2009). 'What's Next for Policy Design and Social Construction Theory?' *Policy Studies Journal*, 37: 103–19.

Scott, J. W. (1990). 'Deconstructing Equality-versus-Difference: Or, the Uses of Poststructuralist Theory for Feminism', in M. Hirsch and E. F. Keller (eds). *Conflicts in Feminism*. New York: Routledge.

Scully, D. and Bart, P. (1973). 'A Funny Thing Happened on the Way to the Orifice: Women in Gynecology Textbooks', *The American Journal of Sociology*, 78, 4: 1045–50.
Sebestyen, A. (1985). 'Britain: The Politics of Survival – While the Work Goes on', in R. Morgan (ed.). *Sisterhood is Global*. Harmondsworth: Penguin Books, pp. 94–102.
Seedhouse, D. (1998). *Ethics: The Heart of Health Care*. New York: John Wiley and Sons (Second Edition).
Segal, B. (2001). 'Responding to Victimized Alaska Native Women in Treatment for Substance Use', *Substance Use and Misuse*, 36, 6: 845–65.
Shapiro, H. (2000). 'Winter Comfort: The Price of Trust', *Druglink*, 15, 2, 4–7.
Shaw, T. C. (1903). 'The Psychology of the Inebriate Mother', *The British Journal of Inebriety*, 1, 2: 58–60.
Sherman, S. G., Kamarulzaman, A., and Spittal, P. (2008). 'Women and Drugs across the Globe: A Call to Action'. *International Journal of Drug Policy* 19, 2: 97–8.
Shildrick, M. (2002). *Embodying the Monster: Encounters with the Vulnerable Self*. London: Sage Publications.
Shildrick, M. (1997). *Leaky Bodies and Boundaries: Feminism, Post Modernism and Bioethics*. London: Routledge.
Sister Joan Elizabeth (1974). 'Helping Women Addicts at Spelthorne St. Mary's, England', *International Journal of Offender Therapy and Comparative Criminology*, 18: 77–81.
Smart, C. (1985). 'Drug Dependency Units in England and Wales: The Results of a National Survey', *Drug and Alcohol Dependence*, 15: 131–44.
Smart, C. (1984). 'Social Policy and Drug Addiction', *British Journal of Addiction*, 79, 1, 31–9.
Smart, C. (1981). 'Law and Control of Women's Sexuality: The Case of the 1950s', in B. Hutter and G. Williams (eds). *Controlling Women: The Normal and the Deviant*. London: Croom Helm in association with the Oxford University Women's Studies Committee, pp. 40–60.
Smith, D. (1990). *The Conceptual Practices of Power: A Feminist Sociology of Knowledge*. Toronto: University of Toronto Press.
Somerset, Lady. H. (1912). 'The Duxhurst Industrial Farm Colony for Female Inebriates', *The British Journal of Inebriety*, 10, 2: 81–5.
South, N. (ed.) (1999). *Drugs: Cultures, Controls and Everyday Life*. London: Sage Publications.
South, N. and Teeman, D. (1999). 'Young People, Drugs and Community Life: The Messages from Research', in A. Marlow and G. Pearson (eds). *Young People, Drugs and Community Safety*, Lyme Regis, Russell House Publishing, pp. 69–80.
Spear, H. B. (2002). *Heroin Addiction Care and Control: The British System 1916–1984*. London: Drugscope.
Spear, H. B. (1988). 'Journal Interview 20: Conversation with H. B. Spear', *British Journal of Addiction*, 83: 473–82.
Spear, H. B. (1969). 'The Growth of Heroin Addiction in the United Kingdom', *British Journal of Addiction*, 64: 245–55.
Spivak, G. C. (1993). 'Interview with Sara Danius and Stefan Jonsson', *Boundary 2*, 20, 2: 24–50.

Stein, M. D. and Cyr, M. G. (1997). 'Women and Substance Abuse', *Medical Clinics of North America*, 81, 4: 979–98.

Stella Project (2002). *Separate Issues, Shared Solutions: Exploring Positive Ways of Working with Domestic Violence and Substance Misuse: Report from the Launch of the Stella Project* 2 December 2003. London: Mayor of London. See: http://www.gldvp.org.uk/module_images/The%20Stella%20Project%20-%20Separate%20Issues%20Shared%20Solutions.pdf. Accessed 12 September 2010.

Sterk, C. (1999). *Fast Lives: Women who Use Crack Cocaine*. Philadelphia: Temple University Press.

Sterk, C., Theall, K. P., and Elifson, K. W. (2002). 'Health Care Utilization among Drug-Using and Non-Drug-Using Women', *Journal of Urban Health: Bulletin of the New York Academy of Medicine*, 79, 4: 586–99.

Stern, R. (1966). 'The Pregnant Addict', *American Journal of Obstetrics and Gynecology*, 94: 253–7.

Stimson, G. V. (1987). 'The War on Heroin: British Policy and the International Trade in Illicit Drugs', in N. Dorn and N. South (eds). *A Land Fit for Heroin: Drugs Policies, Prevention and Practice*. Houndmills, Macmillan, pp. 35–61.

Stimson, G.V. (1973). *Heroin and Behaviour*. London: Irish University Press.

Stimson, G. V. and Oppenheimer, E. (1982). *Heroin Addiction: Treatment and Control in Britain*. London: Tavistock.

Stone, M. L., Salerno, L. J., Green, M., and Zelson, C. (1971). 'Narcotic Addiction in Pregnancy', *Journal of Obstetrics and Gynecology*, 109, 5: 716–23.

Strang, J. (1991). 'Injecting Drug Use', *British Medical Journal*, 303: 1043–6.

Sullivan, W. C. (1903). 'The Causes of Inebriety in the Female, and the Effects of Alcoholism on Racial Degeneration', *The British Journal of Inebriety*, 1, 2: 61–4.

Sun, A. P. (2000). 'Helping Substance-Abusing Mothers in the Child-Welfare System: Turning Crisis into Opportunity', *Families in Society*, 81, 2: 142–51.

Tanne, J. H. (2003). 'Judianne Densen-Gerber', *British Medical Journal*, 326, 7400: 1216.

Taylor, A. (1993). *Women Drug Users: An Ethnography of a Female Injecting Community*. Oxford: Clarendon Press.

Thom, B. (1997). 'Women and Alcohol: A Policy Dilemma', *Policy Studies*, 18, 1: 49–65.

Thomson, A. D. and Young, J. (1996). 'A Review of Treatment Alternatives for Drug Offenders: A Case for Urine Monitoring in Condition of Treatment Orders', *Drugs: Education, Prevention and Policy*, 3, 1: 49–56.

Teeman, D., South, N., and Henderson, S. (1999). 'Multi-Impact Drugs Prevention in the Community', in A. Marlow and G. Pearson (eds). *Young People, Drugs and Community Safety*. Lyme Regis: Russell House Publishing, pp. 99–108.

Terry, J. and Urla, J. (eds). *Deviant Bodies*. Bloomington: Indiana University Press.

Tracy, S. W. (2005). *Alcoholism in America: From Reconstruction to Prohibition*. Baltimore MD: Johns Hopkins University Press.

Travis-Clegg, J. T. (1913). 'The Work of a Reformatory for Female Inebriates', *The British Journal of Inebriety*, 11, 1: 16–22.

Trickett, S. (1986). *Coming Off Tranquillizers: A Withdrawal Plan that Really Works*. Wellingborough, New York: Thorsons Publishing Group.

Tuana, N. (2006). 'The Speculum of Ignorance: The Women's Health Movement and Epistemologies of Ignorance', *Hypatia*, 21, 3: 1–19.

Tuana, N. (2004). 'Coming to Understand: Orgasm and the Epistemology of Ignorance', *Hypatia*, 19, 1: 194–232.

Tuana, N. and Sullivan, S. (eds) (2007). *Race and Epistemologies of Ignorance*. Albany, NY: SUNY Press.

Turner, B. (1996). *The Body and Society*. London: Sage Publications (Second Edition).

UNODC (2004). *Substance Abuse Treatment and Care for Women: Case Studies and Lessons Learned*. New York: UN Xinhua New Agency.

Urla, J. and Terry, J. (1995). 'Introduction: Mapping Embodied Deviance', in J. Terry and J. Urla (eds). *Deviant Bodies: Critical Perspectives on Difference in Science and Popular Cultures*. Bloomington, Indiana: Indiana University Press, pp. 1–18.

US Department of Justice (1989). 'Office of the Attorney General of the United States', *Drug Trafficking: A Report to the President of the United States*.

US Public Health Service Newsreel (1937). National Library of Medicine.

Valentine, K. and Fraser, S. (2008). 'Trauma, Damage and Pleasure: Rethinking Problematic Drug Use'. *International Journal of Drug Policy*, 19, 5: 410–16.

Vaillant, G. E. (1995). *The Natural History of Alcoholism Revisited*. Cambridge, MA: Harvard University Press.

Vaillant, G. E. (1973). 'A Twenty-Year Follow-Up of New York Narcotic Addicts', *Archives of General Psychiatry*, 29: 237–41.

van Wormer, K. and Davis, D. R. (2003), *Addiction Treatment: A Strengths Perspective*. London: Thomson, Brooks/Cole.

Vivian, M. (1927). 'Alcoholism and Drug Addiction', *British Journal of Inebriety*, 24, 3: 129–31.

Vogt, I. (1998). 'Gender and Drug Treatment Systems', in H. Klingemann and G. Hunt (eds). *Drug Treatment Systems in an International Perspective: Drugs, Demons and Delinquents*. London, Sage Publications, pp. 281–97.

Volkow, N. (2004). 'Drug Addiction: The Neurobiology of Behavior Gone Awry', *Nature Reviews: Neuroscience*, 12: 963–70.

Vrecko, S. (2009). 'Justice in Drug Courts: Crime, Punishment and Societies of Control', *Science as Culture*, 18, 2: 217–32.

Waldorf, D., Murphy, S. and Reinarman, C. (1991). *Cocaine Changes: The Experience of Using and Quitting*. Philadelphia, Temple University Press.

Waldorf, D. (1974). *Careers in Dope*. Upper Saddle River, NJ: Prentice Hall.

Waldorf, D., Orlick, M., and Reinarman, C. (1974). *Morphine Maintenance: The Shreveport Clinic, 1919–1923*. Washington, DC: Drug Abuse Council.

Wallach, R. C., Jerez, E., and Blinick, G. (1969). 'Pregnancy and Menstrual Function in Narcotics Addicts Treated with Methadone', *American Journal of Obstetrics and Gynecology*, 105, 8: 1226–9.

Warburton, D. M. (1978). 'Internal Pollution', *Journal of Biosocial Science*, 10: 309–19.

Waterson, J. and Ettorre, B. (1989). 'Providing Services for Women with Difficulties with Alcohol and Other Drugs: The Current Situation and Problems as Seen by Women Practitioners, Researchers and Policy Makers in the Field', *Drug and Alcohol Dependence*, 24: 119–25.

Waugh, B. (1903). 'The Restoration of the Female Inebriate', *The British Journal of Inebriety*, 1, 2: 73–5.

Weinberg, D. (2002). 'On the Embodiment of Addiction', *Body and Society*, 8, 4: 1–19.

Weisstein, N. (1973). 'Psychology Constructs the Female', in. A. Koedt, E. Levin, and A. Rapone (eds). *Radical Feminism*. New York: Quadrangle Books, pp. 178–97.

Wells, S. (2010). *Our Bodies, Ourselves and the Work of Writing*. Palo Alto, CA: Stanford University Press.

Westcott, W. W. (1903). 'Inebriety in Women and the Overlaying of Infants', *The British Journal of Inebriety*, 1, 2: 65–8.

Westermeyer, J. and Boedicker, A. E. (2000). 'Course, Severity, and Treatment of Substance Abuse among Women versus Men', *American Journal of Drug and Alcohol Abuse*, 26, 4: 523–35.

White, W. L. (2004). 'Women Who Made (and are Making) a Difference', *Counselor*, 5, 5: 25–9.

White, W. L. (2002). 'Women, Addiction, and Recovery: A Historical Review', *Counselor*, 3, 4: 52–4.

White, W. L. (1998). *Slaying the Dragon: The History of Addiction Treatment and Recovery in the United States*. Bloomington, IL: Chestnut Health Systems/ Lighthouse Institute.

White, W. L. and Chaney, R. A. (1992). 'Metaphors of Transformation: Feminine and Masculine'. Unpublished paper.

Wilson, E. (1980). *Only Halfway to Paradise: Women in Post War Britain 1945–1968*. London and New York: Tavistock Publications.

Woliver, L. R. (2002). *The Political Geographies of Pregnancy*. Urbana and Chicago, IL: University of Illinois Press.

Women's Drug Research Coordinating Project (WDR) (1979). *WDR Newsletter*, 6, School of Social Work, Ann Arbor, MI: University of Michigan, May.

Wright, S. (2002). 'Women's Use of Drugs: Gender-Specific Factors', in H. Klee, M. Jackson, and S. Lewis (eds). *Drug Misuse and Motherhood*. London: Routledge, pp. 15–31.

Young, A. (1997). *The Harmony of Illusions: Inventing Post-Traumatic Stress Disorder*. Princeton, NJ: Princeton University Press.

Young, J. (1971). *Drugtakers*. London: Paladin.

Zanetti, F. (1903). 'Inebriety in Women and its Influence on Child-Life', *The British Journal of Inebriety*, 2: 45–92.

Zelditch, M. (1955). 'Role differentiation in the Nuclear Family: A Comparative Study', in T. Parsons and R. F. Bales (eds). *Family, Socialization and Interaction Process*, Glencoe, IL: The Free Press, pp. 307–51.

Zelson, C. C., Lee, S. J., and Casalino, M. (1973). 'Neonatal Narcotic Addiction: Comparative Effects of Maternal Intake of Heroin and Methadone', *The New England Journal of Medicine*, 289, 23: 1216–20.

Zelson, C. E., Rubio, E., and Wasserman, E. (1971). 'Neonatal Narcotic Addiction: Ten Year Observation', *Pediatrics*, 48, 2 (August): 178–89.

Index